"A necessary, wide-ranging, preconception-smashing collection of essays by writers who speak from experience within the sex industry. At turns, these essays are devastating, astute, funny, and heart opening. Taken together, they are a welcome antidote to the reductive narratives about sex worker experiences that we hear too often. *We Too: Essays on Sex Work and Survival* is an anthology that honors the humanity, diversity, and depth of insight within the field. Reading it made me want to stand up and cheer."

    **—MELISSA FEBOS**, author of *Abandon Me: Memoirs*

"This incredible anthology has pulled together personal stories of sex work that speak to a reality that only so many of us know. Beyond the buzzworthy story of selling sex is the truth and lived experience, and the understanding of value, self-worth, self-pity, and self-empowerment. *We Too*'s firsthand accounts will give perspective and nuance to the 'sex work is work' conversation in this new era of informed consent."

    **—LOTUS LAIN**, adult performer and sex worker rights advocate

"*We Too* embodies the rallying cry 'Nothing about us without us.' Featuring incisive essays by sex workers of all backgrounds, this vital anthology centers diverse narratives about sex work, labor rights, sexual assault, trauma, and healing that too often go unheard. Raw, gut-wrenching, and transformative, *We Too* is a powerful addition to the canon of books by sex workers and for sex workers and their allies."

    **—KRISTEN J. SOLLÉE**, author of *Witches, Sluts, Feminists: Conjuring the Sex Positive*

"*We Too* offers a sharp indictment of this world and a warm invitation to build another one. Against a #MeToo movement that represents some at a high cost to others, *We Too* places sex workers at the front lin~~ ~~ anti-violence movement for the rest of us. ~~ ~~ state is no ally, that freedom won't come ~~ ~~ cultures of consent will come from the gro~~ ~~

    **—HEATHER BERG**, author of *Porn and Late Capitalism*

"*We Too* is a powerful, engrossing collection of essays, each lending a unique perspective from a courageous and resilient voice. Together, these essays constitute a critical resource for understanding the complex and diverse world of sex worker experience."

—**ISA MAZZEI**, author of *Camgirl*

"The Me Too movement, started by Tarana Burke, was formed to fight for the working class, often left vulnerable to sexual violence with little to no justice. This anthology examines that sexual violence and labor with a lens aimed specifically at how sex workers experience and witness it. Documenting personal accounts of sexual violence in the workplace, *We Too* can be a hard pill to swallow but presents a path toward healing from and combating rape culture from people who have survived on the front lines. This anthology brilliantly showcases the billowing voice of the sex worker community and how it supports and should be supported by feminist movements like Me Too."

—**COURTNEY TROUBLE**, founder of NoFauxxx.com

"In *We Too*, the voices of those within the sex worker community come together on topics that don't get much exposure outside our own private gatherings. This collection is incisive, generous, vulnerable, and insightful with a fair dash of humor and verve. It should come as no surprise that sex workers thinking and writing on harassment and interpersonal violence are much more multidimensional, tender, and thoughtful than most mainstream intellectuals on the topic. It's so important that these stories are heard as told by us."

—**RACHEL RABBIT WHITE**, author of *Porn Carnival*

"*We Too* is a crucial, brutally necessary book that works to create needed intersectionality within the Me Too movement and feminism generally. These stunning outsider voices are thick with inside information, personal and political, and most importantly they're great, gripping reads. I'm very grateful for this collection."

—**MICHELLE TEA**, author of *Against Memoir: Complaints, Confessions & Criticisms*

# WE TOO

## ESSAYS ON SEX WORK AND SURVIVAL

EDITED BY NATALIE WEST
WITH TINA HORN
FOREWORD BY SELENA THE STRIPPER

**THE FEMINIST PRESS**
AT THE CITY UNIVERSITY OF NEW YORK
NEW YORK CITY

Published in 2021 by the Feminist Press
at the City University of New York
The Graduate Center
365 Fifth Avenue, Suite 5406
New York, NY 10016

feministpress.org

First Feminist Press edition 2021

This book was made possible thanks to a grant from
New York State Council on the Arts with the support
of Governor Andrew M. Cuomo and the New York
State Legislature.

First printing February 2021

Cover design by Jacqueline Frances Sawatsky
Text design by Drew Stevens

**Library of Congress Cataloging-in-Publication Data**

Names: West, Natalie, 1985- editor. | Horn, Tina, editor. | Selena, the
   Stripper, writer of foreword.
Title: We too : essays on sex work and survival / edited by Natalie West
   with Tina Horn ; foreword by Selena the Stripper.
Description: First Feminist Press edition. | New York City : The Feminist
   Press at the City University of New York, 2021.
Identifiers: LCCN 2020036576 (print) | LCCN 2020036577 (ebook) | ISBN
   9781558612853 (paperback) | ISBN 9781558612877 (ebook)
Subjects: LCSH: Sex workers--United States--Biography. | Sex
   workers--United States--Social conditions. | Sex workers--Civil
   rights--United States. | Sex-oriented businesses--Social aspects--United
   States.
Classification: LCC HQ144.W478 A3 2021  (print) | LCC HQ144.W478 (ebook) |
   DDC 338.4/73067--dc23
LC record available at https://lccn.loc.gov/2020036576
LC ebook record available at https://lccn.loc.gov/2020036577

PRINTED IN THE UNITED STATES OF AMERICA

# Contents

## THE STATE

## THE WORKPLACE

## HEALING

# *Foreword*

## SELENA THE STRIPPER

During the 2017 resurgence of the Me Too movement, you may not have heard much from sex workers. Were we there? Did you somehow miss us? As a sex worker, I can attest that we were there, and some of us spoke openly about surviving sexual assault, but many of us were also reluctant to come forward. Those of us on the front lines of the fight for decriminalization often hesitate to admit to the abuses we have faced, for fear that our opponents will use our trauma against us to further crack down on our industry. Those of us who perform services outside of the protected spectrum of legal sex work often remain silent for fear of incrimination and prosecution. Considering that society has historically sided with predators, all victims of sexual assault are forced to make the difficult decision of whether or not to come forward. The difficulty of prosecuting sexual assault is only exacerbated when defining it within a commercial sex exchange. And so we look to our community. We share our stories and protect each other. We confide in each other because the rest of the world writes off our assaults as "part of the job." This book exists to create space for our stories. It is where we acknowledge the trauma that has touched so many of our lives. It is also an incredible show of resilience and diversity. This is a safe space, for those of us who are denied safety everywhere else. And so I begin with my own confession.

I began my foray into sex work by failing miserably. I was in my early twenties attending an art school in Baltimore that my family could hardly afford. I was living modestly and committing petty theft to make up for the difference between what I had and what I wanted. I bought into the internship-industrial complex and volunteered my free labor to an artist in Brooklyn, hoping it would open a door to the NYC art community. She was a Black performance artist making edgy work that explored gender and body commodification, who wore masks that made her look like Black Barbie. My portfolio explored similar themes. I scheduled a visit to her studio and asked if I could assist her over the summer, and she agreed. I didn't know where I was going to stay. I had an apartment in Baltimore, but I was homeless in New York. I knew a lot of people in the city, but none of them well enough to ask if I could crash at their place for a few nights a week. Space is a commodity few New Yorkers have enough of to share. I thought sugar dating might solve my housing situation, and I had hoped I would find a friend who might let me sleep on their floor while I searched for a sugar daddy.

One weekend a friend—a pretty white woman—invited me to her gorgeous penthouse apartment in Manhattan where she had just moved in with her older tech bro sugar daddy. I wanted that. I wanted to find one of those. At the time, I was hesitant to even call her partner her "sugar daddy," as if it was a derogatory term. I didn't know how she viewed her relationship: if it was emotional and she was a "kept woman," or if it was an explicit, financially based partnership. Whatever it was, I wanted it, and seeing her proved to me that it was possible.

The veteran sex worker in me cringes at how unprepared I was to begin this journey, but the reality was that I didn't have any viable mentors. My friend happened upon her tech bro daddy at a conference. She didn't have to navigate digital sugar dating and didn't have any tips for me. At that time, there was much more of a clandestine silence around sex work. There weren't a lot of guides aside from what SeekingArrangement offered, and that site is notorious for dodging the label "sex work" for legal and liability reasons. My first profile was full of misconceptions and language informed by porn. My Blackness translated to "ebony"; I was in college, which translated to "barely legal"; and I was small, which translated to "petite." I didn't know what beauty meant for a person like me. I grew up in Oklahoma, where Black did not equal beautiful. I didn't know anything about makeup because I'd never cared to learn. I didn't know what men wanted; I just knew that for whatever reason, they seemed to want me. I'd dealt with sexual advances and overt propositions from men since I hit puberty at eleven. Even with my queer looks, I was subjected to the male gaze. I knew I was an object of lust; the question was how to harness that for my benefit. How could I turn unwanted attention into housing?

I knew her world was different from mine as a Black and Indigenous nonbinary person who had recently shaved their head and refused, for moral reasons, to shave anything else. And yet I felt that her reality was accessible for me. I was naive.

My first foray into sugaring was brash and poorly researched, and I wasn't asking the right questions. What rate did I expect? What services was I willing to provide? What did a successful profile look like? I did have an answer to the last question: a successful profile was white. BIPOC like me were not the faces featured on the website. There was no blueprint for a person like me. Even now, I feel a pang of sadness that there was nobody I could look to for help. And that lack of guidance and support led me into dangerous situations.

I didn't know how to filter for viable candidates. Instead of searching for clues to verify my candidates' financial circumstances, I was primarily concerned with avoiding anybody too old or ugly. Because I was unfamiliar with the economic geography of NYC, I wasn't filtering according to borough or neighborhood. If I had been smarter, I would have narrowed my search to affluent areas. If you can't afford the Upper West Side, you can't afford me. I chatted with a number of possibilities, labeling them in my phone as "Jay Possible Sugar Daddy" and other irreverent names, but as is the case with all dating sites, the number of people actually willing to meet is much smaller than the number of matches you make.

I went on two dates. The first was with a man who owned a carpentry company. He was a tall white man in his midfifties with a substantial gut. He reminded me a little of Dan Conner from *Roseanne*. We chatted over beers. I was terrified, and embarrassed to be seen with him. He was easily twice my age, and I looked young enough that I got carded by both the bouncer and the bartender. I felt as if I were a prop child in *To Catch a Predator*, and Chris Hansen would pop out at any moment. We walked to a park nearby, and he asked if he could kiss me. I didn't know how to say no, so I nodded in agreement and kissed this man in broad daylight without being paid a dime. I was overwhelmed with repulsion and shame. I felt so visible and I couldn't handle the idea of anybody seeing me with him. I made up an excuse to leave and practically ran to the subway.

Ambitious baby heaux that I was, I'd lined up a second date for later that night. I was flustered but undeterred. This round, I was meeting a man who appeared to be at least decent looking. He was Black, in his early forties. I'd picked him for his looks, even though his profile raised a massive red flag: he wasn't looking for "someone just out for money." That's always the most perplexing flex. Why put up a profile on a sugar dating site if you aren't looking to pay a sex worker for their time? But I hoped, contrary to every signal, that I might convince him to pay me. We met at a restaurant on the Upper East Side and he bought me dinner. It was a casual dining spot, nothing that would hurt his wallet. I'd set up our date with the understanding that I would be spending the night at his house. I was desperate. I didn't have the money for a hotel or Airbnb, and I needed a place to stay. I followed him to his apartment in Harlem. It was a rough area, and a tiny apartment. As soon as we arrived, I realized with certainty he would not be paying me. I hadn't negotiated payment, so while it was shitty, it was also my fault. I resigned myself to the reality that I was stuck in a sketchy shoebox of an apartment with a strange man.

He put on a TV show and made his move. He started kissing me, jamming his tongue down my throat, and roughly pulled down my shirt, exposing my breasts. He reached under my skirt for my vulva and I froze. It was too much, and I had at no point consented to any of it. I was a twenty-one-year-old kid just trying to find somewhere to sleep. I somehow managed to articulate that I wasn't ready. When I voiced my no, he became grumpy. He clearly felt entitled to having his way with me. He reluctantly assured me that he wouldn't hurt me—he wouldn't do anything I didn't want. He pulled out a sofa bed for me and went to his room. I began settling in, grateful for a bed. I was nearly asleep when he came back into the room and lay beside me. He started thrusting against me, reaching into my clothes. I felt utter terror. I started whispering "Please don't" repeatedly.

"Please don't. Please don't. Please don't."

Please don't rape me. He recoiled, realizing the line he'd nearly crossed, and left my bed, returning to his room. Before he closed his door, he said, "I don't want to see you in the morning." His hostility was palpable. I couldn't sleep at that point. I didn't know if he would come back again. I lay still, trying to take up as little space as possible, trying not to make a sound. As soon as the morning came and the first rays of sunlight peeked in, I grabbed my backpack and left for the bus station.

Two years later, I managed to develop enough courage for a second foray into the sex industry. The greatest difference was that when I began stripping, I had a community. A number of my friends from college had gotten into dancing before me. They all worked together at a little club called the Ritz. I'd come to know about their work through the art they were making about it. I was entranced by what they were creating, from a pop-up strip club performance art space, to gritty poetry readings, to an installation chronicling one woman's journey from early sexualization to sex work. I felt like I was already woven into the narrative, even though I hadn't had any success.

One of my partners at the time was an experienced stripper. They patiently taught me everything they knew and pointed me in the direction of online resources to research before taking the plunge. They invited me to the club during one of their shifts, and I watched them work. They were in full female drag with a very fake-looking blond wig, and they were killing it. They had a fluidity to their dance style I'd never seen before, and the men were eating it up. I auditioned and another friend showed me around on my first night. The two of them supported me. They told me about Pleasers and helped me pick out my first dance outfit. I was very much a baby stripper, but they protected me. My little community made sure that I would be safe during my first night at the club.

THIS BOOK IS about many things: making complex the otherwise essentialized sex worker narrative of "happy hooker" or "trafficking victim"; advocating for our rights as a diverse labor force; telling our stories, the happy and the traumatic. But it is also about community—the knowledge we pass down to protect the next generations. For a community that is constantly silenced and erased, spoken for and talked over, the gathering of so many voices here is powerful. We create a safer future by speaking and sharing. Too often those of us who are advocating for the dignity and rights of sex workers are afraid to voice these less-than-positive experiences. We don't want to hurt the cause by talking about abuses, assaults, or rapes. We don't want to be pigeonholed into the role of victim, even if we are sometimes victimized. Often it feels like we are fighting for the minimum: to exist without persecution, criminalization, and stigma. But in this fight, there is room to demand more. Yes, I can say I was raped, but that doesn't give you license to take away the place where I work, the means by which I support myself, and my financial independence. Every worker has a voice, even those who have been trafficked. They can say what they want without paternalistic outsiders deciding what they need. We can speak, and it is time people listened. It is time for our perspectives to be treated as legitimate. It is time to include us in all that affects us.

And so, it is with great honor that I introduce this book, a collection of writings by heauxs across the spectrum of sex industries. Their experiences are as diverse as they are. It is very rare to collect an anthology of writing like this about sex work, authored by sex workers—so eat it up, take notes, share it with everyone you know, bring up passages over Thanksgiving dinner with your bigoted family. We're speaking, and it's time to listen.

# WE TOO

# Introduction

## NATALIE WEST

It's 2012. I'm in my midtwenties, struggling to pay my not-yet-skyrocketing Los Angeles rent. I've recently moved from the Midwest, where things weren't really any easier. I'm in graduate school, getting a degree that is unlikely to end in a career that will garner an income high enough to make a dent in the student loans I'm taking out to supplement my meager TA salary. I don't know that yet. Well-meaning people have told me that I will be an exception and I believe them. I'm the first in my family to have gone to college. My mom and dad are excited that, in a few years, they'll be able to call me "Dr."

I meet a woman on a dating site who, an hour into a first date, tells me that she's a professional dominatrix. We kiss. I go home and google "dominatrix." I ask my grad school friends if they think I should actually consider dating a dominatrix. They tell me not to be a SWERF. I go home and google "SWERF." It means "Sex Worker Exclusive Radical Feminist."

Spring turns to summer and academic work has dried up, as academic work dries up every summer. I date the dominatrix. I can't make rent. I resent my colleagues whose parents send them checks in the mail to cover happy hour tapas and new laptops when old laptops break and research trips to the Beinecke Library at Yale. I get bitter, start smoking again, learn to pull a decent shot of espresso, and do that for minimum wage.

I meet my dominatrix girlfriend's best friend: a middle-aged man who calls himself a fetish photographer but doesn't appear to work much at all. On his desktop computer, he shows me photographs of blonds in motorcycle jackets and cheesy red press-on nails. They remind me of the girls in hair metal videos my older brother watched on MTV when I was a kid. The fetish photographer used to be in a hair metal band. Now he's bald. My dominatrix girlfriend often goes over to his house in the afternoon and doesn't come back until two a.m., complaining she was exhausted but he wouldn't let her leave. *You're the fucking dominatrix*, I think but don't say.

"YOU CAN WEAR a wig in your sessions," the photographer tells me. "There are no good blond dommes in LA right now. You'll make a killing." My hair is dark, short, boyish. "Men wouldn't pay for it," he says. I had never worked as a domme and he had supposedly trained half a dozen, so I listen to his advice. He pulls one of his finest blond wigs down over the wig cap he's placed on my head. I look in the mirror and, surprisingly, like it. I look like a Texas beauty queen. I take a sip of the prosecco he's poured me, set it down carefully, and start smoothing down the wig with the palms of my hands. It doesn't shift, but it's hot as hell.

"I'll teach you everything you need to know." He says this nonchalantly, like I should recognize I'm being done a favor, but the man offering doesn't want too much credit for his generosity.

I go alone to the photographer's house to "train," the first time I've been alone with him. He's got a large metal dog cage set out waiting. He's wearing nothing but black boxer briefs and his prescription eyeglasses with transition lenses that have stopped working and never adjust to clear, even inside, even at night. He tells me he wants to assist me in putting on makeup. I already have makeup on—my girlfriend applied some before I left the house because makeup is not yet a dominatrix skill I've acquired—but I acquiesce: I am training, after all. We go into the bathroom and he drops to his knees. He picks up a tray lined with orangey makeup, far too dark for my complexion, and holds it out in front of him.

"I'm here to serve, Mistress. To help you get ready," he whimpers.

I grab the foundation. He lowers the tray, pulls down his boxers, and places his hard cock onto it, its distinct curve to the right making it point directly at a cheap palette of shimmery eye shadows.

"You're so helpful," I say, holding back the urge to laugh.

I realize at once that professional domination is, indeed, a facet of the service industry. That sex work, as the protest signs say, would be real work.

I'M STANDING IN front of the elevator to the fourth floor of a university building that houses the administration offices for the graduate program I've been attending for four years, with two to go. I usually take the stairs, but I'm already sweating. I rehearse my lines in my head before pushing the button to ascend: "He's a jealous ex. No, I don't think he's dangerous."

After the years he spent coercing me into free play by saying it would help "launch" my side hustle in professional domination—and also advance the career of my much-more-established dominatrix girlfriend—the fetish photographer snapped, ended our friendship, and went on a mission to end our professional lives. Jilted on a vacation he attended with her and me and two paying clients—imagine feeling entitled to more attention than the guys who were paying for it!—he returned from paradise to purchase some domain names. He bought NatalieWest.com and redirected it to my grad school student profile, where my legal name appeared alongside a photo of me smiling in front of a bookcase, wearing glasses and the blazer I bought for academic conferences, trying my best to look the part of the young professor. He bought the URL of my legal name and redirected it to my dominatrix website, outing me to anyone who cared to google my name or work.

I knock timidly at the door of the university administrator's office. Going into as little detail as possible, I tell her, "I have a jealous ex." I tell her that he's harassing me online and possibly stalking me and definitely trying to ruin my reputation. I tell her he's taken my photograph. He's taken many photographs. I cry and think that, because she's a woman, she's likely to have been stalked too and so maybe she won't investigate further.

I make it past this incident and out of graduate school, earning a degree they can't take away from me, even if they find the photos of me, even if they find out what I did to feed myself, even well sometimes, and pay my bills while I was there.

READING THE OUTPOURING of #MeToo stories on Twitter and across the media landscape in 2017, I immediately thought of the fetish photographer. And then I thought of the kitchen manager at the corporate chain restaurant where I worked during undergrad, who cornered me in a walk-in freezer and forced me to kiss him and feel his erection through his pants. When I filed a complaint, they transferred me to a location forty minutes away and told me he just wanted to take me out on a date. I thought of the BDSM client who pushed his fingers inside me without my consent. I had experienced sexual harassment and abuse in nearly all the jobs I had done—sex work or otherwise—throughout my working life. I didn't tell any of these stories in 2017, when the #MeToo movement gained traction on social media. I didn't use the hashtag at all.

Many of us—workers in various aspects of the sex industries—didn't use the hashtag. There's a great risk in telling stories like mine. Like ours. But we too live in a world marked indelibly by sexual harassment and abuse. And as sex workers, who among us hasn't been told that we were asking for it?

In the wake of #MeToo, there have been numerous accounts of those workers left out of conversations about workplace sexual violence, and we have been mentioned in those accounts alongside women of color, poor women, domestic workers, and women working in various low-profile industries. In a 2018 *Time* magazine piece titled "'They Don't Want to Include Women Like Me': Sex Workers Say They're Being Left Out of the #MeToo Movement," Samantha Cooney addresses the pernicious myth that sex workers cannot be sexually assaulted. One sex worker who used the hashtag in an act of solidarity reported getting messages saying she deserved to be raped, and numerous iterations of the question, "How can you sexually assault a whore?"

If you think this is the type of question that could only come from some virulent strain of misogyny found in the bowels of the online "incel"[1] community, think again. Consider the 2007 rape of a sex worker in Philadelphia and Judge Teresa Carr Deni's reduction of her sexual assault to "theft of services." After hearing the case of the nineteen-year-old woman who arranged to exchange $150 for an hour of sex with one client, but arrived at the address he gave her to find an abandoned building where she would be gang-raped by four men at gunpoint, Judge Carr Deni justified her court decision by saying, "She consented and she didn't get paid . . . I thought it was a robbery."[2] Clearly our absence from movements against sexual violence isn't simply due to a lack of public attention. The dehumanization of sex workers can render us impossible to victimize, or else it can render us the ultimate victims. This anthology was conceived in response to the outpouring of responses to workplace sexual harassment and violence that began with the revival of the #MeToo movement in 2017,[3] but as sex workers with particular experiences that complicate that movement, we also want to move *beyond* it. For us, that means we must first move past a number of myths about sex working people and activists engaged in the sex workers' rights movement.

A COMMON REFRAIN in the sex workers' rights movement is "sex work is not trafficking." The reason that this refrain is common is that anti-trafficking organizations justify police raids and arrests of sex workers as part of a larger fight against sex trafficking, which US law broadly defines in the Trafficking Victims Protection Act of 2000 as the "recruitment, harboring, transportation, provision, or obtaining of a person for the purpose of a commercial sex act." While it's key to keep in mind as you read this collection that we all have varying relationships to trafficking, pimps, management, and other forms of alliance or association that may be swept under the umbrella of trafficking, we do not advocate for the criminalization of sex work as a means of "rescuing" those populations that are being trafficked in the US and globally.

The term "trafficking" has become too broad to actually help those individuals who most people think of when they hear the term. Most people think of white teenage girls in the suburbs, kidnapped, bound, and taken across state lines, then forced into drug addiction and sexual labor. And it's not as if this type of horror has never happened, but these are not the cases of human trafficking reflected in the numbers that anti-trafficking NGOs often cite. Polaris Project, the central NGO with a mission to end human trafficking, claims that forty million people worldwide are victims of the crime. However, that figure includes people who are participating in arranged marriages and anyone who is working in a foreign country to pay off a debt of any kind. While there certainly are predatory referral agencies that exploit migrants working abroad, these are issues of borders and immigration, not necessarily trafficking—at least trafficking as it is commonly perceived. Even more pertinent to the essays you're about to read in this collection: sex workers who share safety-related information with other sex workers, especially underage sex workers—who are always already considered victims of trafficking, even if their age is unknown to the supporting parties—can be charged and convicted of trafficking or trafficking a minor.[4]

Liam Neeson and the *Taken* movies aren't all we have to blame for these misconceptions of trafficking. Anti-trafficking NGOs rose to power alongside politicized conservative Christianity, anti-immigrant and nationalist responses to globalization, and the radical feminist position that sex work is inherently violence against women. All of these ideologies frame sex work as "modern slavery."[5] As you'll read in personal accounts from sex workers in this collection, those "rescued" from trafficking most often do not get support and safety, but "detention, court fees, and criminal records that only make their lives more difficult."[6]

Anti-trafficking NGOs have worked for decades to convince the public that "if we could abolish prostitution through criminalizing clients and managers, the trafficking of women would end, as there would be no sex trade to traffic them into."[7] This argument ignores the economic need that drives people to enter the sex industries of their own free will, or at the will of another. In the United States, one result of the conflation of sex trafficking and sex work is a 2018 law that attempts to stop sex workers from communicating online with potential clients or within their own communities, putting workers into greater danger without safe outlets for screening potential clients.[8] But beyond the fact that anti-trafficking campaigns do not use their vast resources to support survivors, anti-trafficking efforts are inherently carceral.[9]

Juno Mac and Molly Smith's chapter on "Borders" in *Revolting Prostitutes: The Fight for Sex Workers' Rights* problematizes the move to categorically differentiate between sex work and trafficking. Instead, they urge those of us involved in the sex workers' rights movement to welcome conversations about human trafficking that would take up "how border enforcement makes people more vulnerable to exploitation and violence as they seek to migrate."[10] The problem, then, is the border and the state itself. Melissa Gira Grant, in *Playing the Whore: The Work of Sex Work*, urges readers to question and complicate outsider narratives about the horrors experienced by "prostituted" girls and women: "The experience of sex work is more than just the experience of violence; to reduce all sex work to such an experience is to deny that anything but violence is even possible. By doing so, there is no need to listen to sex workers" who can never transcend their conception as victims.[11] For the purposes of approaching the stories in this anthology, non–sex working readers should keep in mind that we all have different relationships to what the state defines as trafficking, but that we as a collective agree on one central point: criminalizing sex work does nothing to mitigate the exploitation and violence that the most vulnerable among us experience; indeed, criminalization increases violence against us.

THE UMBRELLA TERM "sex work" encompasses a variety of acts, gigs, and professions, with different levels of vulnerability to law enforcement and the criminal legal system: escorts, hoes, dominatrices and fetish professionals, people in the trade, massage parlor workers, porn performers, cam models, strippers, and others who trade in sex and sexuality for money. Many sex workers face the criminalization of their work, and because women of color face the criminalization of their bodies, sex workers of color live at a particularly violent intersection of these processes. As such, the sex workers' rights movement has sought to legitimize our work to the wider public, defend our choices, and fight for our right to make them—all as part of a battle for decriminalization. This fight makes it difficult to make a complaint, to allow the non–sex working public to see the problems within the sex industries, especially when that allowance may confirm what they thought they knew, when what they think they know comes from a culture that stigmatizes sex and criminalizes sex work.

These differences between sex work and other forms of work render movements against workplace sexual harassment and violence particularly vexed terrains for sex workers. The public often considers abuse a natural outcome of sexualized labor, and because sex work is criminalized, sex workers have no access to workers' rights that might mitigate those abuses when they do occur. If you've encountered the movement for sex workers' rights, you've likely heard the refrain "Sex work is real work." Without seeing sex work as work, sex workers cannot be seen as laboring subjects in need of rights, not rescue. This refrain reverberates throughout this collection. As sex workers, we know that sex work is work, and as such, this book makes space for us to speak openly about the harms we have experienced on the job, whatever the job might be. For our non–sex working readers, this may be a new experience. You will hear about labor rights violations, sexual assaults, and shit days with shit managers in shit clubs on shit porn sets. We ask that you to resist the urge to use our stories as symbols through which to criminalize our work, or to turn us into victims in need of rescue. The answer to labor rights violations, sexual assaults, and shit days at work is not criminalization or (re)victimization: putting us in prison or taking away our incomes would not right the wrongs in the stories you're about to read. As Mac and Smith explain in *Revolting Prostitutes*, "In being candid about bad workplace conditions, sex workers fear handing a weapon to political opponents; their complaints about work paradoxically becoming 'justification' to dismiss them as not 'real workers.'"[12]

For the sex worker readers and writers in this collection, the stories here will, unfortunately, come as no surprise.

As sex workers, we are taking a big risk by sharing our stories with "civilians." "Civilian" is the in-group term we use to describe non–sex working people—this book will introduce you to many such words, but it will rarely slow down to explain them to you. We trust that if you can't pick up our language with context clues, you'll do the work of looking it up. The "happy hooker" narrative is the one we have typically reserved for civilians, restricting our complaints about bad working conditions to private conversations among ourselves. That happy hooker narrative is one that works in tandem with sex positivity, and it's worked to yoke the sex workers' rights movement to sex-positive formations in third wave feminism. Mac and Smith describe this narrative as one that blurs the line between paid and recreational sex, creating "the illusion that worker and client are united in their interests." This is a narrative with which many sex workers are familiar, even beyond the bounds of activist practice, because it's a narrative we use in our advertising to clients: "The bored, libidinous housewife, the authentic 'girl-friend experience,' . . . and the powerful, formidable dominatrix are socially palatable fantasy characters designed to entice and impress customers."[13] Certainly, there can be a kernel of truth in these fantasy characters, but there must be room in our narratives for the *unhappy* hooker: the sex worker who chooses to work in the sex industries—compelled by the same economic necessity to work as any other type of worker—but who wants to improve the material conditions of their labor. If we cannot discuss the material conditions of our work, we cannot decrease violence in our industries. If we want to address the problems that sex workers face, we have to stop thinking of sex workers simply as self-directed individuals choosing sex work as a joyful project of selfhood (the sex-positive liberal model), or as victim-criminals in need of carceral reform.

Sex workers in the United States, and in many other places that criminalize sex work, live in fear. But those fears might not be the fears that we, in a culture unaccustomed to listening to sex workers, expect to hear: The pimp. The bad date. The good client gone bad. The sleazy producer on the casting room couch. The exploitative strip club manager. Living in a culture in which sex work is vilified, we all know the stories about what goes wrong in the sex industry and which figures perpetrate those harms. You will encounter these figures in the narratives that make up this anthology. Yet there are other fears within the sex industries that you might not hear about if you're a non–sex working person: The leak in the strip club ceiling, causing you to twist your ankle and lose a week of wages. The cops. The fetish photographer calling himself a BDSM "trainer." The client who tries to slip off a condom. The child welfare court. The fucking cops. The criminal status of many forms of sex work—and the stigmatized status of the rest—makes it difficult for sex workers to take action to mitigate the harms we experience at work. We try our best to protect each other—through community support networks, bad client lists, and sharing best practices to keep us safe from law enforcement—but the state seems hell-bent on passing legislation that keeps us from doing so. But again, we ask you to approach these issues with an open mind: we are not asking for rescue. In this book, we are, as contributor Lina Bembe says, "demystifying" our industries for ourselves. We are allowing our non–sex working readers to sit with us as we do so across the pages of this collection, but the collection itself is for us. We hope that giving voice to our individual experiences as a collective will allow us to heal, and to continue our work toward transforming our industries to become safer, saner, and more supportive in the face of the violence we endure.

This anthology will not offer readers direct argumentation against the criminalization of sex work, but it will offer personal narratives that undergird the logic of decriminalization. Decriminalizing the facets of the industry that are currently criminalized—and destigmatizing the rest—is central to a movement toward compassion and humanity. However, this collection does not exist to convince non–sex workers that we deserve to be treated with compassion and humanity. We have written to and for those who would deny our humanity for far too long.

We have come together to collect the personal narrative essays that make up this collection because we—current and former sex workers—are the experts on the working conditions in the sex industries, and yet our voices are often ignored in favor of politicians, celebrities, law enforcement, and NGOs that claim to know what is best for us. As a collective of voices, we can move beyond the #MeToo movement and other movements to decrease workplace sexual harassment and violence that do not serve us or value our stories. We can build a movement toward healing, by and for sex workers.

Implicating anti–sex work feminism in the dehumanization of sex workers, contributor Lorelei Lee explains, "I'm angry that I could not talk about violence without fueling descriptions of me as an object, written by women claiming to be my allies." This collection seeks to change those conversations in which sex workers are the objects, not the subjects, of their own stories. Listening to the polyvocality of experiences in the sex industries is the first step toward decreasing violence, and that is precisely *We Too*.

## NOTES

1. "Incel" is short for "involuntary celibate," a community of men, facilitated by online community forums, who define themselves by their perceived unjust rejection by women.
2. Catherine Plato, "Escort Rape Case Causes Uproar in Philadelphia," in *$pread: The Best of the Magazine That Illuminated the Sex Industry and Started a Media Revolution*, eds. Rachel Aimee, Eliyanna Kaiser, and Audacia Ray (New York: Feminist Press, 2015), 250–52.
3. Me Too is a movement founded in 2006 by Tarana Burke to help survivors of sexual violence, particularly women of color from low-wealth communities, and bring healing and allyship to the trauma of sexual assault and violence.
4. Ine Vanwesenbeeck, "The Making of 'The Trafficking Problem,'" *Archives of Sexual Behavior*, no. 48 (October 2019): 1961–67.
5. Vanwesenbeeck, "The Making of 'The Trafficking Problem,'" 1965.
6. Vanwesenbeeck, "The Making of 'The Trafficking Problem,'" 1964.
7. Molly Smith and Juno Mac, *Revolting Prostitutes: The Fight for Sex Workers' Rights* (New York: Verso Books, 2018), 59.
8. The House bill, Fight Online Sex Trafficking Act, and the Senate bill, Stop Enabling Sex Traffickers Act—known as the package deal FOSTA-SESTA—serve to make websites liable for what users say and do on their platforms. Intended to curb sex trafficking—despite law enforcement agencies and trafficking survivors claiming that the shutdown of online platforms like Backpage would make it more difficult to arrest traffickers and find survivors—sex workers could find independence, safety, and community online prior to the passage of this law.
9. Jennifer Lynne Musto provides a history of restrictions placed on NGOs receiving state funding and argues that, because the terms of their funding require them to take a stance against decriminalization, these NGOs are necessarily carceral institutions. Musto, "The NGO-ification of the Anti-Trafficking Movement in the United States: A Case Study of the Coalition to Abolish Slavery and Trafficking," *Wagadu: a Journal of Transnational Women's and Gender Studies*, vol. 5 (2008): 6–20.

10. Smith and Mac, *Revolting Prostitutes*, 85.
11. Melissa Gira Grant, *Playing the Whore: The Work of Sex Work* (New York: Verso Books, 2014), 102.
12. Smith and Mac, *Revolting Prostitutes*, 45.
13. Smith and Mac, *Revolting Prostitutes*, 32.

# STIGMA

## That Sliver of Light

ASHLEY PAIGE

There are an infinite number of malicious schools of thought, which we often have shoved down our throats, when it comes to what kind of woman is considered "acceptable." Then, what kind of sex worker is acceptable? What kind of black woman is acceptable? What kind of queer person is acceptable? As a black, queer woman, and a very public and out sex worker who has been in the adult industry for coming up on thirteen years—who has done many different forms of sex work, from escorting to pro-Domming—I have stories of violence, as many of us do. I have been independent and not independent. I have been exploited and dehumanized, in and out of sex work.

I'm hesitant to reveal these vulnerabilities. Nowadays, I identify as a Professional Dominatrix, and Dommes are often seen as these untouchable entities: femmes fatales who cannot be broken or violated because they're so powerful. Clients and the general public tend to dehumanize Dommes in that way sometimes.

Along with that lies this notion that sex workers can't be raped. And black sex workers get it worse. As a black femme, I'm over-sexualized just because I reside in this body. Black girls are seen as sexual beings even at the age of five. I carry that burden. I am thirty-one years old. So, for at least twenty-six years . . .

There are a lot of things that weigh on me regarding how this story will be perceived. How will this affect my income? How will this affect my brand? How will it affect what I am looking to do with my career? Will clients still see me in the same light? See me in general? Will other sex workers want to be associated with someone who is very much spilling the beans? Sex workers paint this picture of perfection, because that's what we sell: this perfect fantasy. And I'm coming up with a big-ass needle to that bubble, like, "Am I gonna do it?!"

I HAD JUST turned nineteen when I did my first porn films in California. Six months after that, I started working for Snaps, back in Texas. By the time I was twenty-two, I was done dealing with him. A lot happened in those three years.

When I started working with Snaps, I was nineteen and homeless. A friend of mine was fooling around with this guy whose best friend was a pimp. I made her set up a meeting between him and me. I grew up with men—uncles and other relatives—who were hustlers as well, so I knew hustlers had a connection to this other world.

My first impression of Snaps was that he was smooth. Very smooth. Seventeen years my senior. But I was the instigator in this. I was very much the one to be like, "I need to get some money up quickly. I can't rely on anybody." I wanted to make sure that he was a valid source of information and education. Because I knew that if I was going to be getting a pimp and I was going to be getting this money, I needed to get an education and it would be for a certain amount of time. I wanted to learn the game.

We met, went to his place. He was in Lancaster, not far from granny's place, which was funny. His place was gorgeous. It was a three-bedroom house. Big backyard. It was very much a Texas home: a lot of space, well-appointed and decorated. His bottom was there. We chop it up. His chick clearly doesn't like me, but it's like, *Well, I guess that this is what he wants to do*. So she's like biting her tongue. I need to make money. I don't give a fuck about emotional shit.

The first call was honestly a con because Snaps just wanted to get me drunk and fuck me. Which is what a pimp does, right? He always tests the product. So he says that he has a call for me. It's at this hotel in DeSoto, not far from mine. I go over there. Call ends up canceling. He's just like, "Let's have some drinks." End up getting wasted. And he fucks me. And the sex was good. Like it was fucking great, honestly.

I WAS WALKING the track in the beginning, so I had a lot of like quick little wiggle outfits that you could wiggle in, wiggle out of really quickly. It wasn't about fashion. It was what makes the titties pop, what makes the ass pop. You need to be able walk by a cop and not get arrested, but you could pull a trick in fairly quickly too.

No one saw me without makeup. Period. It was all high femme. I wore wigs. I wore extensions. And I was miserable in the process because it was uncomfortable. It was like I was wearing a hat in the Texas heat. All the time. I was a thicker girl at the time. It's the Bible Belt. It's Texas. It's the South. Just a thick black chick. Oh god. Heels. All the time. I hate heels. They were like four-inchers or more. They were stripper heels, platforms.

There was this really ugly pair, these platforms with a thick heel. And it had the wrap around the ankle, the band across the toes. I'm a ten and a half, eleven, and that shit was like a nine and a half. Those motherfuckers cut! I've never had bunions as bad as those motherfuckers gave me, and I was in those shoes all the fucking time. So my foot would slowly slide up the peep toe, and then it's like my three toes are suffocating! Oh my god, I hated it so much.

The track was this weird little cul-de-sac off Harry Hines in downtown Dallas, not far from the strip clubs. Just a quick little turn-in. The cars would line up. The pimps' cars would be parked. Tricks would just roll through. I remember this one dude with the most bling'd out white Caddy. He was the most obnoxious fucking pimp. He had this all-white suit, this white hat. All-white everything. He had some badass chicks. But he had snow bunnies—white girls—out the wazoo. And he had track stars. Track stars work a track better than nobody's motherfucking business.

Being a track star was a whole other world of existence. I had dreams of getting there but no ideas of how to actualize it. I was doing survival sex work. I was living at a motel room for forty dollars a day. Even that was a motherfucking struggle. Snaps wasn't really giving me a whole bunch of play at the time. He wasn't sending a bunch of tricks my way. Texas was very much a trick's market. The tricks set the price for what it was that they were willing to pay you. "Nah, you a fat black chick. So, I'ma have to pay you less. And really, that's if I wanna pay you at all."

So I quickly found out I'm *not* a motherfucking track star.

One night, I got held up. I got into the car with these two guys. Go around the corner to the regular hookup spot. Start fooling around with the first guy. The second guy's in the front seat. He gets a little bit too handsy, and he's trying to fuck me without a condom. We're both in the back seat. I give him a blow job. He gets a little bit irritated. And so they switch. I start fucking around with the second guy. The first guy's still irritated that he can't fuck me without a rubber. Things escalate quickly. Before I realize it, they're cutting me up.

I always carried a knife with me, which was supposed to be my protection—but once things escalated, one of the guys lunged at me and took the knife. They both attacked me. One put the weight of his body on me to pin me down while the other cut me up. I remember one kept saying "pistola, pistola," trying to find their gun. All I wanted to do was to get my phone and my wallet and get the fuck out of there. I didn't care about anything else. I just needed my phone so I could call Snaps and I needed my wallet because it had my ID. My ID had my address. And even in the midst of all this, that's where my mind goes. Luckily they weren't stabbers. They were just slicers. Silver linings, man.

I remember there was this little sliver of light. One guy's in the front seat, and the other guy's in the back seat with me. There's this one little sliver where I could push and like dive through it and get at the car door at the same time.

And so I do. I dive out onto the ground, and roll behind the car. It all happens in a matter of seconds. And in the midst of this, they start shooting into the sky. I'm fucking shaking, and I stay on the ground. I got cut on my arm and ribs, but I was able to get my phone. It felt slippery because blood was coming down my hand. I made the dive. Don't get my wallet, leave the bag. Made this dive, and I'm on the ground outside of the car, and immediately running. I remember turning on my phone, and there's blood on the screen. I called Snaps. I don't even remember what I said. I was in such a panic. I'm like, "Come get me, come get me," or whatever the fuck. He was right around the corner. And I remember thinking, *How fucking long can it take you to get here?* Finally he pulls up, and I'm still behind the bushes, holding on for dear life. And I peek through the bushes and see that he's pulled up in the Caddy.

His Caddy was maroon red. Another default Texas staple!

I remember coming from behind the bushes, running and diving into the Caddy. He said something about me getting blood on the handle. Then, "Tell me where they're at. I'm going to go find their asses." And I'm just like, you ain't gonna do *shit.*

AFTER THAT, I took off to the Caribbean to dance. You know how a two-year-old has a toy and is like, "It's mine! I may not be playing with it, but it's mine. And you can't touch it." Snaps's toy had walked the fuck away without his permission. So when I came back, he found me in San Antonio. When he found me, it worked out because I was broke. I went back to Dallas to hustle with him. And that's when shit goes in heavy and hard.

It's in-calls, it's out-calls. I'm traveling. I was posting ads, and developing a website, and getting reviews, and traveling all over Texas and Louisiana. I got busted three times. First time was in Shreveport, Louisiana. I kept telling Snaps I had a horrible feeling.

I end up in jail for twenty-four hours. I got molested by the cops in Shreveport. And they took pictures.

The next time, it's in Dallas about a year later. Horrible feeling. We're gonna be leaving town that night. All I have to do is this session. Keep on telling him, "Something's off. Something's wrong." Gotta do a session. Gotta make the money. He has shit to do. So I do the session, get arrested. I'm in jail for four days. He goes off to Louisiana. Leaves my ass in jail.

The first time I was arrested, he laughed at me. And it broke my fucking heart. And the second time, he just shrugged it off, like he expected it. I am apparently a fucking masochist, because I kept with that shit! After seeing so many negative interactions between women and men in my family, I got the idea that you are supposed to accept it and just turn the other cheek. And so this was just one of those situations that you just turn the other cheek.

I WAS TWENTY years old. Got a call. On Craigslist, you knew when they were doing stings. Back in the day screening was not like it is now, but you could tell when you had a cop on the phone. They're a little *too* something. A little too calm. A little too chipper. A little too eager. Little too willing. Little too ready to pay more. A little too suspect. A little too quiet.

Versus you can tell when it's a nervous trick.

Shreveport is a very small city, a casino city. And even though it definitely was a ho mecca, you got like a certain kind of call. You got a certain kind of caller. And there was a certain frequency. So when all of a sudden you start getting like five times as many calls, you notice. Ten times as many calls, something's going on. Is it because there's a convention? Is it because there's something going on at the casino? Or is it because they're busting bitches left and right? Ninety percent chance they're busting bitches left and right. Plus, it's election time.

I get this call from a Craigslist guy. And immediately my intuition, this gut, this spirit of mine, is very motherfucking in tune. As soon as I picked up the phone, I knew something was off. Soon as he started talking. But I'm not going to give it away. So I'm talking to him. Give him some information. He was a little too Southern. And I'm from Texas. We in Louisiana. I know country. But he was a little bit too Southern. Just a little bit too twangy.

I tell Snaps, and Snaps is tied up. It's late night. Business had been slow. And I remember telling him I'm just uncomfortable. And he dismissed my gut intuition. "You don't know what the fuck you're talking about. We're gonna go get this money." You know you have this responsibility to make this money. You have a responsibility to do this job, because it is a job: One, as a bottom. Two, as a ho. Three, because you're attached to this idea that's outside of yourself. This stable, this pimp, this whatever. This family. You have to meet certain demands. And to pay your fucking bills! And that's why the fuck you came here, to make this money. Craigslist ads are how much? It might be a dollar or two a day, but it's a dollar or two out of your pocket that you're not actually replenishing. You're going out of pocket again. So you need to go make this money.

I remember when we pulled into the parking lot, I felt off the whole time. I felt like we were being watched. I get out of the car. I remember seeing this white van. And I go into the motel. And it's just fucking eerily quiet. This guy asked for a session at like ten p.m., an out-call. And his hotel is seedier than mine. They have the night-watch window with the sliding glass, you can't even talk to a person. Red carpet. That ugly, nasty red carpet that you always see—it's not red, it's maroon. The color of Snaps's car. Smells like cigarettes. There were certain hotels that were safer to work at. As long as you're not causing any problems and you're discreet, they really don't give a fuck.

I'm still telling Snaps this feels off. And Snaps was just like, "It'll be cool. If you feel anything, just don't take the money." That doesn't actually work! If you show up and they want to arrest you, they will fucking arrest you. It does not actually matter. That's a lie we tell ourselves: Just don't take the money.

I was wearing a purple skirt with a little bit of a twirl. And a blouse and a pleather jacket. Shoes were definitely some kind of heel, probably like a peep toe. Four inches. Maybe brown? I had a wig on. No, I had extensions. I had my father's hairline. With extensions, that always fucks me up. It's the worst fucking thing ever, because it doesn't actually match the texture of the hair you have sewn into your head. I didn't know how to really, like, do my makeup. I didn't wear makeup until I graduated high school because I was a tomboy. It was just tacky. The weave was bad. It was probably stringy, because I had too much oil in it. It was a bad look, all right?

I was discreet though. I was never straight-up like ho shit. That was always a thing for me: plausible deniability. The thing about it is—talking to enough hoes—the shoes always give you away. Even if they're brown. They always give you away.

WALKING IN FROM the parking lot into the lobby, which is just a hallway, the camera's watching me and I can see myself. And I have to open this heavy lobby door. It just felt like *The Shining*. I can hear every footstep. And I get to the hotel room door. And I'm having a debate in my head. Not even three seconds go by. And I'm not going to knock. I'm about to turn and the door opens.

It's this very nasty car salesman guy, right? He looks like he hasn't washed. There's a jacuzzi tub that has platform steps up to it. Nasty little couch that you don't want to sit on bare. And then there was the bed. And a sliding glass door. I remember the glass door was cracked. When he opened the door, it registered in my mind immediately. It was cracked. And so he said that the money was on the steps up to the bathtub. I remember thinking automatically, *I'm not taking the money.* And I remember I put my bag on it. I didn't touch it. Smart, right? Except not really. Because it doesn't fucking matter.

And that was the thing! Snaps didn't know how to educate me on what a fucking sting was because he's not the one who's going into the fucking call. He's had bitches get arrested but he isn't like, "Okay, baby, tell me what happened. What were the signs that you knew that this was about to go down? What did they do? What did you do?" It was none of that. I never got any kind of education from any of his girls. And I remember a number of different girls that he introduced, trying to add to the stable. I remember at a certain point thinking, *He's not educating them.* I tried to protect them, even in the midst of being aware that, really, we're not a family and this is just a competitive thing.

The men who arrested me, they were very much Louisianans. They got that drawl. Their energy was very much the dirty cop that caught you on the back roads and is going to pull up your skirt and rape you because you just don't happen to be on the right road. That's the vibe I got. And that's very much the experience I got as well.

I WAS SNAPS'S bottom by the time I knew I had to get out. A bottom bitch is the main chick. The pimp's right hand, first in command. But it's all a fucking con. I was touring all the time. He sent me this girl to train in Philadelphia—she ended up being worthless, got me arrested. My birthday's coming up—he cancels all the plans, he's got a girl pregnant. It was tumultuous, more and more volatile.

He was a suave pimp. He was into *psychological* abuse. Emotional manipulation and gaslighting. You know, just that constant digging. You can violate my body, you can try and break that shit, but you can't break my fucking spirit and you cannot violate a bond. Somebody can do all kinds of horrible, degrading shit, just defile me completely—but you act like you're family and reveal to me you're not, that's a hard limit for me. Me and Snaps were working toward something tangible, like a home—property and land. He had his music business and I wanted to go to school. But it became clear that he was abusing me. And it became clear when it was past my tolerance for abuse. I was struggling with my gayness and presentation. He would attack my masculinity. He would say that I look like a man, too muscular, too buff. That's part of what eventually led me to cutting ties and going independent.

I went up to New York. I saw some clients. Did some overnights. Got treated really well. Within a month, I was out. I had a shared Airbnb in Alphabet City. The owner of the apartment and his dog were in the other room, and I had this screaming match at three o'clock in the morning with my pimp about how I was done, saying, "I can't do this shit anymore!"

Snaps emptied my apartment back in Houston by the time I got home: the safe-deposit boxes, all the money I sent back, everything. And I was a fucking dedicated-ass bottom! I had this hippie I was friends with pick me up from the airport. We rode over to my place, this gorgeous two-bedroom apartment with a garage. Walked in. It was fucking empty. My hippie started crying. And I said, "Well, at least it's fucking done now." I could have called to change the locks in the apartment. But I know I would've still been in debt to him. So I just let Snaps empty the apartment because that was the safest way to be done.

I called Snaps. "So you got everything you need? We're good? The debt's settled then?" He says, "I'm cutting your phone off. Just know it'll be off in the next hour." And I say, "There's no reason for you to contact me, right? You're good? Okay. Then we're good." And my fucking hippie, he's bawling. I'm just like, "It means I'm out. He can take whatever. It's fine. I'm out."

I was no longer associated with a pimp. I was independent, and I left by way of buyout. Typically the only way you're going to break loose from a pimp is if you buy yourself out. Which means you pay your debt and move forward. But the debt is an arbitrary moving target. My debt was what he deemed it to be.

For a good year, I was getting phone calls, all kinds of harassment. It was like, *I'm watching you, bitch.* That year, I lived in absolute terror of anybody knowing who the fuck I actually was. I was living in New York at the time, but if anybody had any connections to folks in Texas, I wouldn't let them know where I lived.

He knows my family. He knows everybody. He knew where my mom lived. I was afraid he would pop up. The thing about having a pimp is you're ten toes down—meaning you are in the life. You're grounded in that shit.

I used a different name then. I was Amazing Asia. I felt like Tina Turner, because he gave me that name, right? I kept my fucking name. That name was fucking money. If I ran into him now, I have no fucking clue what I would say to him. I probably wouldn't say shit. The fuck. For what? Hell. Waste another fucking breath? Nah. But in the midst of all the inhumane shit I experienced with Snaps, I can still see his humanity. I will never give him another ounce of my energy, but he's a human with flaws. I want to reconcile who I was then with who I am now, but I don't like the idea of giving a platform to prove his humanity.

IT'S FUNNY BECAUSE now that I'm further into the fetish world and pro-Domming, I love a good mindfuck. Never having to lift a finger to fuck with someone, to really get them in this place of just, *ugh*.

But I *always* get consent. I'm not dehumanizing them beyond their limits. I'm not diminishing someone's value. I'm not engaging in emotional manipulation. Those who I have mindfuck arrangements with, boundaries are discussed and limits are respected. There's ongoing communication. There is ongoing checking in to make sure that, even though you might be a dirty little fucking hole, you're genuinely present and excited to be here with me. And there's a separation of what is fantasy and what is reality. Because when you walk away, you have to walk away whole. I can't play with anyone who does not get that. That's what a psychological abuser does, and Snaps excelled in that realm.

BDSM feels empowering. I am a person who is aware of my trauma, other people's trauma, and do not want to perpetuate that. It feels really fucking good to be able to hold space for someone who wants to go into the space of being abused, defiled, humiliated.

To be aware and present and empowered in that. We can go there and there is no judgment. And even if it goes past the point of desire, there is a safety net. We are able to come back and gently reintegrate into normal life, without all the shame and the guilt and the stuff that comes with wanting to indulge in a desire that is taboo.

On the top side, I have been the instigator (with consent) of abuse. I have been on the bottom side as well. To bridge those two places, it feels fucking wonderful. It feels like the shit that I've endured has given me some kind of understanding as to what I will or will not endure going forward. And being able to weave that into something that is positive for me and someone else—I really like kink for that shit.

WHILE I'VE WORKED in sex work, my family has mainly worked in the government. All different branches of the military and the IRS. They have suffered, experienced abuse in dealing with these institutions that are totally fucking legal.

My father is a brilliant man. But working with the Marines broke him psychologically and spiritually. He was an abusive piece of shit for a long time. He is no longer that man. The Marine Corps exacerbated his ability to disassociate and disconnect from anybody else's humanity. To be able to perpetuate certain things upon those he says he loves. To just do things that are honestly atrocious. My father, as much as I love him—there are certain parts of him that are dangerous. I'm processing some of that still to this day.

My mom, my grandmother, and many aunts worked for the IRS for all of their adult lives. Last year my mom didn't get paid for six months out of the year because she was on furlough. She's had to do pretty much free labor at the expense of all of her bills. I'm lucky that I'm privileged enough where I can give my mom money if she needs it.

My mom is being exploited by the government—legally. The bullshit keeps her blood pressure in the stroke zone: taxpayers calling in and cussing her out, the boundaries she has to make sure she doesn't cross because she's being listened to. They'll dock her pay if she acts like a human, tells someone, "I wish the fuck you would" over the phone. She has arthritis and her job is a detriment to her body: walk up the stairs, walk down the stairs to get to her car. That's legal though. It's just regular-ass bullshit that you have to deal with when you have a job. Everybody wants to say, "Oh, because it's sex work, it's this whole thing." People are exploited every fucking day. People are abused every day. And it's legal. It's just because it's sex work that we're deemed dirty—but also holy and sanctified at the same time. No, it's a job, man. I've had more #MeToo moments of exploitation outside of sex work.

The impact of the circumstance is definitely felt more intensely when it's at the end of a knife. It is an automatic life-or-death situation. But if you survive it, it's over—versus having to experience abuse again and again, not being able to get out of it because you need the paycheck, and it's the only paycheck you can get.

That night in Dallas I got to dive out of that tiny little opening from the back seat and get out. I ran. I hid. I escaped the end of the knife, dodged those bullets, and mended my wounds. But I've also had jobs where I've been stuck, where I couldn't even see that sliver of light, that tiny little hole to just dive out and fight for another day. And in the end, those were far graver times.

## Your Mother Is a Whore: On Sex Work and Motherhood

JESSIE SAGE

Violet* is at home with her daughter and boyfriend when she hears a knock at the door. She opens it to find five police officers and a social worker. "They went through our laundry, our bag of adult toys, all of our cupboards," she tells me over the phone. "They said that my mom called and told them that I am a prostitute and that I am subjecting my daughter to it."

Violet does work in the sex industry, but she isn't a prostitute; she is a cam girl. And though this work may be highly stigmatized, it is legal. So she was shocked when the judge granted Violet's mother full custody of her daughter. She says, "It blows my mind that you can lose a child like this. I haven't been charged with anything. I've never been arrested."

Violet's story stands out to me because, as an online sex worker who is also a mother, this is my worst fear. I started doing a mix of phone sex, cam modeling, and clip production when I was going through a divorce. Online sex work offered a flexible schedule that allowed me to take care of my kids. Divorce, as it turns out, is time consuming and expensive. Sex work was a good fit for the circumstances. It was also a good fit in many other ways that I didn't anticipate: the work, while challenging, can be interesting, rewarding, and meaningful. But beginning a sex work career in the midst of

*Name has been changed to protect privacy.

32

a divorce made me particularly attuned to, and afraid of, custody issues such as Violet's.

This fear is not unfounded. Sex workers who are mothers often find themselves in the middle of such battles, even if they're engaging in perfectly legal behavior. Juniper Fitzgerald, a former sex worker and author of *How Mamas Love Their Babies*, understands this all too well, having faced her own custody battle related to sex work. "Not a day goes by that I don't hear of a sex working mother crowdsourcing funds for a custody lawyer. It's heartbreaking," she says.

The fact that sex workers who engage in legal work face these challenges points to something important regarding attitudes toward sex work: our fitness to parent is seen through a lens of the stigma that surrounds sex work. Mothers who engage in sex work are perceived as lacking the judgment and boundaries needed to be good parents. This stigma is injected into our legal system. While the law may not forbid stripping or cam work, judges have a lot of discretion, and if doing stigmatized work leads them to believe that we have poor judgment, they can slap us with consequences that, for mothers, can feel worse than being arrested.

Fitzgerald notes that she has it easier than most in her position. "I have a great deal of privilege as a white woman with a PhD," she says. "Even given those privileges, the court wanted detailed explanation of my work and a good-faith testament that I was no longer engaged in sex work." This becomes an even bigger problem for those who do not carry such privilege. suprihmbé, an online sex worker and artist, observes, "As a Black woman who has run into many problems with the law, I avoid the court." And in the case of prostitution, Bella Robinson, executive director of COYOTE Rhode Island, a sex workers' rights organization, remarks in a phone conversation, "You are more likely to go to jail for prostitution than you are for drugs."

And yet, despite the fact that society portrays motherhood as incongruent with sex work—scrutinizing our judgment and credibility—sex working mothers continue to parent our kids in a way that is not only appropriate but radical in its power to destabilize these narratives and destigmatize our work for future generations. In other words, sex working mothers are at the front lines of a radical sexual politics, as these front lines begin in our own homes. Because we occupy professions that are highly stigmatized, sex working mothers are pushed to parent with a thoughtfulness and a courage that undermines the perceptions of unfit motherhood that society wants to insist upon.

For myself and the other mothers I spoke with, this begins with figuring out how to talk to our kids in an age-appropriate way about both sexuality and sex work. But more than this, we also have to talk to them about the stigma we—and, they, by extension—face. This is never simple. suprihmbé notes that while she is not secretive about what she does, her son is only five and she hasn't yet decided how much she will tell him. Part of her worry is that other parents aren't having the same conversations with their children about the nuances of sex work. She says, "Probably once he's a little older we will discuss it more, but I don't know how in depth I want to be. Because I'm a single mom, and I don't want him running off at the mouth to other kids' moms and dealing with their bigotry."

Fitzgerald describes the way in which she has talked to her four-year-old daughter about sex work. "I have told her many times that I used to dance naked for a job. My former work is very normalized in our household." Porn performer Lotus Lain hasn't yet told her children what she does for work, but she is laying the groundwork for these conversations. "My kid is still elementary age, but they have a healthy view of sex, they know what sex is," she says. "They're not judgmental at all. I've talked to them about different types of sexuality and gender, and they've completely understood without challenging the concepts." She hopes this will set them up to be understanding when they're old enough to learn more. "I know that once they're high school age they will be able to fully understand the type of sex work I have done and why."

Yin Q, a Dominatrix, writer, and educator, says that she is also preparing her kids to understand sex work as they grow older. "My kids are too young to understand sex work at this point," she says, "but I raise them to be accepting of different sexual lifestyles and orientations and am already very careful not to slut shame." Yin Q has also written and produced a series based on her career called *Mercy Mistress*, and her kids have seen some of the footage of the main character, a Domme in fetish gear. "They've asked me what she does, and I answered that she helps people face their darkness. 'So she's a superhero?' they said. 'Yes,' I answered, 'Sex workers are superheroes.'"

This conversation seems to capture what many sex worker mothers are doing in their parenting. Because I have older children, I was able to have very direct conversations with them about my work, and this became more urgent when I started doing sex work writing and local activism. When I explained to my preteen what phone sex is and why people call phone sex lines, he responded with, "So you are like an online therapist but you talk to people mostly about sex." I laughed, because it is closer to the truth of what this kind of sex work looks like than most people realize. I was proud to have raised a kid who could see past the sensationalism of the "sex" in sex work (unlike most adults) and see the bigger picture. But for this to happen, a foundation had to be laid: a sex-positive foundation which included a respect for personal autonomy and for women, including those who have made choices that fall outside of cultural norms.

Indeed, Ramona Flour, an art model and sex worker whose mother also worked in the industry, exemplifies this, tweeting, "I have been advocating for sex workers my whole life because my mother has been a sex worker my whole life." On the phone, she expands, "The thing I want people to understand is that there are a lot of single mothers [in sex work], mothers who are struggling to take care of their children." Of her own mother she says, "I am thankful, above everything else, that she was so selfless and provided for me and took care of me. She used sex work to take care of her kid and that is so commendable."

While the image that we have of sex work activists is that of the most public and most visible sex workers—those who march on the streets and stand at the forefront of political action—sex working mothers are also engaged in a radical activism at home. They are teaching their children to see sex workers through their own lens and not through a filter of shame and stigma. This is important political work. "We need more representations of sex workers that are authentic, complex, and generous," says Yin Q. "Culture change happens before policy change."

*Originally published on the* Establishment *on July 18, 2018.*

# Bifurcating

## JUNIPER FITZGERALD

I was sixteen the first time I stepped into a strip club. The threat of parental disownment loomed over me from a young age, creating an almost obsessive concern with labor and income.

"Get out and never come back" was repackaged in myriad ways. Sometimes, it was those exact words. Sometimes, it was my little brother's toys piled into trash bags with threats of being kicked to the curb. Sometimes, it looked like physical violence. Once, my uncle forced me to watch as he tortured his own son—punishment for my failure to adhere to the strict Catholic code of femininity in which we were steeped. It was also a warning: conform or *get out and never come back*.

Although I started working at the age of fourteen—seven, actually, if I include uncompensated childcare and the emotional labor of protecting my newborn brother from our parents' drunken brawls—I never amassed enough cash for an apartment deposit. As such, I was perennially suspended between here and there.

The threat of disownment and subsequent fears about self-sustainability are omnipresent even now as an adult, and the sex industry remains the careful arms into which I fall. This is my contradiction—the thing that most alienates me is also my reprieve from alienation.

THE STRIP CLUB manager was nothing more than a sentient patina of slime, a thick moss grown from years in the moist shade of greed and entitlement. A cloud of cigarette smoke hung over him with a darkness in his eyes that I would later see in myself. He took my baby fat and fake ID as an invitation to humiliate. "What are your favorite sex toys?" he asked. "What's your favorite sex position? You spit or swallow, baby?"

I was a virgin.

Leaving smaller than when I had entered, I decided to get a job washing dishes instead. I showed up to my first dishwashing shift in a floor-length pink dress from Goodwill, which was the source of even more humiliation. Somewhere along the line, I was told that one must look sophisticated at work, and the pink dress was the most sophisticated thing that I owned.

As I attempted to carve out space for myself in the workplace, I quickly learned that it didn't matter if the workplace commodified femininity or devalued it; either way, men orchestrated the work.

I wouldn't be brave enough to set foot in another strip club for a few years. But when I did, I found home: women—lots of women. It wasn't that this home was unproblematic. The women had scars. It was patriarchal and abusive in all the ways that my childhood home had been. But at least in my chosen home, the women were brave enough to name things: bad dates, time wasters, undercovers, sleazebags, dirty managers . . . thieves.

I learned how to hustle. More importantly, I learned how to take what has always been rightfully mine—what has always been rightfully *ours*. I took it and apologized to no one. I learned how to break a man's nose in one fell swoop. I was Dotty on stage and Jenny in the sheets. I was Juniper on paper and Jennifer in lineups, and somehow all of that felt unbending and unwavering. I was a wide-eyed midwestern girl, eager to learn. I was a multiplicity, but not yet bifurcated. I wasn't yet a mother.

Graying with the age of a life a little more than half gone, in *Feminism and Marxism*, feminist sociologist Dorothy Smith identified what is known as the "bifurcation of consciousness." Women, suspended between our own truths and those "realities" imposed upon us by men, are forced to reconcile the contradiction between the two. We have insight into patriarchal ways of knowing while sometimes also knowing that our empirical realities are much different. Patriarchal ways of knowing further bifurcate women's consciousness by chopping us up into digestible versions of ourselves—we are either Madonnas or Whores. We are either public property or the singular property of a man.

Of course, patriarchal values do not just penetrate masculinity. People of all genders are susceptible to its charms. But for those of us who straddle identities of Mother and Whore simultaneously, the demand to bifurcate one's consciousness is even more profound.

Over the years, eagerness turned to resentment. A pregnancy turned into a botched abortion and a lover turned into an abuser. So I ran away to the desert. I ran until I was pregnant, again.

The Mojave had suffered a spasm of blossom, which was preternaturally beautiful even as it signaled grave environmental decay in the desert. I was blossoming too, and decaying somehow.

The sunrise in Las Vegas is bookended by replicas of replicas, what sociologist Jean Baudrillard identified as simulacra, a culture of infinite regress where the world rests on the back of a turtle who is herself atop another turtle. *Turtles all the way down.* On speedy nights saturated in booze and cigarettes and the kind of loop-de-loop rooftop monologues that accompany such dreamy conditions, I wondered aloud if the sunrise was, in fact, real. "In the future, they will knock down mountains to build casinos that look like mountains," I told my lover.

There was a particular sunrise, though, that swam in with the silence of stilted mornings and I knew at that moment I was pregnant. It had become intolerable to swing around a stripper pole. It felt like gravity was swallowing my swollen breasts. I'd convinced myself up until this point that my body was simply gearing up for an epic period or perhaps just tired from all the drugs. My lover was strung out beside me.

I can say with unwavering certainty that until this particular moment, the series of events I called "living" were merely loose ends, tied together with prurient, fleeting, and bodily interests. They suddenly seemed meaningless when measured against the pulsating anticipation of my child. And then, the emergent question—Mother *or* Whore? Was I a collection of seedy underbelly stories? Or an angelic mother, reborn with purpose?

I could no longer strip on a stage, so I marketed my pregnant body. I advertised my breast milk as a fetish but quickly recoiled from the enterprise upon meeting a man who wanted to make me his "submissive pregnant slave." He detailed his fantasy: as his slave, I would offer up my engorged tits whenever he pleased, from which he'd take his fill. I would bear his children and we—our children and me—would be his property.

My maternal body was still whorish to this man, still property. Sliced down the center of my personhood, I was to become singularly owned like a Madonna but publicly available like a Whore. It is this cultural inability to see sex working mothers as committed to our children *first and foremost*—this cultural desire that instead sees Whores as *Whores* first—that causes so much pain and aggression against our bodies and being.

BIFURCATION IS A form of violence. It shrinks femininity in size and raises it in pitch. We are asked to be accommodating, but to raise our voices an octave or two. Sex working parents are told, *Shrink your infinite unknowability for the pleasure of men or for the raising of your babies!* Bifurcation asks, *Does your body produce property inheritors, or does it produce pleasure?* It cannot produce both.

Sex workers have always produced pleasure—not pleasure for ourselves, of course, but for those who seek our services. Feminist movements have largely ignored sex workers for this reason—many assume that women who commercialize their bodies for pleasure are complicit in violence against other women. This approach assumes that sex workers are to blame for their own bifurcation. Sex working mothers are twice bifurcated, then. First as unsavory women, and then, in the eyes of other women, as administers of pain through the production of pleasure.

All of that happens in theory. In practice, this looks like sex working mothers losing their children to the state or to violent partners. It looks like sex working mothers engaging in riskier sex for fewer resources. It looks like sex working mothers leaving behind children, either through death or jail time or both. It looks like the ultimate form of violence: a fleshy, mental, and metaphysical kind of violence that burrows so deep it is reborn again and again in the cells of our children's children's children.

I AM A sort of tragicomical stereotype. I was sexually abused as a child, later abandoned, and repeatedly traumatized. I am unapologetic about my former drug use; I still occasionally take mushrooms because, *fuck it*. I have no qualms admitting that I downed a bunch of speed after defending my PhD dissertation. I am twice divorced. I am a mother.

I am the fucking personification of a cautionary tale.

The mixture of abuse, drugs, sex work, and motherhood makes a lot of people uncomfortable for many of the same reasons that sex workers are left out of mainstream movements toward mitigating violence against women: too much baggage ostensibly signals to civilians that perhaps sex workers are partially responsible for the ways we have been harmed. Sex working mothers are allowed social capital only if we renounce our multilayered experiences. It is a secular form of penance: the Mother must reject the Whore, and all her agency in her whoring, in order to be legally and socially accepted—*acceptable*—as Mother. We cannot say, "I took drugs to ease the pain" or "I sold sex to live" because a woman's pain, just like her will to survive, might implicate a man.

And so bifurcation is mandatory. We bifurcate our consciousness and split womanhood right down the center into "pure" women who can lay claim to victimization and "bad" women who cannot.

PETITE JASMINE WAS just one example of a "bad" woman. She worked as a full-service sex worker in Sweden and despite the father of her children having a collection of domestic violence charges, he was awarded sole custody of their children when the pair split. The court commented that working as an unapologetic sex worker was evidence enough of Jasmine's parental unfitness. She could not lay claim to victimization at the hands of her former partner just as she could not lay claim to her own children. Her refusal to bifurcate her consciousness cost her not only her offspring but her life. Jasmine's former partner and father to her children murdered her shortly after being awarded custody.

I knew this story, and other cautionary tales that sex workers share in the silence of our own homes, when I chose the man who would later become the father of my child. I knew all of these stories when the Mojave was exploding in blossom, when he lay trembling at my side, when my unborn child announced their presence under a desert morning sun.

I called another sex working friend and mother to say, "Holy fuck, girl. I'm pregnant." She had just one reply. "You better make sure he won't take you to court for being a whore."

Two short years after the birth of my child, I was told that the conservative midwestern court system would undoubtedly use my sex work as evidence of parental unfitness.

DISSOCIATION FEELS LIKE sinking inside yourself, watching as your flesh is suspended between two planes of reality; men are often the architects of these planes. Dissociation feels like being a citizen of nowhere, exposed to the elements of lawlessness as your body gets tangled up in things you don't understand. It's when you can *feel* the bifurcation.

"Are you now or have you ever been a prostitute?" the lawyer asked.

I fell silent and she repeated herself.

"I said, *Are you now or have you ever been a prostitute?*"

BAUDRILLARD ENJOYED Las Vegas, that impossible desert town, the way it seemed to unfold just for him, a submissive slave of a town, pregnant. Casino girls and LSD, the stifling brass body of the desert lends itself to an unlikely expansion. This place is not supposed to exist, but it does, so the people who live or visit or play under its canopy either expand or contract with the unlikeliness of it all. For Baudrillard, it was easy to sway with this impossibility. A writer and philosopher, language was the tool with which he explored the world, a world where he was an uncontested citizen. On the other side of the globe, Dorothy Smith felt language itself prosthetic—not unlikely, but unreal. For Smith, language was not a casino built to resemble a mountain. Language was, in the first place, a destruction of the natural landscape.

We must make space for the feminine self that is both agent and victim, empowered and marginalized, Mother and Whore all at the same time. We must interrogate space and language as static and as neutral. We must dismantle the imperative to squeeze women into a singular point of existence, whether that point is sexual or maternal or something else entirely. If we are coerced into choosing between Mother *or* Whore, then our complexity is whittled down and the beneficiary of that belittling is patriarchal. If we are left out of conversations about violence, then it is assumed we cannot be victims of violence.

I AM INFINITELY unknowable like the dark and scarred crevasses of my body.

I have been harmed by men; I have loved them.

My body has been a space of both creation and destruction, sometimes at the exact same time.

I endure the threat of violence, even as some feminists claim that I am immune to pain.

I *endure*.

I am Mother *and* Whore.

# Sex Working While Jewish in America

ARABELLE RAPHAEL

Being the person that I am is not easy in the United States right now. It's not easy for my friends, my family, or millions of Black people, Jews, and LGBTQI people.

I'm an Iranian, Tunisian, French, and Jewish sex worker. I'm queer, a drug user, and a sexual abuse survivor. I immigrated from France to the United States as a child. I still hold a large amount of privilege; my skin is light, unlike that of many of my family members, and I am a high-income sex worker. With that, I'm still confronted with Islamophobia—many people assume I'm Muslim because I'm Middle Eastern—and anti-Semitism both in my personal and professional lives.

I was raised with Judaism but I'm a secular Jew. I'm a Hebrew school dropout. My feelings about religion are very complicated and, honestly, it often makes me quite uncomfortable. Every time I walk around New York and see white Hasidic Jews, I feel otherness—we are culturally different and I'm not a nice Jewish girl—as well as a connection to them.

The thing that makes me feel most Jewish is knowing how much people hate us. People hate them as people hate me. I've been to Nazi death camps and I remember looking at a flyer in one camp's museum. There were excerpts from a pamphlet the Nazis passed out during the war. It was titled *How to Spot a Jew*, containing several highly racist caricatures presented as what to look out for. Those racist caricatures all looked like me. I don't need to have religious garb on to be recognized as Jewish, and I still see those caricatures being used in reactionary media today.

I've been conflicted about saying anything about anti-Semitism under my work persona. I struggle with being politically vocal while still trying to make money and remain appealing to clients.

But when I'm faced with these prejudices at work, being silent gets complicated. I feel like I've lost. My racial identities come up too often at work to ignore. I once posted a photo online of myself post–menstrual sex, and someone's response was, "Now I know why Hitler gassed the Jews." People frequently point out my big nose. I've been called a "terrorist," "camel pussy," and "kike" on client-facing social media quite a bit.

When I was younger and new to sex work, I was afraid to set boundaries and money was scarce, so I took jobs that I wouldn't take now that I'm in a better financial situation. I think all performers of color are faced with this experience. I've been in a movie called *Women of the Middle East* and have been cast as a belly dancer many times. I was always given the information that I would be participating in a racial fetish scene only after I had traveled, paid for testing, been booked, etc. I've had a director make jokes about needing machine guns as props for Middle Eastern vibes, and I've had to fuck a white man as he was in a turban wearing black eyeliner. Clients and fans still ask me to wear hijabs.

I'm afraid of racist attacks when doing in-person sex work. Sometimes I see clients and have fans who support Trump. They are fine consuming my sexual labor but do not care about my safety or my rights, or they look at me like they would an "exotic" bird or rug.

The Far Right thinks pornography is a Jewish conspiracy to turn white men into cuckolds. In contrast, I've had many deep conversations and connections with my Middle Eastern clients. I don't see that side of my family much. I do not have the Irani community present in my life. I was even outed as a sex worker by my cousin to the Irani side of the family after I posted an anti-Zionist article on Facebook. Middle Eastern clients are one of the very few ties to the culture I have besides my family.

My work doesn't escape the realities of identity, racism, and anti-Semitism—that is not a privilege I have.

I've seen many articles on the rise of anti-Semitic harassment popping up in the news. As a stereotypically Jewish-looking sex worker, this is nothing new to me. I've spoken a lot about how sex workers get to see human beings without their social masks on. Sex workers of color have known for quite some time just how prejudiced and racist people are. Many clients feel no need to pretend around us. Many people, including Jews, were surprised when the Tree of Life synagogue shooting happened in Pittsburgh in October 2018, but many of us knew it was only a matter of time. It doesn't make it less painful.

The Israeli government's response to the shootings wasn't a surprise either, and it proved that they don't actually care about Jews—surprise, their priority is colonialism! In 2018 Israeli leftist leader Avi Gabbay said the attack should inspire "the Jews of the United States to immigrate more and more to Israel, because this is their home." Then it was widely reported that Israel's Ashkenazi chief rabbi refused to use the word "synagogue" to describe the Tree of Life, because it is not Orthodox but Conservative, part of one of the more progressive branches of Judaism rejected by the Israeli state's definitions of Jewishness. It turned out that this was a distortion of what the rabbi had actually said, but the divisions this misreporting revealed run deep—Israeli Orthodoxy has often disavowed Conservative, Reform, and Reconstructionist Jewish practice, alienating millions of Jews. Naftali Bennett, the Diaspora Affairs Minister at the time, visited the United States only to offend American Jews by implying that anti-Semitism is overblown here and we have nothing to fear. He also staunchly defended Trump, the person responsible for inciting these white nationalist attacks in the first place. Israel chose its political ties over American Jews. It is more interested in furthering white supremacy.

Israel did not show up for Jews, but you know who did? Two Muslim organizations, Celebrate Mercy and MPower Change, raised more than $130,000 for the victims of the attack and their families. This has been my only sliver of hope—hope that Jews, Muslims, people of color, and gay and trans people create ties. Hope that marginalized communities will fight back, that we will acknowledge that our communities intersect and that we have no choice but to fight for each other's rights.

That being said, I hope such unity will include sex workers. The sad fact is that sex workers also need to fight for legitimacy within their intersectional communities even as we all are forced to fight white nationalism. It's quite a lot of work to do simultaneously, but the only thing we can do in order to continue to survive is to try.

*A version of this piece was originally published on* Tits and Sass *on November 5, 2018.*

## How to Not Be an Asshole When Your
## Sex Worker Partner Is Assaulted at Work

MAGGIE McMUFFIN

All right folks, there's no sugarcoating it: people get sexually assaulted. Some of those people are sex workers. While you of course want to be there for your loved one right after an assault, it's all too easy to let the internalized stigma against sex workers cloud the conversation and the language we use to discuss it. Based on experiences with my exes, my coworkers, and other people's partners, here is a quick list of how to be supportive when clients go bad:

### 1. DO NOT BLAME THE JOB

People are assaulted all the time. Sex work also intersects with every other marginalized identity, which means the chance for assault goes up. Have I been assaulted by clients? Yes. I have also been assaulted by lovers, partners, and friends. But an assault does not mean you should give up on relationships, marriage, or movie nights.

It is not sex work's fault that sex workers are assaulted. It is the fault of people who choose to assault sex workers and a society that considers sex workers less than human.

### 2. DO NOT GO VIGILANTE

It is understandable to be angry that someone hurt someone you love. But railing about how you need to know who did this so you can beat them up is making it about you. Someone you care about was just assaulted. The last thing they need is to start talking you down from your feelings.

### 3. HAVE YOUR OWN SUPPORT SYSTEM

You are allowed to have feelings here. You are not allowed to make the person who was just assaulted perform emotional labor for you. Talking about how their assault has affected you can heap guilt onto your partner at a time when they already feel awful. This is, again, making it about you.

But just because you aren't throwing all of these emotions on your partner does not mean you should suppress those emotions. You may feel helpless. You may feel like a bad partner. You may— regardless of your gender identity—be dealing with some shades of toxic masculinity that you're ashamed to face. This all happens. Find someone who can be there for you personally or profession- ally. Have someone who you can talk to who will be sympathetic to what you're feeling.

### 4. BE THERE

Sometimes all someone wants is their partner to be there for them. It may feel ineffectual to hold someone while they continue to cry, but if they asked you to come over and that's all they've asked for, then keep doing that.

Yes, you will eventually have to leave. Yes, you may have to can- cel some plans. It's okay. As long as you are doing the one thing that was requested of you, that's fine. Chances are you don't have the resources to actually take care of anything else. Which brings me to the final point . . .

### 5. LET THE SEX WORKERS HANDLE THIS

We have multiple whisper networks: bad date websites, black- lists, email chains—hell, even just texting photos and information to our closest peers. These are resources that a civilian will not have.

You may have noticed that *nowhere in this did I say to call the cops*. This is because in most places, a sex worker cannot report an assault without fear of being arrested (also sex workers are statistically far more likely to be assaulted by law enforcement than clients). In most places, law enforcement won't even believe us; this is how serial killers like Gary Ridgway could operate for years. Because of this, sex workers have developed ways to seek our own justice and safety.

## SO WHAT CAN YOU DO?

If you really want to help, then start before assaults happen. Speak up when someone tells a dead hooker joke. Call out your friends when they slap a woman's ass at the bar. Destroy the idea that seeing a sex worker is more of a taboo than killing one. If women say they're uncomfortable around your friend, don't just insist he's "really a good guy." These clients are your brothers, friends, fathers, roommates . . . and if they get to a point where they assault someone, then there were a million ways you could have stepped up before then. You cannot be upset at strangers who hurt people you love, but ignore when people you love hurt strangers.

But most of all, talk about it. Not as a badge of honor for being the best ally, but because it is a reality we have to live with. Violence against us is a direct consequence of stigma, and in attempting to combat that stigma we often paint pretty pictures that downplay the ugly parts. If you're going to date us then you need to join us in confronting that stigma and you must remember to love us even when things get rough.

*Originally published on* Slutist *on January 29, 2018.*

# THE STATE

## How to Rape a Sex Worker

AK SAINI

### FANTASY

Richard was my favorite client. He hired me twice a month and paid extra to pretend to rape me. He enjoyed the struggle but I refused to risk injury by staging a fight. My body is not in small part how I earn my income. Moreover, there is an element of trauma, even when you know it's pretend. The extra money would not compensate for the lost income I would endure if I found myself physically or emotionally immobilized by his fantasy.

We negotiated scenarios that played more to my interests: submission, taboo, and the lazy luxury of playing unconscious on the job. We played make-believe that he slipped a drug into my drink, that he used a rag of chloroform to force me to sleep. Once, he got creative and used his doctor privileges to supply needles for a staged injection. When he pulled them out of his bag mid-session I panicked without breaking character. I wrenched the still-packaged needles from his hands and threw them into the abyss of a bedroom dimmed for seductive effect. He could not know, I rationalized, of my needle phobia. He represented too much of my income to even consider ending the session. When I raised the issue of my phobia during our post-session pillow-talk debrief, his response was simply, "I figured." I told him in the future I don't want any more surprises.

He complied. For a while. Until, like many men, he chose to stop complying. A few sessions later I was splayed wide with my hands tied above my head. He placed an exposed switchblade on my chest in between my two breasts bouncing from the cowardly force of his fucking. I knew he would not hurt me and yet I knew he already had.

FETISH

The best and worst thing about working at an agency is that you never talk to the client until he shows up at your door. The "agency girl" takes care of answering phone calls and booking your clients. You'd like to think the agency girls thoroughly screen everyone but you also know that they work mostly—if not entirely—off of commission, so their primary goal is to close the deal. She will likely never meet you—much less care about you—and probably feel little to no accountability for whatever happens to you as long as she gets her cut.

When my agency girl tries to set me up with a trick that I don't want, it turns into a grudge match. "I've got a great client for you," she says as a preface to giving me a client that she knows I'll find undesirable. "An easy domination guy." I don't do domination. She knows this about me, and I know she knows this about me, but I tell her again. "Oh c'mon," she says. "You don't even have to *do* anything. Just hit him and call him names. You really want to say no to easy money?"

Yes, I reiterate, I really want to say no to "easy" money. I don't explain why or why not, I never explain why or why not—it should be enough for her to know my boundary. She responds too quickly that it's all good and he will come see me anyway, meaning she went ahead and booked him without telling him anything about my boundaries, and I would just have to deal.

"I don't do domination." As soon as he walks through the door I tell him and can see in the expression on his face that he was not informed of this fact prior to arrival. "Oh c'mon," he says. "You don't even have to *do* anything. Just hit me and call me names. You really want to say no to easy money?"

Yes, I reiterate, I really want to say no to "easy" money. He responds too quickly that it's all good and let's do the session anyway, meaning he will spend the next hour pushing my boundaries, and I would just have to deal. But I don't do domination; it triggers memories of child abuse, so I tell him to leave.

There is a glint in his eye, and with it I now know that he's folded my resistance into his fetish. He says he won't leave, asks me what am I going to do about it, tells me he won't leave unless I do something about it. He reaches into me to extract the rage he wanted all along, using a combination of aggressive obnoxiousness—repeating that he wouldn't go no matter what I said—and passive-aggressive feigned ignorance—pretending he didn't understand that I ordered him to leave at all. I know what he is doing, and I know he knows I know what he's doing, but it is still working.

Finally I give in, everything blurs, I am my father, I am the abuser, I hit until he is on the floor, then I kick and kick, until I am sick and sick wells up from inside and overflows along with the rage, and I vomit and vomit. He leaves satisfied. He tips extra for the vomit.

## BAREBACK

The wealthiest people are the ones who will haggle with you the most. This one is relentless. I wrench an hour-long booking from him with a fifty-dollar discount. For screening purposes, he provides his name and instructs that I call him through the front desk at the Four Seasons to confirm it is real. It checks out.

He doesn't seem as much of an asshole in person. He sports a long mustache curled at both ends. He spends the first half of our session telling me of his rise from the slums to riches.

Once in bed he immediately tries to enter me bareback. I block him with one hand and use the other to toss a condom at his dick, which is instantaneously rendered flaccid. "But why can't I??" I just glare at him. "Please??"

I tell him either fuck me with a condom on or I'm leaving, and I make it clear that even that is a gift. "Okay, fine," he says, and turns me onto my side to spoon. I let him rub his raw cock between my asscheeks long enough for him to get hard and then reach back to put on the condom with or without his support. I feel his erection fizzle again, him fumbling to jack it hard again, eventually giving up, removing the condom, and again trying to enter me bareback. "Are you fucking serious!?" I exclaim and pick up the semi-used condom to slap him with it several times in the face. Furious, I dress, take my money, and leave while he pleads with down-turned eyes for me to stay and pretend what he did was not a violation.

I get to the exit and realize my coat is still upstairs. I consider leaving it up there in spite of subzero Toronto winter temperatures, but my phone is in the pocket. I never want to see him and his stupid mustache again, but my phone is the foundation of my business.

I can't remember his room number. I am in shock. *This is what shock feels like*, I contemplate at this most inappropriate moment, *you can't remember basic things like the number of the room in which you were just sexually assaulted*. I go to the front desk and ask that they direct me up to his room. I am visibly shaken and stuttering about my missing coat with the phone in the pocket. The front desk person calls up and, to both our surprise, he agrees to have me come back up to collect my coat.

When I get back to him, he is waiting at the door with my coat and a look of guilt, but not remorse. He is sad that he was caught and about the potential consequences. He says he is sorry for upsetting me and wishes me the best. The shock has yet to wear off, I think, so I just grab my coat and go.

A couple months later I am with my "Captain-Save-A-Ho" client. A "Good Guy"™ who asks with saccharine concern whether

I've ever been raped in this line of work, as if discussing such topics in the company of virtual strangers is the kind of intimacy for
which you can pay. I shrug, shake my head no, and say, "That must
be awful, though. I'm thankful it's never happened to me."

When the Captain is in the shower, I glance over to the bedside
table and see Stupid Mustache staring back at me from the cover of
a magazine, featured as a paragon of the Horatio Alger Myth of the
American Dream™, an immigrant who built himself up from the
working-class slums of his home country in the Third World™ to
becoming one of the wealthiest people on the planet.

## ENFORCEMENT

He emails saying he wants to see me for the whole night at the Ritz.
He says he doesn't have references but I can meet him at the bar
in lieu of screening. Typically I require at least one reference from
another escort to verify that the client is safe but I am too broke to
be picky so agree even though I know no legitimate client would
book at the Ritz (the room is too expensive to waste on a date with
a hooker you've never met) and I doubt this will end well.

Without the luxury of feeling overwhelmed, I navigate the
chandeliers and marble of the expansive Ritz lobby to the hotel
bar with an artifice of self-confidence. I saddle up beside the one
single man that I profile as my guy—dressed business casual and
conspicuously alone among a panel of couples—and ask him if he
is waiting to meet me. He says no, he is not who I think he is, but
let's have a drink. I tell him no thank you, I'm waiting on someone,
and relocate to a seat on the other side of the bar. Over the course
of the next hour, diners ebb and flow from the surrounding stools,
none of them there for me, and it becomes clear that he is almost
certainly my guy. I sit back down beside him and ask, "Are you sure
you're not looking for me?"

Again he says no but with the open-ended intonation of someone with an agenda. He's too calculating to be a trick. *He's a cop*, I

realize on a subconscious level. I can't let myself know this in real life because I want the money bad.

We spar back and forth about whether he will buy me dinner or if we will proceed directly to his room. Of course, he needs to not have dinner with me, because it muddles the prostitution charge the more it looks like we are on a date rather than a simple exchange of sex for money. And he needs me to name my price, to solicit him, because the criminal justice system will call what he's doing to me entrapment only in the narrow circumstance that he explicitly proposes we engage in criminal prostitution. Still not having named a price, I follow him up to his room. I rationalize I am safe as long I don't initiate anything, knowing full well that this idealized sense of safety is a chimera in a reality of crooked cops.

On the couch of his suite at the Ritz, my mind's eye confirms everything my conscious mind was denying: this is a sting operation. They were, and are, common in Michigan. Exhausted, worn down by the dance we were doing, the swirling temptation of a payoff in the context of poverty, I name a price. I mutter it, let it trail off my tongue at the end of a run-on sentence.

He leans in and asks me to confirm my fate, "Did you say you want XXX dollars for us to spend the night?" Everything stops now, whirs to a halt. I disassociate and float overhead to observe the situation. From this bird's eye view I can see the rest of his team poised to act in the adjoining bedroom of the suite. I could see that they might take turns raping me before taking me to the station, where they would realize I am an undocumented immigrant and I would face the threat of deportation or jail time, or jail time followed by deportation. I saw my life further unravel from there into homelessness and, when there was finally nothing left, suicide. I was not going out like that, I decided, and sprang into action.

I knew the story of Sodom and Gomorrah. I knew that if I stopped to look back at the scene of sin, these ignorable boars foraging for an innocent kill, I would dissolve into a pillar of salt, finished. And I knew, just as when you are dealing with a wild animal, not to run away or signify fear.

I walked briskly out of the suite and down the hall as his calls for me to return burned into my back. I willed the elevator to arrive before he could catch up to me and before I could look back or run or signify fear. I didn't look at myself in the mirrored elevator; I just stared at the numbers as they approached "G" for the ground floor and when the doors opened I kept my pace and gaze forward, nodded goodbye to the concierge, and pushed forward to the parking lot. *Good I didn't valet my car,* I thought, *otherwise . . .*

But I couldn't consider that, couldn't look back, couldn't signify fear.

## Victim-Defendant: Women of Color
## Complicating Stories about Human Trafficking

CHRISTA MARIE SACCO

Current discourse around prostitution forces people who work in the sex industries to identify as either passive victims of sexual slavery, or as happy and empowered sex workers. The following stories are intended to envision sex worker self-determination for the purposes of building new social identities that honor our embodied and experiential ways of knowing. They challenge the victimized/empowered binary.

The three vignettes that follow are partially fictionalized accounts of real people in real situations, each of which, according to current definitions in a US context, could be considered "human trafficking victims." They consist of my own narrative of sex work and critical feminist ethnographies of others. They are partially fictionalized to protect those involved; there could be consequences for survival if street workers come forward for a standard interview. Character vignettes illustrate the issues faced by these populations while also protecting research participants who have little to gain and much to lose from openly and directly telling their stories. I collected these stories as a peer member in various support circles of people with experience in the sex industries, as well as various annual and one-time events for current and former sex workers, including dinners, summits, and vigils. I also collected stories through my professional role as an outreach worker, group facilitator, advocate, and peer counselor for women with experiences in the sex industries at a local rape crisis center, as well as participation on Los Angeles's human trafficking task forces. These stories are meant to provide a counternarrative to mainstream accounts of human trafficking.

These sketches are the stories of at least three real people whom the media, social service providers, or legal professionals might label as human trafficking victims or survivors. However, when we hear their stories, they present complex identities and define themselves very differently than the media hysteria surrounding them does. They identify as a singer, a ho, a student, an entertainer, a hustler, a condom lady, and more. Each person I have met in the sex industries has their own worldview, their own world, their own ethics and imagination, and we who wish to learn from them have to take time to appreciate the nuance and the wisdom in their different perspectives. After the sketches, I have included a conclusion to this essay that puts the narratives into a framework for understanding why mainstream narratives about human trafficking "victim-defendants" harm women of color like those whose voices can be heard here.

## SMOKE BREAK, 2017

I'm just here in the park smoking. Haven't seen a trick in the park since the early morning. I think the last tipo was from Guatemala or somewhere like that. Not that that matters anymore. All that matters is he came quick. I want to go take a break but I can't leave the park right now. Even though it's not really safe in the park anymore. I haven't felt the same since Lucy died. I feel fucked up now. I have this repeat dream now, like there's some urgent crisis that I am forgetting about and sometimes I'm in the back seat of a car that has no driver. Lucy got stabbed to death by a rapist in the park. I think I was in a car with someone when it happened. She probably thought he was a trick. He slit her throat wide open. The day we all found out, the cops came and questioned us about it. We tried to hold a little vigil for her in the park a couple nights later. The condom lady came. She was the only one. We're not really safe to talk to anyone else. Now, when I don't feel safe at night, I talk to Lucy.

I glance over toward the bus stop and there she is, the condom lady sitting on the bench like a fuckin' mirage or something. I learned that in eighth grade. We had this science teacher who told us about mirages and shit. Sometimes I feel like I'm *in* a mirage and I'm just gonna wisp away like vapor if people come too close. Fuck if I don't need some condoms right now, but I don't want to approach her. My folks is watchin'. Then I see the end of my cigarette getting small and I think, *Might be worth it to see if she has a cigarette*. So I throw my eyes over at her and catch her attention and lean toward the bus station. She doesn't nod back or anything, but I know that she understood and sure enough after a few minutes, she starts to shuffle off to the bus station. She gets there and leans up against a bench and lights up a cigarette. As I watch her smoke, she kind of reminds me of some of those cholas on my old block. After I approach and ask for a cigarette, I stand a little away from her and we face away from the park so no one can see that we are talking. Just sharing a smoke, waiting on the bus.

I saw her get stopped by the cops the other week. They fucked wit her and asked for her ID and work badge and questioned her like she was breaking the law. Then she said they told her some shit about how she has to keep those condoms hidden away, and if she gives them out, only one or two at a time and the person who receives them has to put it away immediately, otherwise it's solicitation. Fucked up that this little piece of latex that saves lives could become such a deadly weapon in the hands of the puercos.

I can't afford to get stopped. I'm not eighteen yet and for us underage girls what we get is worse than jail sometimes. At least in jail you eventually get out. I don't ever want to go back to another placement again. By the time I got out of the last one and was able to come back to the neighborhood, I had to pay dues before they let me back in. I had to swear I never told those motherfuckers anything. They made me do things, I had to prove to them, you know. If the cops get me again, they will drag me back to one of those child-molester homes. They call it "AWOLing." Like I'm a soldier who left the battlefield, but I'm not. I'm just a ho. I got a fake ID now but some of 'em know who I am. They want to rescue me and shit and have me snitch, but they can't protect me from the people who would come for me. They don't even have a decent place for me to live to get me off the streets. They're bullshit.

One of the girls I work with is twenty and she got a ticket. She said they won't help you unless you snitch your people out and they never offered her the classes. They said it was 'cause she had priors. She said she will probably never get her kids back by the time she gets out this life. There's a trans girl who works with us too. I saw her get into it physically with some punk who tried to rob her in the park last night and I was thinkin' like, *Damn, I wish I was trans.* But sometimes shit happens to her in that park that I'm like, *Damn, at least I'm not trans.* And then, *no mames,* when they are always throwing her in jail with all those big hairy mens. First thing they do is snatch the wig off. It's like they see a Black woman or a trans woman walking and they just can't wait to snatch her wig off, for whatever reason or no reason at all. Guess that's why we started sewing 'em in. Weave, motherfuckers, what you know about that!

The condom lady's bus came before my cigarette finished. She managed to slip me some condoms and cigarettes before she left. She is kind of slick with it in a way that lets me know she's been on the streets before, and I'm left to finish smoking in silence and a little bit of peace washes over me.


## MOVING ON PIZZA PARTY, 2019

Oh hey hun, thanks for coming. Did you get the soda? I don't know if there's any pizza left, but the cupcakes should be here any minute. I used to live off these fucking cupcakes. I would eat two of 'em every day. That was when I was homeless, I would just walk and walk and walk. Everywhere. Now I got 'em delivering these cupcakes to me, and I told 'em, "You gotta call when they get here," 'cause I live in a Catholic home for women now.

Okay ladies, thank you for coming to my pizza party. I'm René! I think most of yas I know—no wait maybe some of yas I don't know yet—but anyways I'm René and I just wanted to do something nice for you ladies since Friday is my last day here.

*Sing! Sing something!*

What? Okay, I'll sing something. What do you want me to sing? I'm really a singer.

*Are you a celebrity, Miss René? You never know, she could be a celebrity.*

No, I'm not a celebrity. I can sing though. I got a standing ovation at the Apollo on amateur night. That's in Harlem. That was pretty much the highlight of my career. Then I went to Vegas. Yeah I'm from Vegas!

*I heard you make a lot of money in Vegas!*

Yeah, that's about the only good thing about Vegas: the money! Everything's different there, it sucks. The cops, the cops are different in Vegas too. I used to live in this building, you know, one day I was coming home and I saw this girl outside crying and her nose was all bloody. And the cops showed up and they found her boyfriend and they had him out in front of the building and they asked 'em, "Did you do this to her?" He said yea and they beat the shit out of him. I mean they beat the *shit* out of him. As they're leaving they asked me, "You okay sweetie?" I said I didn't see nothin'. They said, "Yea we know you didn't. You okay though?" I said yeah I'm okay.

Huh? Okay what do you want me to sing? I'll sing some Mariah Carey.

*Ooo. I love Mariah Carey!*

"'Hero,'" that's my song. *"There's a hero . . . if you look inside your heart . . . you don't have to be afraid of who you are . . ."* Thank you. Thank you. What? No, I can't chew it. I need to go to the dentist.

I'm supposed to be in the studio on Saturday. I told 'em, "My teeth hurt, you gotta wait till I can sing again." They said, "I don't care, you can really sing, I want you in the studio."

*Do you have a boyfriend?*

No, you know, I've had a few husbands and I love love. I've always loved love. But I love me more now. You see these legs? I made a lotta fuckin money on these legs. I'm forty-six.

*You look great!*

Oh thank you. Yea, these legs made me a lot of money. I been every kinda dancer there is: jazz dancer, tap dancer, club dancer, showgirl, exotic dancer, nude dancer. The young girls used to come up to me in the strip clubs, the new ones, and try to tell me their name and I'd tell 'em, "Sweetheart, please, don't tell me your name, 'cause in a few days, you'll be on coke and on your back. So just try to stay not dead!"

Oh, hold on, I think it's the cupcakes! Hello? Hello? Yes. Okay thank you. They're here ladies! They're here! I'll be right back!

Do you want chocolate or vanilla? Chocolate? The chocolate ones are more moist, but the vanilla ones are really good too! You still want chocolate? Okay, here take a vanilla one too! I want yas all to try both and we'll leave the extras on the counter for the others, you can eat 'em all night. Do you want more soda?

*Yeah I'll take a hit!*

Here you go. Have a little more soda. Do you want more soda?

*Yeah, René, pass that Courvoisier!*

How about you, do you want more soda?


PUTTING ON MY FACE IN THE MORNING, 2008

Oh good, I still have a little time to finish getting ready before I'm late for class. I split the Xanax in half before I take it 'cause it's still morning and I'm already fucked up. But I need that little half though, things are getting too heavy. When I go to pick up, I will need the shit just so I will be able to tolerate Keni's ass and put on the face. I'm not sure how I got this deep in, I was just trying to make enough to pay rent and stay in school, now I'm flippin SIM cards on the reg and moving fluidly through the city from the flea market on Northwest Seventy-Ninth to the high-rises on Brickell. Shit is complicated. I kind of wish I could go back or slow it down some, but everything is already in motion. Everything is leading up to tonight, then I hopefully won't have to work for a while. I wasn't even gonna do this one. I didn't even tell them I got hired to work that after-hours party to the Bacardi gala, but they found out. Or maybe I got hired because of them. Anyways, I'm committed now. The goal is to get to the pad on Brickell by ten p.m. to pick up and get dressed. I just have one stop to make after class. I want the white sunflowers. That's my spiritual side hustle. It's like my gift to Miami, giving back to all the travelers on the sexual underground. Purest X you'll ever find.

I remember how I got involved like this with Keni. I had gone on a tear after getting paid for my last gig and ended up robbed and bleeding on the curb in the middle of the night in a bad part of town with no memory of how I had arrived there or with who. Knowing myself, I probably split from whoever I was with in a hostile way and came by myself trying to score. There are only a few people who will come far to pick you up in questionable places in the middle of the night, no questions asked. I definitely wasn't gonna call anyone from school, not that I had that many friends from school to call anyway. So I called Keni. I met him a while back with my friend at a weekly amateur striptease contest that she liked to be a contender in. We had spent a lot of time late nights, so I knew he wouldn't be asleep. When I got in the car, he saw I was upset and I explained that I had blown all my rent money. He quickly presented a solution, said if I come work for him, I will never have to worry about rent again. He said all I have to do is bring his product into "all those crazy sex parties I hustle at." I told him I wasn't sure about if I was gonna get another gig like that any time soon because networks had changed. The last time I worked with those folks, I left in a bad way and Nico is back in the Dominican right now. He said, "You never know, baby, you could get another gig tomorrow. We do all kinds of things."

Holy shit, that phrase, that simple phrase: "We do all kinds of things." That changed my life in so many ways. Now, when I free-style by myself on South Beach, I use that phrase and it unlocks so many doors for me. "What do you do?" "I do all kinds of things. Que te interesa?"

The next day, after he spoke that prophecy over my life, a man in a suit approached me while I was having a square lunch with a square friend. Of course, I know now that Keni sent him, but at the time I was caught off guard. I thought it was divine intervention. He gave me his card and what do you know? When I called he had a gig for me. And after that gigs were steady, and I made so many contacts that I felt I almost didn't even need Keni anymore, but always I was able to slide his coke like a credit card to gain entry wherever I wanted. With Keni, I make money just by being on the scene. The party host or production company would hire us to be there or be available or perform, not to mention extras. There's real value in being involved in that way and the key is *relationships*. It is all connected. Not that everyone is nice to each other all the time, there's plenty of smaller power struggles. But in terms of economics, everyone works together. If you make money, they make money. If you do well, they do even better.

I still do feel the pull of my DNA to follow my ancestral purpose and find love, but that shit just has very little to do with my survival right now. It keeps going. It has to keep going. In order for me to stay in it, everything has to just keep going. It's out of my hands now. My only escape, besides when I have to be on campus doing data entry, is when I'm rolling or when I'm lost in time. 'Cause I black out for days at a time sometimes on that Xanax, but they give me the three-for-fives so I feel special. There's always another trick, there's always another cash deal, there's always another gig, another pound to move, another filthy rich foreign businessman, another score, another party. More . . . more . . . more, more, more! It's exhausting. Sometimes I cry a lot. Sometimes I just sleep for days. Maybe I'll have time to sleep a little before I pull this last job.

## CONCLUSIONS

People with experiences in the sex industries are a lot like other everyday people, only more fabulous. We are just doing the best we can with fucked-up circumstances. This is especially true for the more marginalized realms of the sex industries that live deep in the shadows, which some people might think of as trafficking. Due to the legacies of white supremacy, cisgenderism, and heteropatriarchy, society is unable to recognize the dignity of those people who are experienced in the sex industries.

A significant number of people who become human trafficking survivors do not initially consider themselves as such. Many only learn about the definition of human trafficking after they have initial contact with law enforcement. Many of the major human trafficking or commercial sexual exploitation service organizations in Los Angeles get referrals solely from police and obtain or recruit clients by doing police ride-alongs and collaborating with law enforcement and district attorneys on prosecutions. The receipt of coercive services, like an emergency shelter to get you "off the streets," depends upon your cooperation with law enforcement and prosecution—including sometimes testifying in court. Testimony is negotiated in exchange for "diversion," i.e., removal of the ticket and the permanent criminal charge. Thus, it is law enforcement who plays the central role in deciding who are victims and who are criminals, and how emergency services are distributed.

The 2017 revision to the Trafficking Victims Protection Act stipulates that the only way to gain federal funding through the Office of Emergency Services for the provision of holistic services to trafficking victims is to convene a local human trafficking task force led by law enforcement agencies. It also bars any organization using the language of sex work or decriminalization from receiving said funding for "holistic services." This means that in order to access services, an individual or organization must come into contact with the police. Law enforcement agencies have placed themselves on the forefront of human trafficking interventions, using this cause to police the sexual, political, economic, and migration choices of women and other vulnerable groups, like gender nonconforming people, youth, and immigrants. Both the FBI and Homeland Security have offices within the Human Trafficking Bureau of the LA Sherriff's Office. In addition, "victims" are subject to a filmed police interview, in most cases before they have access to an advocate. In comparison, sexual assault victims are protected by penal codes which give them the right to have an advocate present when they report the crimes against them.

It becomes crucial that the authorities verify potential survivors as legitimate victims before they can access any official services related to trauma recovery or victim compensation. The authorities have solidified their place in the victim-defendant-survivor pipeline, which they themselves created. It is not impossible, but very unlikely for anyone to get services or victim compensation unless they have documented police cooperation. For example, I am familiar with two stories of older women who later discovered they had been victims of human trafficking and were turned away from case management by several diversion services because they did not have police referrals. Their response was to start their own alternative and culturally-authentic programs to mentor survivors. Furthermore, the belief that law enforcement deploying state-sanctioned violence is the only legitimate response to the complex problem of human trafficking—a problem rooted in centuries of racism, colonization, and financial exclusion—is an extremely problematic and deadly stance for many groups vulnerable to criminalization and mass incarceration.

The consequences of being on record as a human trafficking victim-defendant, even if testifying to obtain services or expungement, range between mandated classes, years of surveillance by the court system, an arrest record that follows you forever, child welfare or custody issues, immigration issues and detention, and additional charges for related crimes such as drug possession—which can further damage employment opportunities, family unification, or the ability to participate in government funding for college through FASFA.[1] Other crime victims or crime witnesses are not systematically coerced and bullied in this way. This is all in addition to the danger of being forced to testify against your trafficker in court, likely without witness protection. The nature of sex work in coercive environments that can be mediated by criminal networks makes it dangerous if not deadly for a person to disclose that they want out, who their traffickers are, or that they are being exploited—even once legal or criminal justice repercussions are removed for that person. But the current discourse only transitions that person from criminal to victim if they make that life-endangering "choice."

For economic, relational, and survival reasons, it often doesn't make sense to testify against a trafficker, since emergency homeless shelters hardly seem like a viable alternative for many. Not to mention that police have a track record of being abusive, racist, homophobic, and transphobic with sex workers and are not seen as an authentic source of relief or escape from the sex industries. So, if you are waiting for someone "in need of help" to tell you that they are a human trafficking survivor, or to go looking for a police referral for "services," it is possible that you are missing the boat completely.

There is no one-size-fits-all solution to trafficking. But we can stop trying to place people involved in the sex industries in categories of "guilty" or "innocent," leaving all of us prey to intersecting categories like "victim-defendant" that force us to cooperate with law enforcement despite great collateral consequences. Sex workers' life histories offer voices of resistance to these very structures that seek to control and define them. Sex workers construct their occupational fields as sites of resistance to stigma and criminalization. We need to listen to them and support their existence, rather than trying to define them out of existence.

## NOTES

1. Meredith Dank, Jennifer Yahner, and Lilly Yu, *Consequences of Policing Prostitution: An Analysis of Individuals Arrested and Prosecuted for Commercial Sex in New York City*, Urban Institute, April 2017, https://www. urban.org/sites/default/files/publication/89451/legal_aid_final_0.pdf.

*The author has developed these characters into a full-length solo theater performance called* Don't Tell Me Your Name, *which is performed live for social justice and training purposes.*

## Hustling Survival

BRIT SCHULTE
with contributions from
JUDY SZURGOT and ALISHA WALKER

Incarcerated survivors have had little to no voice in mainstream movements against sexual violence. This is an unacceptable elision, as sex workers—who too often face both sexual violence and incarceration—have among the most nuanced and considered senses of consent in sexual encounters, whether transactional or personal. Those in the trade ought to be some of the first to whom we look for insight into combatting sexual violence both inside and outside the criminal legal system. Judy and Alisha, two formerly and currently incarcerated sex working and survival-hustling women, lend their voices to this book to find a place for themselves in building the movements against sexual violence.

WHEN I WAS forwarded Judy's petition and affidavit, I had to read it almost a dozen times. I couldn't believe it. I actually thought the case details had been typed incorrectly. I reread it aloud. As someone who's worked on popular defense campaigns of criminalized survivors, I should not have been surprised. The system of punishment is working exactly as designed: to punish cash-poor women, to punish Black people, to punish drug-using people, to punish sex working folx. To punish survivors.

Judy and I started our letters frequently by sharing favorite quotes of inspiration and hope. Our correspondence had an intentional positivity that at times strained against the respective terrors

72

on either side of the wall. I signed her up for the Sex Workers Outreach Project (SWOP) Behind Bars newsletter, which she was eager to receive. She wrote to me about missing her daughter most of all, about the separation being unbearable. Being connected to community on the outside, coupled with a larger-than-life imagination, helped Judy distance herself from the violence of the everyday; the evil banality of prison life.

Judy wrote:

> *Thanks for signing me up for the newsletter. I'd like to get involved with something bigger than me. I like keeping busy and speaking up for things I believe in. I wish I could start a newsletter or some type of outlet in here for women so they know they ain't alone. Court for my daughter was this morning, they ended up excluding me from the conference call so now I'm waiting 'til this afternoon to know what's going on.*

Judy is a thirty-four-year-old working mother, a former drug-using person (at the insistence of her ex) who was engaged in survival work and straight work while living with domestic abuse. She did what she had to do to take care of herself and her daughter. Like so many other criminalized survivors, Judy was forced to labor against her will. Judy became dependent on the substances her ex pushed to dull the mental and physical pain of abuse. Her ex and one of his acquaintances ensured she had little to no independence. Much like the violence that would come from being incarcerated by the State of Illinois, her movements were dictated and restricted, and her ex punished her for resistance.

## CONSENT

Consent in survival work is often mischaracterized as nonexistent: no agency, all exploitation and violence all the time. Providing for yourself and your family while surviving abuse means your ability to consent is under constant threat of attack, but that doesn't mean that it disappears. Lines, boundaries, and thresholds shift, flex, and alter based upon what would immediately reduce harm toward yourself and your loved ones. People do what they have to do to be as okay as they can be. We need to talk about what creates these conditions, rather than victim blame folx who make day-to-day decisions in order to survive.

Judy describes her survival in the face of abuse, and her description reinforces the shifting nature of consent in survival work:

> *Now with strangers, when I was on the street, I was extremely shy. I didn't even know to call strangers "baby" at first, to sweet talk them. Then the more I hustled, the meaner I got. Though, looking back, I never put myself in (well, in my mind) complete danger . . . I hated being touched, and would cringe and flinch when I'd have to allow a vic [trick] to feel me up to prove I wasn't a cop. And if they didn't give me the money within a few moments of being in the car with them, I would leave; all my intentions were of taking the money and running, so too much chit-chat or touching would make me physically sick.*

Throughout Judy's marriage, her life was characterized by acts of survival, punctuated with emotional, physical, and financial abuse. Her ex would regularly hit her in public or berate and attack her in front of close family members. When money ran out, he would force her to pick up clients as a sex worker. Judy was arrested for prostitution numerous times. Sometimes, Judy's ex would pose as her pimp, showing up and robbing clients who paid for a date.

Even though she never wielded a weapon and was a survivor of domestic abuse at the time, Judy was convicted of armed robbery and sentenced to fourteen years in prison.

## RESISTANCE

In the face of the deadening evil of the carceral system, Judy advocated for herself, researching Illinois domestic violence law, searching for ways to survive this punishment no one should have to face.

Using the prison library, Judy found the law that would eventually aid in her own release from prison: a provision that protects defendants who are or have been victims of domestic violence from being punished for criminal acts committed while living through that abuse. Their conduct can be justified by their status as "victims."

Section 15 099-0384, a new domestic violence provision of the Illinois Public Act, went into effect on January 1, 2016. It reads: "At the time of the offense, the defendant is or had been the victim of domestic violence and the effects of the domestic violence tended to excuse or justify the defendant's criminal conduct. As used in this paragraph (15), 'domestic violence' means abuse as defined in Section 103 of the Illinois Domestic Violence Act of 1986." This new domestic violence provision should have been invoked at the time of her trial, but she had inadequate counsel who did no research or advocacy on her behalf. She had also been assigned to a court-mandated substance abuse program at Cook County Jail, but a Sheriff's deputy refused her admission, citing her high bond and "violent crime" conviction. She received no support while incarcerated to manage the substance use into which her ex had coerced her.

Judy writes about her release:

*To my knowledge, I'm the first person released under this new domestic violence law. I set the precedent. It was by chance that I read about it in the prison library. Can you believe that?*

When I received "the word" from my contact, I literally screamed out loud and shook my phone wildly in the air. "She's fucking out!" I said to no one but myself in my apartment. That first text from her—"Hey girl hey it's Judy —made my month, my year. Even still, it was a sobering moment amid the celebrations as we both acknowledged that post-release (the inevitable parole and probation period) would come with different methods of confinement and punishment.

Still, Judy is out. She woke up free from prison on November

30, 2018. There is so much new work to be done supporting her and her family as she builds a new way for herself, with the State of Illinois attached to her ankle. Mainstream movements against sexual assault have little room for such an "imperfect victim," but Judy's experiences with her abusive ex-husband, the police, and criminal courts show us why women, femmes, trans, and gender nonconforming people do not report sexual assault through law enforcement channels. The carceral system suspends your consent, disallowing you from actively participating in healing and justice as a survivor. It demands your re-traumatization, revictimization, your money, your time, your freedom, your children.

What happened to Judy remains unexceptional and to be expected from a system founded upon the cruelty of carcerality. Judy was released but her friend, and mine—Alisha, whom Judy met when she was incarcerated at Decatur Correctional—is still behind bars for an act of self-defense.

## "JUJU, LELE IS LOOKING FOR YA": FINDING CONNECTIONS

Judy describes how she connected with Alisha:

*Alisha heard about me and my case through you, Brit. I went by JuJu inside and people kept saying "JuJu, LeLe is looking for ya." But I didn't know LeLe yet so I stood her up the first few times she tried to get in touch. Finally one day at the gym, she came up and was like "Girl, I've been trying to meet up with you. Brit says we should talk!" We became fast friends. Ended up we knew a lot of the same people outside, so it was amazing that we never bumped heads. She was very adamant when we first met, "You better be down with hos, I just wanna make sure you won't be doing any ho-bashing." I told her, "Oh no! Whores are my best friends! No ho-bashing here. You know what I'm in for? You don't gotta worry about me." But I didn't want to socialize a lot in general because of my depression. I didn't leave my room a lot. I didn't want to accept the fact that I was there. I wish I could've but it was too much inside, and missing my daughter. LeLe and I have very similar stories and life history. I even told my Dad about her. She's awesome.*

Judy and Alisha have both characterized their life stories as similar even though they identify with their respective hustles differently. Their differences are less important than their camaraderie. Perhaps it was the violation of consent that renders them so similar: both doing what they needed to do, proficiently. When they failed to acquiesce to the demands of men who did not share their level of risk or need for survival, they were both subject to the bootheel of the state.

Judy and Alisha had the same original counsel, two men notorious for their predatory behavior toward women facing criminal charges in Cook County. Judy remarked that one of them made unwanted sexual advances toward her. Alisha attests to the same aggressive, sexist behavior, such as being asked to wear a "schoolgirl uniform" for him during one of their meetings. These were men who were supposed to defend Judy and Alisha in court, advocate for them, not sexually harass and intimidate them. They both remember feeling torn between refusing, reporting, and dismissing these men because of the charges they were facing.

Judy lost at trial because her lawyer forced a plea deal of fourteen years. The judge was set on sentencing her that day and didn't want the "hassle" that goes along with picking a jury—something Judy was originally insistent upon. The attorney attempted the same with Alisha, but she refused the deal. In turn, he never requested bond for her. According to the Chicago Community Bond Fund, "Inability to pay bond results in higher rates of conviction, longer sentences, loss of housing and jobs, separation of families, and lost custody of children. Paying bond . . . restores the presumption of innocence before trial and enables recipients to remain free while fighting their cases."

## THE PARADOX OF "VICTIMHOOD"

Because Judy was married to her abuser, the title of domestic violence survivor was extended to her, and was sufficient to win her petition for release. She was deemed a "victim" deserving of freedom, support, and access to community. Alisha would not be afforded the same. Victimhood is conditionally offered to sex workers when society deems us in need of rescue. Alisha—surviving an attack on her life—was an affront to a society that already believed her disposable. It bears mentioning that both men who were violent toward Judy and Alisha were white.

Like Cyntoia Brown, Alexis Martin, and Chrystul Kizer, the details of Alisha's case have been misrepresented by a host of mainstream publications. Alisha is a twenty-seven-year-old artist, poet, and sex worker from Akron, Ohio. In January 2014, when she was nineteen years old, Alisha was attacked by a client in his Orland Park home. He became angry when Alisha refused unsafe services, punching her in the face before grabbing a knife from the kitchen. Alisha managed to wrestle the knife from the client, stabbing him. He was found dead in his house three days later.

Despite that no physical evidence had been recovered from the scene, Alisha was arrested and charged with second-degree murder. At her trial, the prosecutor portrayed her as a manipulative criminal and spoke disparagingly about her profession. A jury convicted her of second-degree murder, and Alisha was sentenced to fifteen years in prison. Her counsel was inadequate, failing to file crucial motions which have since been major impediments to even initiating a proper appeal. Currently, advocate organizers in the Support Ho(s)e collective coordinate the Justice for Alisha Walker Defense Campaign to fight for her freedom and materially support her while she's inside. Other grassroots organizations, like Survived & Punished and Love & Protect, have continued to raise awareness around Alisha's case and connect it to other cases involving Black, Brown, and Indigenous survivors, both trans and cis, who have been criminalized for acts of self-love and self-defense.

Alisha was sex working largely of her own volition (compelled by capitalism to labor), though a third party managed her bookings. Her attacker was a known client. Sex workers have their own harm reductions tools—like bad date/dog lists—but they aren't foolproof. Alisha essentially experienced workplace violence and because of racism, whorephobia, and the criminalization of sex work, it was inconceivable that Alisha was acting in self-defense. The judge essentially said she shouldn't have fought back and lived. It did not help Alisha's case that the sister of the deceased was also a Cook County judge, and the brother of the deceased a prominent lobbyist in Illinois. His sister was even given access to the judge's chambers during sentencing. Alisha remembers watching the sister holding the purse of the forensic specialist who took the stand for the prosecution during her trial.

Alisha does not characterize her work experiences as inherently exploitative. She was proud of her self-sufficiency and ablility to support her family (mother, father, little sister, little brother). She felt empowered, learned self-love and confidence, but also experienced violence and messy management situations. She contends that yes, all those things are possible to feel and experience at once.

Alisha reflected on consent, work life, and her current incarceration:

*Consent for me has always been the same: if I don't want to do it I don't, or if I'm not sure about the risk I don't do it. With clients in particular, I won't even allow kissing—it's too personal, nor do I allow finger penetration or any unprotected contact while I'm working for that matter. Those are my hard boundaries when I'm working. However, in my personal relationships, I'm pretty open to whatever would make my partner happy, but that of course comes with how much trust I have in that relationship and how affirming it is for me. Listen, prison has sent my body to shit. I'm not offered adequate food or nutrition that I (and all people) need to be healthy; nor do I have the right to do with my body as I please—from being outdoors in the sun, to sex, my hair color or hairstyle, they dictate every choice of change. I cannot care for myself by seeking medical attention when I actually require it, and I've gone without much human touch (platonic or otherwise) for over five years. I did not consent to that. I did not consent to losing loving touch and embrace. I do not consent to these strip searches and their violent cavity searches. Consent does not exist in prison; you are state property.*

Alisha's unapologetic working identity lives in her visual art and poetry. Her organizing on the inside, and her own political education, have gotten her in trouble with correctional officers, prison counselors, and the prison administration. She's taken time and care to meet with people who have had similar life and work experiences, doing that essential and difficult work of breaking down stigma and shame. Through those acts of self-love and care she's expressed becoming more emboldened in her personal commitment to organize toward destigmatizing sex work. Her thoughts around prison abolition, state violence, consent, and decriminalization of the sex trades seem to be ever deepening and informing one another.

## THE VIOLENCE OF THE STATE

*Prison reminds me of warehouses for people who society doesn't want anymore . . . they just throw them, us, away.*

*—Alisha*

To me, there's no clearer cause for Judy's and Alisha's incarcerations than the hatred and contempt judges have for criminalized survivors, especially those who are cash-poor, drug-using, mothers, and sex workers of color. These systems of punishment are designed to cage and remove from public view all of the above. It is not shocking to me that both Judy and Alisha were and are incarcerated. What is shocking is how Judy escaped a punishment designed for her. What can sometimes take years of outside-inside collaborative organizing, popular defense campaigns, petitions, direct actions, and astronomical legal fees, Judy managed to coordinate and discover, and then self-advocate for new legal representation. This tenacity in the throes of incarceration is incredible and worth celebrating.

Judy comments on the punishments that followed her outside of prison:

> *The second night in the halfway house, I asked my roommate if she thought I would wake up at Decatur [Correctional] if I went to sleep. She said, "You better not because that would mean I'd be right there back inside with you." Immediately after getting out, I went to Walmart with my dad, and somebody named "Judith" was announced over the PA. I had a panic attack. I knew they had made a mistake and were coming for me. For days afterward I kept waiting for the knock on the door. For there to be guards. It's very unreal. I'm still scared to believe it.*

Since winning her release, Judy has encountered trouble accessing food stamps and other assistance programs. There have been numerous difficulties surrounding her driver's license being reinstated and determining responsibility for parking tickets and moving violations incurred by her former counsel, after leaving her truck in his possession. After she was released and we were able to correspond via text, she characterized this as another kind of prison—one with a lack of access to movement, existing at the whims of probation. There have been issues with employment under these restrictions, common to those on probation and parole. Judy asks, "When is it a good time to say you're a convicted felon when you're interviewing for a job?" Despite all of these imposed obstacles, she remains committed to working and saving up, as well as dedicating herself to the fight to free others like herself from prison.

I'm able to sit with Judy at cafe tables now. We can text and call as long as we can both afford to pay our cell phone bills. Judy and I mostly get to choose (insofar as there remains the illusion of "choice" under capitalism) when and how we see each other. I have to travel almost one thousand miles to be searched, patted down, and then told where to sit to visit Alisha. Our calls are monitored, our letters read and sent back, deemed contraband, our emails screened and approved or denied on a whim. These are not conditions we consented to endure, and yet, this is how we negotiated a friendship and organizing relationship. I'm left with rage and love and a fierce sense of the need to fight to end confinement of all kinds. For Judy's part, she "want[s] to be able to be a mom again. A good mom." She said, "I wanna help volunteer and do whatever I can [for criminalized survivors]. I really do."

To conclude, Judy and Alisha offer their thoughts on consent and violence.

Judy:
*My ideas of consent are still pretty screwed up too. I've allowed people closest to me, especially a sexual partner, to take complete control and advantage of me. My mother was a wonderful woman, the best mom I could ask for, but she never gave the best advice. My first sexual relationship I wanted to stop was when I was sixteen. I was too young, and didn't enjoy it. I talked to my mom about this, and she said I can't just stop having sex now with my boyfriend, he would leave me. She said that all men want is sex, and if you don't give it to them they will leave you for someone who will have it with them. I know now that's wrong, and not true, but fifteen years later this is still instilled in me.*

*As far as consent in prison, besides the strip and cavity searches, which after three years became almost second nature, I never felt invaded or abused per se. I, unlike others, am very adaptable, I guess. A couple days of one thing becomes the norm to me; even uncomfortable scenarios become less and less uncomfortable. That was my defense mechanism for prison. Consent in prison is tricky. I never felt forced to do anything except stay there. I even had a run-in with a CO [correctional officer]—it started out as flirting and then went a little further, but when I didn't wanna go all the way, we didn't. So no, in my experience I had full consent over my body as far as anything sexual happening.*

Alisha:

*The #MeToo "movement" is supposed to give women a voice, and sometimes it does, but it does not give everyone a voice. Especially sex workers and prisoners. I was almost raped and killed. For defending myself, I am sitting in prison. "Me too" doesn't cover me. I think it's great as an idea, but sex workers are left completely out. I'm ready to get to work. I want to be an advocate, I don't want anyone to ever have to experience what I did. I want to fight to decriminalize sex work and stop the victim-blaming, anti-survivor mentality that makes up this whole court and prison system.*

What do our movements to end sexual violence offer Judy, Alisha, or any of the many others in similar circumstances? Radical community is almost certainly the only venue in which either woman will ever have the opportunity to air their grievances and offer support, sympathy, and empathic experience to others with similar survival narratives. Even the dream of full decriminalization of sex work is far from a guaranteed destigmatization of sexual violence against sex workers—a climate in which their (our) experiences are seen as equivalent to trauma and resistance outside of the trades. If our activism fails to recognize this, it risks becoming a hollow, respectability-driven movement that gatekeeps, polices, and filters out those whose stories are seen as somehow inadequate, sullied, or otherwise less-than.

*Special thanks to Aaron Hammes for editorial work on this essay.*

# Context for "Undercover Agents"

## VANESSA CARLISLE

When Norma Jean Almodovar wrote and posted "Undercover Agents" on her personal website ten years ago, it was not only common practice for cops to have sex with sex workers who were under suspicion or in custody, it was tacitly assumed to be legal, because there were very few state laws prohibiting the practice. In the intervening time, both civil and criminal cases have emerged to challenge this practice. In 2014, despite police efforts to protect their ability to have sex with suspects during prostitution investigations, the Honolulu department had to bow to political pressure and concede that it was an abuse of power, if not institutionalized rape. By 2017, the state of Michigan was the last to create legislation making sex with people suspected of prostitution or solicitation a no-no. In other words, the policy change for which Almodovar seemed to have been calling has in large part come to pass.

An irony: while policy changes that prevent cops from having sex with suspected prostitutes/victims of trafficking *seem* to protect sex workers from rape by the police, the continued criminalization of sex work coupled with anti-trafficking rhetoric and claims of victimhood across the board actually keep sex workers shrouded in confusion—just the place where they are most vulnerable.

What hasn't changed in a decade is the fact of police corruption. The case of Celeste Guap is one example: in 2017 she was able to name nearly thirty officers in multiple departments in California's Bay Area who were either participating in, or knew about, sexual contact among police and sex workers. When Alaska's violent policing tactics in human trafficking and prostitution cases were revealed in Tara Burns's 2012 research study, lawmakers scrambled to create new policies. After a three-year investigation, seven New York City cops were indicted in 2018 for running a "prostitution ring"—the very thing they were supposed to be preventing.

One reason Almodovar's frustration is so intense in "Undercover Agents" is that she has seen the cycle repeat itself ad nauseum since the 1970s. Her writing seeks to illuminate the ways in which the criminalization of sex work allows—perhaps even requires—law enforcement to twist the narrative and propagandize the dangers of sex work to keep the money flowing toward their investigations. This creates circumstances ripe for corruption, violence, and even trafficking by the police themselves—in other words, police create much of the danger sex workers face. Almodovar doesn't have time for policy changes that do anything less than fully decriminalize sex work, and she knows law enforcement sees the sex industries as cash cows.

When revisiting her writing from ten years ago, readers should keep in mind that, despite legislative changes, the basic structure for the sting operations Almodovar described in 2009 has not just stayed intact—it has been expanded via federal monies, legislation like FOSTA-SESTA, increased cooperation among law enforcement organizations, and AI technology. "Reverse stings," in which women cops pose as sex workers, and online surveillance of both workers and clients, are both more common now.

Sex workers are still subject to predatory police tactics, cast as either criminals or victims depending on the needs of law enforcement coffers, and the public is silent: presumed to be too ignorant, too sexually squeamish, or truly supportive of efforts to rescue victims in a "NIMBY" sort of way. And the rescue of trafficking victims is no more effective now than it was then—often involving deportation, detainment, forced rehabilitation or diversion programs, sometimes a backpack with a pair of flip-flops and a handwritten note saying, "I believe you can learn to love yourself." What's changed is that anti-trafficking efforts now have the full support of federal law and more grant money than ever before.

Almodovar scoffs at the notion that women making more money in an hour than police officers make in a day is exploitation, but she also knows both the gravity of the stigma and the difficulties street-based sex workers face. She worked both for the Los Angeles Police Department and later, disillusioned and gorgeously sassy, as an escort. She did time in prison and then devoted her life to the pursuit of freedom from stigma and oppression for sex workers. Do not be distracted by her dark humor or use of words like "skanky," "hooker," or "ho"; for Almodovar, decriminalization is deadly serious. Her life's work has been to help and support sex workers from diverse corners of the industry and the world.

In "Undercover Agents," Almodovar's use of "victim" as a stand-in for "prostitute/sex worker" does double duty. First, it exposes the fallacy that all sex workers are de facto victims of trafficking via the exchange of sexual service for money. But perhaps even more importantly, it addresses the ways in which sex workers are experiencing real victimization due to criminalization by the police. Notice how "victim" works throughout Almodovar's scenarios—where it rings true or false, but especially where it appears simply unfit, because it indicates an overly-simplistic understanding of the complexity of lived experience in sex work. Almodovar takes an already twisted narrative and twists it up again, revealing how little sex worker experience is valued in the rush to make arrests.

# Undercover Agents

## NORMA JEAN ALMODOVAR, 2009

HELP WANTED (Anywhere, USA): Hey guys—looking for that perfect job? Something that will give you access to hot babes who are always available? You get to party at upscale hotels, unlimited free room service including booze AND you get paid to get laid! Sound too good to be true? No—I am not talking about becoming a gigolo! This is a vice cop job! But if going through the academy and walking a beat is too much work, there's also the exciting opportunity to be a high-paid undercover police informant! You get the same great benefits of parties and girls without the risk of being shot at by real bad guys! And we aren't talking skanky street hookers either! We got laws to round up those hos without having to say a word! Ever priced those Emperor's Club gals? Think they are out of your league? Not when you are working for the government! We got you covered! It's all part of the package! All we need is your testimony in court that you had sex with these poor victims and they asked you for the money. That's it! Case closed! Not only will you have the opportunity to get laid by the same high-caliber call girls but you will be doing your community a great service by rescuing these poor gals from a life of exploitation and degradation where they get paid upward of $5,000 an hour. After their arrest and conviction, thanks to your testimony, they can find societally approved employment which is more appropriate for them, like cleaning toilets at Motel 6 for minimum wage! Call your local police vice unit for details! Get in on this exciting career now!

This help wanted ad may be fictitious, but its content is not. While sex workers' rights activists like myself have known for many years this was happening, most people out there, including many of the women who advertise on the internet, don't have a clue that vice cops and undercover informants can actually have sex with a suspected prostitute before the cops arrest her. Some police departments actually hire men from the community to carry out the necessary sex act to make their arrests of the prostitute stick.[1]

Imagine, our tax dollars going to pay some lucky guys to have sex with women who are suspected of being "victims of exploitation," also known as sex workers. You should be warned though—if you go out there and attempt to conduct a rescue on your own, you might get arrested for solicitation and sent to your local "John School" where you will learn how awful you are for exploiting those poor gals by paying them instead of just forcing them into sex for free![2]

Stopping the exploitation and degradation of women is the motivation behind the heavy enforcement of prostitution laws, according to the religious right and radical feminists who have persuaded liberal legislators to pass laws that give cops cart blanche to make their arrests. These groups of moral and social busybodies insist that all prostitutes are victims, regardless of their age or consent. In what follows, I will substitute their term, "victim," for "prostitute/sex worker" to expose just how ridiculous the enforcement of the laws really is.

California's liberal Democrats passed a law that allowed an undercover cop to suggest an act of sex for money and all the suspected victim had to do to get arrested was to "manifest an acceptance" of the offer, as detailed in Section 647(b) of California Penal Code. If she smiled or winked at him, that was an indication, according to the cops, that she was accepting the offer to be exploited and could then be rescued/arrested on solicitation charges. When the poor exploited victims learned they could now be rescued/arrested for just making any sort of facial or body gesture (sex workers called it the "use a smile, go to jail" law), they thought they could outfox the cops by requesting that the potential exploiter/customer drop his pants and show his genitals. Surely the cops weren't allowed to show their dicks, were they? As many of those victims discovered after the fact, the cops could do that as well as go all the way if necessary.

Even with the ability to make an effortless arrest, cops still conduct sting operations when they want to arrest in volume. Some undercover sting operations last as long as three to five years before any arrests are made. During that time, the vice cops (or their paid civilian helpers) visit the suspected den of victims over and over again, just to make certain those women are actually prostitutes and that someone else is in charge.

Prostitution is, after all, "worse than rape or robbery" for the victim because prostitutes are often lured into a "lifetime of shame and degradation which progressively rapes their spirit, character, and self-image" . . . or so the LA District Attorney claimed when he appealed my probation sentence for one count of pandering a number of years ago, successfully overturning the judge's sentence and forcing him to impose on me the mandatory three-to-six-year prison term California law required.

In Los Angeles in 2003, the LAPD conducted a prostitution sting called "Operation Silver Bullet." According to the *LA Daily News*: "In one of LAPD's largest prostitution stings in several years, vice detectives fanned out across the San Fernando Valley on Wednesday and simultaneously raided seven suspected prostitution dens fronting as legitimate businesses." The LAPD proudly reported that "approximately 100 officers took part in Operation Silver Bullet, netting 14 arrests . . . which were all for solicitation, operating a house of prostitution, and residing in a house of prostitution."[3] Anyone who can do the math will figure out that if it took one hundred officers to bust fourteen suspected victims, that's seven cops per prostitute/victim. Oh yeah, and the cops were later given an awards banquet to honor them for their heroic work in making these dangerous arrests. Makes you wonder how they can hand out those awards with a straight face.

When notorious Hollywood Madam Heidi Fleiss was on trial, I had the opportunity to sit in court every day with my friend Sydney Biddle Barrows, the equally notorious Mayflower Madam. During the trial, a number of interesting facts were disclosed, such as how the cops set up the women and what they did to signal their comrades waiting in the other room that a violation of law had taken place and it was time to make the arrests. I guarantee you that for real crimes, the police do not deploy seven officers to the scene of the crime unless it involves a bank robbery or homicide! It is crucial to reallocate the scarce police and government resources used to pursue these victims to pursuing real criminals who have real victims.

The pretend exploiter/client/vice cop will call the madam and claim to be a friend of one of her real clients, and tell her he has a bunch of buddies coming into town. He wants to arrange for her best girls to provide their services for himself and his friends, and he throws around huge numbers at the madam to pique her interest. He will also mention particular sex acts that he wants these "victims" to provide him or his buddies, which he may also repeat to the alleged "victims" over the phone prior to the assignation. A real client generally has a lot more class than that, so this should be a tip-off, but the potential payday can cloud the judgment of even the most paranoid pimp or madam. Another tip-off should be when the client/cop insists on having the madam or the victims bring along illegal drugs for him and his friends.

To set up high-class call girls and their madam, you cannot rent a room at the local Motel 6, so the cops work out deals with upscale hotels that agree to provide comped luxurious suites in which to conduct these stings. Although they are oppressed victims who cannot think or speak for themselves, these women are quite capable of discerning an inappropriate situation once they arrive in their exploiter/client's hotel room, and clearly if the exploiter/client was who he said he was, there would be expensive champagne and perhaps hors d'oeuvres available! To sell this undercover operation to victims who are used to being wined and dined at the very best restaurants and hotels and paid upward of $500 to $5,000 an hour, all the accoutrements of wealth and power need to be visible. And yes, the vice cops get to partake of the food and alcoholic beverages as part of their job to deceive these wretched souls into believing they are about to be exploited/paid for having sex.

Quite often, the undercover cops will request a "double": two victims at a time. For one thing, it speeds up the process of making the rescues/arrests but it also provides entertainment for the other cops, who may get to watch a show of the two women kissing and fondling each other. For while the vice cop acting as the exploiter/client sets up the victims for their arrests, in the adjoining suite, his colleagues are videotaping everything so the jury will see just how degrading being a prostitute really is.[4] May I remind you again that it is necessary for a multitude of vice cops to be deployed for these takedowns as the victims may attempt an escape, not realizing of course that they are better off getting arrested so they can get on with their rehabilitation and transition into the appropriate careers waiting for them in the fast food industry.

The farce continues until every last victim has been identified and caught and the sting has gone down successfully. Now the victims are herded into police cars or vans and taken to the nearest jail facility where they will be processed. Here again they will be strip-searched, given a delousing shower and matching jailhouse pants and tops, and put into lockup until they can make bail. They will also be interrogated and told that if they cooperate with the government and testify against their pimp or madam, most likely they will not be put on trial or go to jail. If they are from out of state or another country, their employer will undoubtedly be charged with violating human trafficking laws—a federal offense. Victims from other countries will be threatened with deportation if they refuse to cooperate. Regardless of their cooperation, most of these victims will still have arrest records that may prevent them from ever finding other employment. At best, they may find work earning minimum wage, which they will have to spend paying off legal bills and fines.

One could say that these laws are turning the taxpayers into johns because they are paying to get screwed. The cops are themselves turned into prostitutes, because the very definition of prostitution is getting paid for getting laid, isn't it? How do we stop the exploitation of the vice cops who are forced into prostitution by their sergeants, lieutenants, captains, and even local prosecutors who instruct them to have sex with those poor victims so the victims can be arrested?

And what about those civilian males who are paid by the cops to have sex with suspected prostitutes/victims? Under the law, aren't they also prostitutes? And wouldn't the hiring of them be considered "pandering" just as it is when a madam hires a prostitute? "Pandering" in most states is a felony and defined as "encouraging a person to commit an act of prostitution." So when the average citizen requests the continued enforcement of these laws to "protect women from being exploited," should we arrest the cops or the taxpayers for pandering? Gets rather complicated when enforcing laws based on subjective concepts like "exploitation" and "degradation," doesn't it?

It gets even more complicated when cops are encouraged to use prostitution laws to recruit victims and even pimps or madams to become informants. For many police departments, such informants are invaluable. And in exchange for being an informant, they are allowed to practice their profession/exploitation without fear of being rescued/arrested. In fact, if they don't continue being victims, pimps, or madams, they would have nothing to offer the cops by way of information on other suspected victims. But you can be sure that the cops let these individuals know that if they cease being useful, they will be rescued/arrested.

There have been so many cases of cops forcing victims to have sex with them in order to avoid being rescued/arrested that it is considered by many to be a cost of doing business. Occasionally the cops get caught, such as the Long Beach, California police officer

Bryon Ellsberry, who was charged with rape after he continually coerced a victim/prostitute to have sex with him. She filed a complaint and was given an opportunity to wear a wire to record their conversation the next time he extorted her for her sexual favors. He was arrested and convicted, but given a probation sentence rather than sent to jail.[5]

I can understand why a man might want to be an undercover agent—especially men who like to brag that they "don't have to pay for it," even though everybody does pay for it, one way or another. And as long as society looks the other way at whatever cops have to do to "stop the exploitation" of women and children, there will be guys who seek out such work. They tell themselves that they are helping the poor victims escape a life of degradation. So don't be surprised if someday soon you see a real help wanted ad just like the fictitious one above. But also don't be surprised that we "victims" are fighting back any way we can.

## NOTES

1. As detailed in *Commonwealth v. Sun Cha Chon* 983 A.2d 784 (Pa. Super. Ct. 2009). https://www.criminaldefenselawyer.com/resources/how-do-police-uncover-prostitution-rings.htm.
2. Almodovar's work at PoliceProstitutionandPolitics.com includes "Operation Do the Math," in which she compares arrest rates and solve rates for reported rapes, and arrest rates for prostitution and solicitation. A major takeaway from her research is that local police departments make many more arrests for sex work than they do rape.
3. Ryan Oliver, "Cops Hit Suspected Prostitution Dens," *Los Angeles Daily News*, June 26, 2003, https://www.policeprostitutionandpolitics.com/images/images_px_3/operationsilverbullet.jpg.
4. Hidden camera footage of undercover stings is now readily available on YouTube through archived news stories. Due to the fact that people who are caught up in these stings are often identified by photo and legal name, none will be referenced here.
5. "LONG BEACH: Officer Gets Probation in Sexual Battery Case," *Los Angeles Times*, January 18, 1995, https://www.latimes.com/archives/la-xpm-1995-01-18-me-21375-story.html.

# The New Orleans Police Raid
## That Launched a Dancer Resistance

MELISSA GIRA GRANT

On a quiet Thursday night in mid-February, just two days after the revelry of Mardi Gras, the narrow gutters and treacherous potholes lining Bourbon Street are nearly empty. Only days earlier, tangles of gold and purple and silver beads, drifting like sea foam trapped by French Quarter curbs, were swept away before Ash Wednesday services began.

Cutting easily through the thin Bourbon Street crowd was Lyn Archer, with pale blond hair and an efficient walk. She turned us right onto Iberville, past the Penthouse Club and its cool blue spotlights, to stop at an adult establishment called Gentleman's Quarters. It was closed. Next to Gentleman's Quarters was Dixie Divas, also shuttered. This whole stretch of Iberville, just a block away from the mayhem on Bourbon, heading in the direction of the Mississippi River, was hushed in the dark, and for a few minutes we were all alone.

Archer has worked as a stripper in New Orleans for two years, after growing up in California's Central Valley and dancing in Portland and Key West. She had dreams of one day taking over Dixie Divas, imagining it as an establishment run by dancers. Dixie Divas was one of the smaller clubs that wasn't connected to a larger corporate brand, like Hustler or Penthouse. It shared a wall with the equally modest-in-size Gentleman's Quarters. "You could drill a hole through the wall and hit the stripper on the other side," Archer said.

But Dixie Divas was closed—permanently—after state and local law enforcement raided it and seven other clubs in late January 2018, putting hundreds of dancers out of work just weeks before Carnival season kicked into full swing.

Law enforcement portrayed the clubs as fronts for human trafficking, but their evidence was thin to nonexistent. Prior to the January raids, undercover agents posed as club customers, itemizing conduct—such as a dancer touching their own body—that they said was in violation of the regulations that clubs have to follow to maintain their liquor licenses. But these alleged regulatory violations, documented in notices of suspension from the Louisiana Office of Alcohol and Tobacco Control (ATC), were not indicia of trafficking. So why the highly publicized raids and the club closures that followed?

Prior to law enforcement's undercover club visits, the local paper, the *Times-Picayune*, ran a three-part investigative series purporting to reveal trafficking in clubs on Bourbon Street and in the French Quarter. Reporters said the head of a local arm of an international charity, Covenant House, with ties to the Catholic church, was "integral" to their reporting. While the *Times-Picayune* stories included two previously reported cases of potential trafficking, they offered no examples of trafficking inside the clubs. The *Washington Post*'s Radley Balko criticized it as a "three-part newspaper series in search of a problem" but the *Times-Picayune*'s editorial board claimed "the French Quarter's most famous street is a hub for sex trafficking."

Then came the raids. Over the course of a week in late January 2018, ATC agents along with officers from the New Orleans Police Department (NOPD) entered the premises of eight different clubs during business hours, corralling and questioning dancers. Officers refused to let them change out of their work attire. They read dancers' legal identification aloud in front of customers, and photographed them—partially undressed—on their mobile phones. "I witnessed women weeping until they vomited," one dancer said.

At a January 29 press conference, Louisiana ATC Commissioner

Juana-Marine Lombard acknowledged that no trafficking arrests had been made, yet NOPD Superintendent Michael Harrison deemed the undercover investigations and raids a "first step" to "confront human trafficking." Meanwhile, the New Orleans City Council was prepared to vote on a proposal to cap French Quarter strip clubs, with the goal of limiting them to one per block. That meant more clubs would share the fate of Dixie Divas.

From the charities to the editorial pages to the politicians, backers of the campaign against alleged human trafficking in New Orleans clubs failed to take into account the harms they perpetrated against the dancers they claimed they were protecting. Official explanations of the raids caricatured strippers as, at best, unwitting victims, and, at worst, willing participants in a "hub" of human trafficking. But most important, and what most city officials failed to acknowledge, was the raids put hundreds of strippers out of work.

Within days of the raids, dancers and other workers in the French Quarter clubs led an "unemployment march" to protest the club closures. They sold dollar bottles of water labeled "stripper tears," carried signs reading "twerking class hero" and "your political agenda shouldn't cost me my future." They chanted: "Strippers' rights are human rights!" and "My body, my choice!" and "I am not a victim! I do not want to be saved!" The large and passionate protests brought media coverage that was starkly different from the pre-raid pieces with narratives guided by Covenant House: actually acknowledging that the dancers could speak for themselves.

The *Times-Picayune* was now covering the protests, somewhat sympathetically, and so was the national media. An energized and powerful protest movement of dancers trained its sights on a January 31 press conference at which departing Mayor Mitch Landrieu was to announce Bourbon Street's infrastructure progress. Dancers gathered behind local tourism officials and drowned them out by chanting "Sex work is real work!" and "Workers' rights are women's rights!" Landrieu himself appeared to be a no-show even though he was scheduled to speak at the event, leading to speculation that he had been scared off by the large and boisterous protest.

Dancers organizing under the name BARE—Bourbon Alliance of Responsible Entertainers—had taken the attention off of Bourbon Street infrastructure and onto club closures. It was an action that tapped into BARE's roots: some dancers had been organizing back in in 2015, after another series of ATC strip club raids, dubbed "Operation Trick or Treat." That's when Lyn Archer began working as a stripper on Bourbon Street. By the January 2018 raids, Archer was BARE's most visible spokeswoman.

When we met after Mardi Gras, Archer explained a theory that her colleague, Devin Ladner, had about the 2018 raids: if the clubs raided closed for good, then the city would have achieved its one-club-per-block plan. "Let's just drum up the grounds to raid these clubs anyway, and then we'll just say it happened through 'natural attrition,'" Archer said. "They died on their own."

Ladner was getting ready to return to work at the Penthouse Club on Iberville when we met that same week. The club is on the same street as the now-shuttered Dixie Divas, but on the brighter end nearest Bourbon. Ladner took a seat on her living room floor in her house in Uptown, her long legs in thin over-the-knee socks. Though the Penthouse Club was not raided, she said she has to go to work and interact with patrons under the assumption that any one of them could be undercover with the ATC or NOPD.

Despite ATC Commissioner Juana Marine-Lombard's claim that "we have no issues with the dancers," it was the dancers' conduct that officers monitored, not the conduct of the club owners or management. "It's been hard to be a fantasy anymore," Ladner said. "I'm worried that it could incriminate me for a solicitation charge, even if I'm not facilitating." For example, if customers want her to engage in dirty talk, purely as a fantasy—a common request—she's concerned that could be misconstrued as facilitating prostitution.

Ladner brought over her makeup kit, spreading out eyeshadows in their lidded black plastic pots on the glass-topped coffee table next to copies of the books *Striptastic!* and *The Modern Herbal Dispensatory*. Her mobile phone, wrapped in a pin-up skin, was at her knee. She hasn't been stripping for long, she said—almost a year and a half. But the idea of losing her job frightens her, because that would mean a return to the work she used to do.

Before dancing, she had been a bartender and a waitress. "The hours that I was working and the emotional abuse I put up with being in the service industry as a woman," she explained, "and making shit for pay and not ever being respected and always being something that can be easily replaced . . . I can't go back to it. Because I know what something else is like."

## A HISTORY OF AND AGAINST VICE

Despite its reputation for perpetual, decadent decay, New Orleans—which celebrated its three hundredth birthday during the BARE uprising in 2018—has a history of running vice out of town, especially when political opportunity and sensationalism collide. "This is what they used to shut down Storyville," said Christie Craft, a New Orleans dancer and writer who had been documenting some of the protests on her Instagram account, as she sipped a lemonade that Mardi Gras week. She sat in a French restaurant on Rampart Street, which separates the French Quarter from the historic African American neighborhood, Treme.

One hundred years ago, Craft explained, the city's legal red-light district, Storyville, was shut down in a swirl of wartime propaganda about venereal disease, bolstered by a national campaign by social reformers attacking "white slavery." Brothels shuttered and workers scattered. "What's there now," Craft continued, "is leveled public housing and dilapidated buildings." Storyville had been bounded on one side by Iberville, now home to several newly closed strip clubs, and had run along the legendary Basin Street, parallel to Rampart. Craft notes the irony that Covenant House sits right between Rampart and Basin. Covenant House, of course, is the Catholic-affiliated charity that helped shape the media narrative that the French Quarter was a trafficking "hub."

The executive director of Covenant House New Orleans, Jim Kelly, has long campaigned against the clubs, claiming that stripping leads young women to become victims of trafficking. In 2016 Kelly offered to help the New Orleans city government hire an attorney who specializes in creating city ordinances that regulate adult businesses, according to emails obtained by BARE and shared with the *Appeal*. That attorney, Scott Bergthold, has been working at least as far back as two decades to tightly regulate strip clubs and other adult businesses. Bergthold describes his law practice as "assisting communities in protecting their citizens against the detrimental impacts of the sex industry." A few months before the raids, the city hired Bergthold.

Covenant House's anti-club campaign, which helped drive the raids, Craft explained, was an extension of a long, historical arc beginning with the moral panic about "white slavery" that helped take down Storyville a century before. But this time, sex workers would not be so easily disappeared.

Hundreds of dancers, far beyond those directly involved in groups like BARE, organized in resistance. "It was a turning point," Ladner said, adding that one of her friends who had not been politically active told her, "I have to say what is going on in my life because I don't know how else I am going to feed my kids."

By targeting so many dancers—one owner said they had fifteen hundred contract workers across two clubs—there was simply no way to ignore attempts to erase them from the French Quarter. On the black gas lampposts along Bourbon, stickers fast appeared and remained through Carnival season: a dancer's bright red heel crushing an NOPD patrol car, captioned "LEAVE US ALONE—NO PIGS IN OUR CLUBS."

And when dancers took to the streets in the days after the raids, they marched under that simple, yet powerful slogan: "Leave us alone."

"That's actually all we want," Archer told me as she joined Craft at the Rampart Street restaurant. "All you have to do is leave us alone. And it's not possible for them, for law enforcement and even city officials, to comprehend that that could be a possibility."

If what public officials really want is to prevent trafficking, Archer continued, then they "need to create a space where people can report their crimes. And every human rights group in the world has said that." Among those groups who support the rights of sex workers by calling for the decriminalization of sex work are Amnesty International, Human Rights Watch, and several UN agencies including the World Health Organization.

But with the raids, New Orleans is moving in the opposite direction: instead of decriminalizing prostitution in order to protect sex workers, law enforcement is trying to link dancers to prostitution. "They are taking the biblical shepherd's crook," Archer said, "and pulling you into criminality."

In the wake of the raids, Dixie Divas closed permanently. According to the ATC, another club, Lipstixx, surrendered its liquor license, while another, Temptations, lost its permit. The remaining clubs submitted to temporary license suspensions and hefty fines while also agreeing to hold mandatory human trafficking trainings for workers. Some clubs even agreed to fire workers for "being involve [sic] with prostitution or drugs" on the first offense.

Now, according to Archer, "there's a bunch of new rules, rules that aren't going to protect the worker or make them feel better. It's kind of like TSA." And club owners and management have just shifted the burden of protecting the club from crackdowns onto the dancers themselves.

## A SURPRISE WIN

About one month after Carnival season concluded, the New Orleans City Council finally voted on a cap on Bourbon Street strip clubs—a variation of the measure which had been introduced several months before the raids by Councilmember-at-Large Stacy Head, except without the one-club-per-block restriction. As written, the proposal would allow existing clubs to remain. But in capping "through attrition," the proposal meant that if clubs were cited for new violations—like those shuttered in January after the NOPD and ATC raids—they would not be allowed to reopen.

But it was a very different political moment when the City Council convened on March 22: with their disruption of Mayor Landrieu's press conference in late January, the dancers had scored a significant direct hit on a popular Southern politician, who, with a popular new memoir, was making the rounds on national television and garnering talk of a 2020 presidential run. The dancers' protests themselves also received surprisingly sympathetic coverage in the mainstream media. BARE and their supporters packed the meeting, with Archer the first to speak. "I'm here standing for a group of strippers and nightlife workers that was founded because of these measures," she said. "Please take us at our word that it is us—we are the people being hurt by this . . . Please don't look at us and take our jobs away, and just say, 'Let them eat cake.'"

Proponents of the club cap like Stacy Head called it "merely a land use matter," but no one from the community showed up to speak in its favor.

The hearing then took a stunning turn when Councilmember-at-Large Jason Williams said he could not support the cap because the raids by the NOPD and ATC raids were carried out "seemingly in conjunction" with the legislative effort at the council. "I do have some deep concerns with why we would have wasted police manpower on those raids," he began. "I understand that there were a number of what I believe were clear constitutional violations: having people line up against the wall that are workers, and patrons are just sitting there watching, using their real names, taking photographs of them wearing their dance attire. That's horrible, it's offensive, it's misogynistic."

Williams's broadside against January's club raids, along with Archer's passionate protest about the harms that would come to sex workers because of the cap, moved other council members to vote against it. "I assumed I was going to walk in here and vote for it, and it was an easy vote," Councilmember James Gray said. "And I am going to vote against the proposal . . . and what convinces me is the statement that a grown person has a right to do what they want to do, with themselves and their bodies and their lives."

Minutes later, the cap was defeated in a 4–3 vote, the clearest sign yet that the protests had made their mark.

## THE NEXT FIGHT

In the months after the raids, the NOPD and ATC still did not announce any alleged human trafficking in the French Quarter clubs. Meanwhile, despite those saying they have the best interests of dancers at heart—like Councilmember Kristin Palmer who, in a 2016 petition in support of dramatically curbing strip clubs in the city, suggested she spoke for women in the clubs "who have no voice and no resources"—more deep-rooted and long-standing challenges faced by New Orleans dancers remain unaddressed. This has only been exacerbated by the raids: the dancers have expended so much energy on simply keeping the clubs open and keeping their jobs that day-to-day struggles have been ignored.

The issues dancers actually face are far less sensational than fears of human trafficking. Some of the clubs in the French Quarter possess beautiful historic architectural details like "medallions on the ceilings," as Archer told me, and solid wood stages. But their age often means that they are decaying and unsafe to work in. In one Bourbon Street club where Archer worked, rainwater leaking into the building produced "a waterfall coming down into a trash can at the top of the stairwell."

"I stopped working there," Archer continued, "because I saw a rat in the dressing room that was literally the size of a cat, and faced it off on the dressing room counter. There's no respect here."

And just as before the raids, there's no incentive for club owners to improve working conditions. "They don't have to care about their workforce because they are always going to have a workforce," Archer said. "No matter how bad it gets, it's always going to be better than the minimum wage here." When Archer worked at the rat-infested and problem-plumbing-plagued Bourbon Street club, she could have gotten a job tending bar. But she remained at the club nonetheless. "It was still better," she said. "Rat world was better."

City officials clearly grasp the often rough conditions at the clubs, but have yet to understand that their crackdowns merely make things worse for dancers. "You want to be treated like other workers," Councilmember Head told one speaker at the club cap hearing in March. Then she asked why dancers weren't fighting the clubs when they didn't respect their rights—like the lack of workers' compensation. "That is something you should be fighting for."

"We don't have any time to fight for this," the speaker responded, "because we are here fighting you."

*Originally published on the* Appeal *on May 30, 2018.*

# Whores at the End of the World

### SONYA ARAGON

O ne of the last times I saw a client in person, before New York City's shelter-in-place order hardened in response to COVID-19, we met in an oddly decorated hotel room in downtown Brooklyn. It was our second meeting, but I had the keen sense that he would become a regular. This, because following our first meeting, we had begun the complicated dance of declaring our feelings—our "connection"—as being out of the ordinary for the transactional circumstances that brought us together. And this was true, to a degree, for me. At our first meeting, I'd earnestly wanted him, something I had never felt with a client prior. He was young and tattooed, a former anarchist punk. He still went to shows sometimes, he said; based on his description of a new DIY space, it seemed like we had attended the same benefit a couple months prior. I liked the idea that someone I could have met as me—a me without the pretense of a different, more appealing me—was paying me, and I liked tracing the skulls and knives on his chest with my fingers, and I liked his implied antipathy toward authority, even if it seemed like he was probably aging into a quieter liberalism.

When we met for this second time, a few weeks prior to the shelter-in-place order, it was pouring in Brooklyn. I arrived late and disheveled, having jumped out of a cab stuck at a standstill to run the last three blocks in the rain. As we warmed to one another again, he remarked on the room's decor. I hadn't yet noticed it.

The walls were *Breakfast at Tiffany's* themed, papered in kitschy drawings and scrawled script reading, over and over, "By Truman Capote." My client found this eerie: "I just read *In Cold Blood* for the first time," he said. "How did they know?" I asked if he liked the book and he had, but the short distance between us suddenly felt impassable, expanded immeasurably by his implicit mention of murder, done by unstable men. (Alone in the room, we both try to forget that popular understanding of our arrangement makes savior types fear for my life and judge his. He tries to forget that he could murder me because he wants to forget that he hired me; I try to forget that he could murder me because, otherwise, I cannot get through the appointment.) "Like, I know my phone is recording everything I say and read and do, but the front desk knowing what room to put me in . . . ?" he trailed off.

"No, totally!" I worked to bring us back on equal footing, to reestablish us as lovers in a secret meeting place, having an affair, even if it was ultimately a prepaid one. I asked if he'd ever read *1984*. I rambled about the frightening scene toward the end, in which Winston and Julia, the protagonist outlaws, think they're alone in their rented room and repeat to one another, in acknowledgment of their inevitable capture by Big Brother, "We are the dead." They're not alone though, and a voice repeats it back to them—"You are the dead"—revealing the telescreen that was hidden behind a painting all along. I said that I feel like Winston and Julia in the room every time my phone advertises something I've only spoken about—like the walls are repeating the fact of my total and inescapable surveillance back to me. My story worked twofold, making us, also, Winston and Julia in the room, our enemy not each other but a common one: the state. We moved back toward one another. He kissed me, and I pretended we were them, doomed but happy, at least, to steal our last moments away from the Thought Police.

I overstayed our appointment by an hour. We texted all weekend, planning to meet again the following week. His girlfriend was away and he offered to have me over. He asked if I would sleep over—in their bed—and I said no. I pretended to say no because I felt too complicated about the circumstances, but it wasn't exactly that. I wanted to maintain a sense of unrequitedness, to delay the extinguishing of either of our desires—but also, he just wasn't paying me enough.

As our date neared, the city grew more concerned about the virus. Rumors swirled: the city would shut down on Friday; no, on Sunday. From three different people I heard the phrase, "No one in, no one out"; some suggested bridges to and from Manhattan would be blocked, and police checkpoints installed on the roads. That Tuesday, a different client—a real-estate developer I'd met once before, who'd spent half our first meeting on the phone with his lawyer—asked me to meet him, last minute, at his office. As I rode the elevator to the thirtieth floor, my friend, a therapist, texted me: "omg someone in my clinic has it." I swallowed dryly. A Jesus pamphlet stuck in the elevator's metal bannister stared at me: HOW DO YOU KNOW IF YOU'RE SAVED? I posted a photo of the pamphlet to my Instagram story, typing "lol who knows bitch!" above it. When the doors opened I rang the bell outside of his office, entered, and left a mere ten minutes later with $700 more to my name. I texted my friend, "do u know the person who has it? Are they ok? This is getting so crazy!!!" I got on the bus home, trying, more than usual, not to breathe on anyone, or let anyone breathe on me.

On the morning of the third meeting with my new client—the one who seemed to want to be my boyfriend, the one whose girl-friend was away—I sat on my roommate's bed and debated cancel-ing. It had become clear the virus was overwhelming the city, and that an order to shelter-in-place would be inevitable. I wanted to go meet him, and my roommate wanted me to stay. What would be the difference, I wondered, if I saw him one more time, and made a little more money, to provide a little more peace of mind, financially, in the ensuing chaos? "I mean, are you going to work tomorrow?" I asked of her after-school teaching gig. She said she didn't know. She hesitated, and then she said it: that my work *is* different, that it's impossible to take distancing precautions when you're swapping bodily fluids, and that it is, inherently, more dangerous with respect to the spread of a sickness. My face got hot and my voice broke a little. "But I need to make money," I said. "I know," she said. I didn't go.

Almost a year prior to the pandemic and to the questions of contagion it highlighted, a client booked me for six hours one night. He, too, was young, and wanted a date for a rave of sorts. I met him in the room first, where we had sex with the television on in the background, tuned to some kind of sports recap. I wore ugly combat boots I bought secondhand years ago, and stuffed the wads of cash he paid me between the zipper and my fibula—I didn't want to leave the envelope in the room, nor carry it at the party in my tiny purse. We danced and kissed under the strobe lights, bobbing to the relentless music. I went to the bathroom and texted my boyfriend a photo of the drone cameras circling the venue, gathering promotional footage for future events. He wrote back that he could see the lights of the warehouse from the roof where he was drinking with friends, less than a neighborhood away.

Eventually we took a cab back to the hotel, stumbling into the room. We had sex again. He finished, pulled out, and told me the condom had broken. I took another cab back to my boyfriend's house. When I got there, I told him what had happened.

HIV won't show up on a test until a month following exposure. "We could use condoms this month," I suggested half-heartedly. He laughed. "I mean, we're just not going to do that," he said flatly. He was right, and I felt grateful for his framing of our refusal as mutual—something neither of us would do. It's easier to care for someone else's life than your own; risking his health worries me far more than risking mine. I can't explain why we wouldn't use condoms that month, other than the fact that our desire to feel good and close outweighed our averseness to risk.

Ezra and Noah Benus—two halves of Brothers Sick, an artistic collaboration on illness, disability, and care—write, "To be scared of the sick is to be scared of [the] living."[1] It's important to me that my boyfriend isn't scared of me. I think it's important to him, too, and so he chooses not to be. Arguably we should be more fearful, but to take on risk with a partner—to alleviate the loneliness of their anxiety by making it both of yours—is an act of dumb love. Thinking about that month now, I feel stupid, and lucky, which is how I feel about a lot of things I've done.

More than a week into shelter-in-place, a client emailed me: "I am a nurse who will be traveling to NYC to help with the COVID Crisis. I was wondering if you were doing physical visits? I have been social distancing for weeks. I was looking to meet before I started working because after I step foot in that hospital I will be knee deep in quarantine." I wrote back, saying how grateful I was for his line of work, and how unfortunate that I was no longer doing in-person sessions. Seeing him wasn't worth the risk, for me, then criminalized two-fold: in the usual ways, plus the added $500 fine, which the NYPD was newly empowered to mete out to anyone they encountered breaking social-distancing guidelines. You can't fuck six feet apart.

Some of us had already done virtual sex work, prepandemic; some of us were suddenly doing it for the first time. I started texting one guy elaborate, forced-bi fantasies every other day for $300 a week, and someone else sent me $1,000 seemingly out of the kindness of his heart. Alongside selfies with bandanas over their mouths and videos of their pets, my friends posted to their private social media updates about their generous and ungenerous online clients, and questions about which cash transfer apps were the most reliable. Prior to COVID, a financial submissive offered to send me money for text humiliation. I instructed him to use GiftRocket but was promptly kicked off the app, receiving the following message: "GiftRocket's Compliance Team identified your account as having sent or received gifts associated with a prohibited use case.

We encourage you to find another payments provider as we cannot process future transactions for you. Going forward, any gifts sent to or from your email address will be automatically canceled." GiftRocket addressed me as Princess, the moniker my sub had used.

I don't know how the Compliance Team knew I was a hooker, but I know from Twitter that in the previous weeks they had done sweeps, banning sex workers from their payment processor. Since, I've found nothing as anonymous. I started trying to calculate, based mostly on intuition, who was safe to give what information through which platforms, like an absentee parent choosing presents for children he doesn't really know: this gentle old man who loves poetry gets access to my full legal name via PayPal; this young banker to the list of contacts I can't figure out how to hide on Venmo; this demanding philanthropist to my real iPhone number, through ApplePay.

These concerns are minor. I was so lucky. Many people were still working in person and outside. How is anyone to turn down work, to stay inside, if they have no savings, no access to financial relief, or no home? In a 2020 essay for *Tits and Sass* called "Coronavirus and the Predictable Unpredictability of Survival Sex Work," Laura Lemoon wrote, "I hear other workers complaining about the lowball offers they are now getting from clients and I think to myself that I've never had the luxury of setting a target fee and turning away anyone who won't meet it . . . I still can't say with certainty what my HIV or STI status is because all of my clients wanted bareback and I was too scared they wouldn't want to see me if I made them wear a condom." To prioritize one's own health in the sex industry is a luxury many workers can't afford. This is true of workers in every industry. Uniquely though, sex workers—particularly those who use drugs or work on the street—are always already seen as vectors of disease, and blamed for any affliction they contract.

A 2020 *New York Post* headline declared, "Sex workers feared to be spreading coronavirus in Tokyo's red-light district," with Lee

Brown reporting: "The intimacy involved makes the spread almost inevitable—and almost impossible to trace, with the sex workers refusing to cooperate about whom they have been in contact with." Good, I thought. No one's snitching.

Online and restless, I googled different combinations of words, curious about the tone of every article on the topic: "sex work"; "prostitution"; "coronavirus"; "COVID-19"; "disease"; "infection." One such search, a few pages in, turned up an academic paper on the Contagious Diseases Act, passed by British Parliament in 1864. The Act was an attempt to eradicate the spread of venereal disease in the military through widespread arrest and forced vaginal examination of women suspected to be prostitutes in port towns. If infected, the women were incarcerated for up to three months. Parliament conceived of prostitution as a threat to the military both materially and morally: the prostitute was both sick and responsible, the otherwise moral soldier merely a victim of temptation. Amended two years later, the legislation sought to regulate prostitution among the civilian population, too, and extended the length of incarceration for the sick prostitute by up to a year.

An escort I follow on Twitter announced she tested positive for COVID-19 and attempted to shift public health responsibility to clients, admonishing them for continuing to seek out sexual services under pandemic conditions. She implored clients—the majority of whom are older men with preexisting conditions—to take their health more seriously.

Some workers on Twitter gloated about their strict adherence to social-distancing mandates, while simultaneously shaming others for continuing in-person work. This became yet another class signifier on what amounts to a client-facing advertising platform—those who could afford it stopped working immediately, announcing indefinite hiatuses. Many outside the luxury class did not.

Ever punitive, Governor Cuomo quickly doubled the fine for failure to socially distance to $1,000. Such a fine punishes those who cannot afford to pay it: those who cannot afford to not be on the street. Access to indoor and online work is classed, gendered, and racialized. The inability to protect one's own health and the health of one's clients is not the product of individual moral failing but of state-sanctioned violence: the criminalization of harm reduction, of poverty, of Blackness, of nonnormative gender expression. Nonetheless, it is the sick prostitute who will be punished, rounded up in a vice raid by the armed and moralizing police.

Whore is an orientation. Not a sexual one; a political one. Miguel James writes, "My entire Oeuvre is against the police."[2] As is mine.

I had a video call with a client for the first time during shelter-in-place. I'd never cammed before, but the financial reality of social distancing had started to set in. I wasn't wearing my glasses or my contacts, so when I held my phone far away from my face for a close-up of what he had paid to see, I had no idea what I was actually showing him. The thought crossed my mind that he could be screen-recording me, but I didn't care very much. I thought about the likelihood that my faux-masturbation performance would end up on PornHub or XVideos, and it seemed truly fifty-fifty. I would feel violated, certainly. I would ask the company to take it down. They probably wouldn't do anything about it. I wouldn't involve the law. I would move on with my life.

I PERIODICALLY ASK my boyfriend to promise to avenge my death, should it ever occur at the hands of a client. "Don't involve the police," I say, every time, as he waves me away: he never would. "But kill him!" I say, and again, he waves me away: of course he would.

Even before the pandemic, the world felt structured by a certain amount of physical paranoia. I remember a time years ago, when I went to see my friend and her client in her new apartment, which the client was subsidizing. He was my first client by way of her, and though it wasn't our first meeting, it was our first in that place: a large, one-room studio. She took a polaroid photo of us, I forget why, and I laughed about it later—how young I looked, swallowed up in a hug by his voluminous figure. I remember the day as a warm one, but I might be misremembering, transposing in my mind the feeling of free movement into warm, easy air. In reality, it could have been raining. A week or two after our meeting, my friend called to tell me she had trichomoniasis, a sexually transmitted infection. She said it wasn't a big deal—easily remedied by antibiotics—but encouraged me to get tested, so I did. I explained the circumstances to my doctor, leaving out any mention of money. (I've only ever told the truth about my income stream to one doctor—a psychiatrist—and in our next session, she said she would be remiss if she didn't circle back to the profound alarm she felt at my desire to engage in such highly risk-taking behavior—meaning, escorting.)

I tested negative. My friend texted me again a few days later, asking if I had heard from her client, which I hadn't. "I told him I had it and since then, radio silence," she texted. "I'm kind of freaking out though, like that's my whole income??" I told her I was sure he would get back in touch, even though I wasn't. He was married, and I could imagine that the suddenly immanent threat of disease transmission destabilized whatever tale he'd been telling himself to make his infidelity acceptable. Their arrangement was a relatively standard sugar-dating setup: discreet meetings a few times a month in exchange for a monthly payment. He was generous and indefensibly wealthy, but he couldn't allow himself to think of his romance as her job. An STI for him would signify, simply, that the affair had run its course. He would see no need for sick pay or severance, and she couldn't very well file for unemployment.

A month into the pandemic, the Philadelphia Police Department announced they would delay the arrests and detainments of people caught for nonviolent offenses, including prostitution. Amid increased risk for many workers, the virus also made plain what we already knew, already dreamed up: the police could simply stop arresting people. They're not going to, of course—at least not for any sustained period—but they could.

I read an interview Fran Lebowitz gave to *Aperture* in 1994, in which she described her friend, the artist David Wojnarowicz, who died of AIDS in 1992. Asked if he was political, Lebowitz answered, "Very. Very. Although not always in a direct way . . . But his basic take on things was an adversarial relationship between him and institutions, or himself and authority, and that's a totally political way to look at life. You know, he hated cops. Not this cop, or that cop. Cops." The interviewer clarifies, "Because of what they represented?" and Lebowitz answers, "Because they're cops."[3]

Wojnarowicz sold sex as a teenager to survive. He raged against a state that had the blood of his loved ones on its hands, a state that would soon have his blood, as well. After his diagnosis, he told us, with everything he made, "fags and dykes and junkies are expendable in this country." Fags and dykes and junkies and whores—criminals, each and every one of us.

I often think about what brought me here. There are plenty of other things I could do to make money, and plenty of practical and impractical reasons I've chosen sex work: lower time commitment than a straight job; insatiable curiosity about the sexual proclivities of others; inherited neuroses I have yet to work out in therapy. Lately, though, I've started to think I became a whore because I wanted to align myself with criminality, and in doing so, to solidify my societal position as materially anti-state.

I say "align myself with criminality" and not "become a criminal" because one cannot become a criminal, one can only be labeled a criminal by the state. And it is exceedingly unlikely that I will ever be labeled a criminal, because of my white womanhood and relative wealth and privilege. When police see me, they see innocence. They have historically committed, after all, their most heinous acts in the name of protecting women who look like me. Nonetheless, I disalign myself with them. I want decriminalization, but I never, ever want police on our side.

The focus on decriminalization within the mainstream sex workers' rights movement necessitates positioning the work as a job like any other—necessitates a struggle for workers' rights, as bequeathed by a legislative body. Workers in this country are treated like shit. It's not that I don't stand with the working class—of course I do—but that I don't view assimilation into state-sanctioned professionalism as our end goal. M. E. O'Brien writes, "When refusing their imposed disposability and isolation through revolutionary activity, junkies and their friends move towards a communism not based on the dignity of work, but on the unconditional value of our lives."[4] I want the same to be true of whores and our friends. What would it look like to move on from the project of demanding that sex work is work? To move on to a politics of crime? I don't want to relinquish our criminal potential. I want underworld bonds, and coconspirators, and money hidden in shoeboxes, to be redistributed to enemies of the state—the ones who will never receive a stimulus check, because they've got nothing on the books to begin with.

I am an anarchist. I suppose it's obvious by now. When I was little, I pored over an edition of Robin Hood with hand-painted illustrations, reading and re-reading the page on which he married Maid Marian. Theirs was an outlaw wedding in the woods, with only animals as witnesses.

During the first months of the COVID pandemic, I lived in a room with my boyfriend and his cat, and I thought about crime. I made a spreadsheet listing every client I'd received money from since the quarantine began, and I calculated amounts I could give to bail funds, and to sex worker mutual aid funds, without feeling acute anxiety for my own financial future. I didn't know when I'd be able to return to full-service work. I supposed we would meet strangers freely again some time, but it was hard to imagine when or how.

I don't know if a criminal kind of class traitorship is valuable, or even possible. But I know whose side I want to be on if and when the world ends, and it's not the one that's blue-uniformed, pristine and cashless, fearful of the sick and the dead, holding on, with some vain hope, that the law and its enforcement have any meaning at all beyond this world. I want to be on the side of covert phone calls, and no paper trails, and networks of care, populated by those of us who would rather die than tell—on the side that has already been blamed, and already been sick, and already been masked.

## NOTES

1. Ezra and Noah Benus, "An Army of the Sick Can't Be Defeated: Reflections on Care Work in Perpetual Sick Times," Visual AIDS, April 2020, web gallery, https://visualaids.org/gallery/caretaking-web-gallery.
2. Miguel James, "Against the Police," *TYPO* 18, http://www.typomag.com/issue18/james.html.
3. Melissa Harris, "Interview with Fran Lebowitz," *Aperture* 137 (Fall 1994): 70–83.
4. M. E. O'Brien, "Junkie Communism," *Commune* 3 (Summer 2019). https://communemag.com/junkie-communism/.

*Originally published in* n+1 *on April 30, 2020*

# THE WORKPLACE

# Dispatch from the California Stripper Strike

## ANTONIA CRANE

It's nine on a Friday night and I'm headed to Crazy Girls, a topless club in Hollywood—the same busy intersection that, two days from now, will be blocked off for the Oscars where Regina King, Hannah Beachler, and Ruth Carter will be celebrated this 2019 season. Lady Gaga will encourage female artists to stand up no matter how many times they get knocked down.

Crazy Girls has a metal detector outside that customers and dancers walk through, like airport security. This one is flanked by two bulky male bouncers in white Pumas. I won't walk through the metal detector tonight because I'm not here to strip or to watch the dancers, even though I'm standing in my sky-high stiletto work shoes with red rhinestone hearts carved into the soles.

Nine on Friday is early for a stripper but not for our allies, and we need our allies tonight. We're staging a wildcat strike action to interrupt the unfair labor practices at Crazy Girls. I dump a big red plastic tub on the sidewalk—it's filled with bottles of water, chocolate almonds and protein bars. Our friends from Democratic Socialists of America (DSA)-LA, Sex Worker Outreach Project (SWOP)-LA, Me Too, 5050by2020 and other groups hold bright pink signs we made together the night before. We ate a home-made dinner while making the sparkly neon signs that read, "Heels On, Walk Off." We gathered in an art gallery where we learned how to make silkscreen T-shirts with bright pink stilettos that say,

"Stop Wage Theft" in Russian, Spanish, and English. Domino Rey, one of the other Soldiers of Pole—a trio of organizing strippers of which I am one third—is already speaking to a local news channel. Her black hair is pulled tightly into braids and her eyes blaze in the lights flooding down from the media van. She's talking to the seasoned news anchor, a striking brunette, about wage theft and our strike.

"We no longer should have to pay to work. We shouldn't have to pay house fees. We shouldn't have to give any sort of percentage of our tips to management or any other employees and we want to stop the sexual harassment and assault in the club," Domino Rey said.

In all radical labor movements, history is made when ordinary workers disrupt the system that seeks to exploit and silence them. In our case, because of social stigma, wage theft, and sexual assault, the strip club has always been a difficult and dangerous work environment. Today, the stakes have reached a desperate tipping point, even though technically, thanks to a recent court ruling, we have more legal rights than ever: we have the right to discuss the job while on the job, the right to organize and gather, and we have the right to unionize, which will give us a voice in the workplace—instead of only a body to be gazed at.

Tonight, we strike. As employees, we can do so because of a California Supreme Court ruling that changed the classification of employees in California: *Dynamex Operations West, Inc. v. Superior Court of Los Angeles.* The ruling makes it harder for employers to classify their workforce as "independent contractors." The Dynamex case involved a workforce of delivery drivers but is only the latest in a long history of misclassification-of-employment cases fought by seasonal workers, car washers, and others.

While the Dynamex ruling gives us the right to strike more easily and organize more publicly, the ruling has also forced California strip club owners to reckon with the fact they have to pay us minimum wage as well as pay federal and state taxes. The way they have implemented the new law has fostered desperation and fear. They've been doling out paychecks for zero dollars or with fictional hours worked. They have created a hostile environment by targeting "problem girls," ones who dare question the random fees and fines, coercive "release of claims" contracts and confusing bribes from management. In essence, strip clubs are charging strippers more fees in order to get us to pay our own minimum wage. It's not the fault of the Dynamex case and the new labor law itself, but the way employers are implementing that law, which makes being an employee seem like a bad deal.

What this looks like on the shop floor is management demanding we hand over the first hundred dollars we earn for the night, or the income from our first five lap dances. Strippers earn the great majority of their income not from their stage performances, but from individual lap dances. Imagine you are an employee at a car wash. Your boss tells you to hand over the cash you earned for the first ten cars you wash. After those ten cars, you get paid. Strip club owners, managers, and bouncers steal our earnings like it's the most natural thing in the world. Now that we're employees, they are snatching and grabbing every last dollar they can before we workers revolt. And we are revolting. The rumblings of revolution begin small: a tiny flickering lamp shedding light on a system designed to keep an almost entirely femme workforce vulnerable and voiceless.

Rebelling against oppressive, exploitative, racist companies and being frightened of losing my job is nothing new to me. Back in 1995, when I worked at an all-nude peep show called the Lusty Lady in San Francisco, we punched time clocks and took ten-minute water and wig-change breaks. Back then, although we aimed to stop blatant discrimination in our workplace, our main rallying point was to stop customers from filming us naked without our knowledge or consent. Imagine your legs spread wide, showing every layer of pink in front of a window with a stranger's head bobbing up and down. Then imagine a red light glowing from a camera recording your clit for a nonconsensual closeup. We wanted management to remove the one-way glass in certain booths and wanted them to ban cameras. After a two-year labor war, we became SEIU Local 790: the Exotic Dancer's Alliance.

Where we were then and where we are now are not much different.

This is what it's like to be a stripper today: lap dancing for free and being pressured to hustle faster to pay your own wages and then sent home if it doesn't happen fast enough, being coerced and bullied by bouncers and managers to hand over money that you've earned with your time and body while employers continue to avoid providing any employee benefits that we are legally entitled to—like a safe and sane work environment, free from wage theft, assault, and abuse. A moneyed man who is a government official came into the club where I still dance topless. He grabbed me and held me in a choke hold. I grabbed his forearms. I tried to elbow him. I said, "Let me go," over and over. Management was nowhere to be found. When he laughed and released me, I told him to give me $200. Then I walked away. To be clear, there is not enough money in the world to be this exposed, disposable, and unprotected at work.

This is the very business model that we need to explode—the one that club owners have operated for decades under an assumption that strippers' bodies are their product that they are pushing: a product of which they are owed a cut. We strippers do not rent a space or a chair, like hairdressers. We don't rent a stage or a room. We don't sling alcohol. We are not working on commission. We are entertainers. As lap dancers, we have more in common with actors and comics than with bartenders and barbers because we are a live show. There is no question whether or not strippers should be classified as employees—we are employees. And now we can unionize. The question is: How are we going to protect workers from abusive labor practices, like employers charging women to work for them? It's not audacious for the state to regulate the private sector, but audacious for these strip club owners to get away with wage theft, racketeering, assault, labor violations, tax evasion, and abuse for decades. Our bodies are not the property or product of strip clubs and never have been.

Corporate strip clubs like Déjà Vu (where Stormy Daniels is the current spokesperson) are the worst offenders. They are notorious for taking a 60 percent cut—or more—of dancers' tips. Daniels and other strippers who dance at Déjà Vu have voiced their preference for independent contractor status, which is contrary to the current change of law in California. However, the term "independent contractor" is intrinsically deceitful. Independent contractors cannot legally discuss money while on the job. They cannot cooperate to set prices due to antitrust laws. The Labor Commissioner's Office has no jurisdiction over independent contractors. Management is under no legal obligation to comply with contractors' demands. The economic incentives for employers to misclassify workers as independent contractors are colossal, as employers under this model evade regulations governing wages, hours, safe and sane working conditions, and other legal protections all workers have under the law.

Most importantly, stripping is women's work. We rely on our tips, which invites different questions that have to do with how we value women's physical and financial autonomy in the workplace. Critics of the Dynamex decision consider regulating the private sector a bad thing, but it can be a useful and powerful tool for workers. And there is nothing suspect about forcing clubs to allow workers employee status.

It's time we ask better questions, like how would strippers like to experience autonomy in their workplace? And what does a safe and sane workplace look like in a strip club? I ask these questions of young strippers who are vibrating with rage, and it's as if they've never been asked what they want before. The thing about normalizing stigma and exploitation is that eventually, you accept your powerlessness, which is a kind of death. Or, you stand up and resist.

It's almost ten p.m. when a petite Latina in sweats and an extra high ponytail approaches the main entrance of Crazy Girls. I reach into my back pocket, in which I've tucked tubes of clear lip gloss with "soldiersofpole.com" written in black sharpie—an offering to alert her and her co-workers who *are* on the schedule tonight that we are here, and we can unionize. As I walk toward her to hand her the lip gloss, two bouncers stand between us. One of them interrupted our chant earlier, yelling out, "You girls can come back and audition on Tuesday." I meet the dancer's eyes, then the bouncer quickly spirits her away, inside Crazy Girls where she may be told to ignore us, and later her tips will be confiscated by a "counter" and she will have to wait until four a.m. to get a miniscule portion of her tips. She may be drugged by a customer, sexually harassed by a manager. And she may be fired if she speaks up. I suppose this is why I'm still here, in red glitter stilettos, still stripping and still fighting, twenty-three years after we successfully unionized the Lusty Lady—to keep reaching my hand out—to remind her and all strippers we can change things again. We can, we can, we can. We are.

# What Media Coverage of James Deen's Assaults
## Means for Sex Workers

CYD NOVA

## INTRODUCTION

When I wrote this piece, shortly after the news of James Deen's sexual violence broke in 2015, it felt to me like something that would force the porn audience and industry to take stock of how things were done, and who they idolize. Years later, it is clear that isn't what happened. James Deen has continued to shoot films for his own and other companies. A year after the story broke, he was nominated for thirty-three Adult Video News (AVN) awards, winning two. A couple of companies broke ties with him, and introduced new consent practices, but a couple of companies is not a cultural shift.

Serial rapists target sex workers. The only reason that this time seemed notable was that the sex workers targeted were white celebrities, and the offender was one of our own. That difference wasn't enough to change the dangerous misconception that sex workers invite our own abuse, and it didn't reward those who stood up to state otherwise.

What would it take for the sexual violence that sex workers face to become the impetus for outrage and solidarity, instead of blank shrugs or undesired rescue missions?

I GOT A call from a reporter from *Mother Jones* the other day, her voice nervous. She was one of the many journalists who called the sex worker health clinic I work at, St. James Infirmary, looking for comments about the public sexual assault accusations made against James Deen over the past week.

She told me, "I'm learning about this world from this story, let me know if I say something wrong." We tried in stops and starts to lay a groundwork of understanding about what Stoya's tweets meant. On November 28, 2015, internationally known porn performer Stoya tweeted: "That thing where you log in to the internet for a second and see people idolizing the guy who raped you as a feminist. That thing sucks." And then: "James Deen held me down and fucked me while I said no, stop, used my safeword. I just can't nod and smile when people bring him up anymore." It seems hard for people outside the industry to digest this story. This time around, most journalists seem to want to be survivor centered, and they want to be clear that they know a sex worker *can* be raped. But their understanding of the environment of porn is always one with contracts which, once signed, mean that anything can happen to you. Where all men on set are lurid in their gaze, and the sadistic domination they demonstrate is heartfelt and misogynist. It's a worldview in which porn shoots are a battlefield where women try to keep as many of their boundaries up as possible.

For the survivors of James Deen, whose stories are told and untold; for the sex workers whose perpetrators used the stigmatized environment of the profession to prey on their vulnerabilities; for the sex workers who have been assaulted and then continued to work, sometimes with the same person who assaulted them, because at that moment that was what they had to do to survive; this news cycle has been hell. The only thing more unrelenting than the new stories of James Deen's violent misogyny cropping up every day is the understanding that these reports are only the tip of the iceberg, that there will be more stories of his attempts to "break women."

There is a way in which these revelations are also exhilarating. I've never seen such public furor around the assaults of sex workers. It's left everyone I know drained thinking, talking, or reading about it. Waiting to see what direction the narrative will take—will the news coverage continue to slant in favor of the survivors? What will the consequences be for Deen after the scandal of this story is dusted over by another? Will any long-term systems be created to ensure worker safety, and will those be driven by performers themselves or by an outside enforcement agency?

These questions will take a long time to answer, but what is clear is the deep breath many took after Stoya's two tweets were posted. It spread across my Twitter feed and it felt like witnessing a spell break. Arabelle Raphael said in a 2015 *Guardian* interview with Melissa Gira Grant that "it was a big relief. Finally, someone had put it out there."

Although I'd always hoped that someone would out him publicly, I understood why, for a long time, no one did. I've been a sex worker for thirteen years and have performed in or produced porn for most of that time. The world that Deen existed in is one I barely touched before gender transitioning my way out of porn that catered to straight audiences. However, I know that being a porn performer means living a life open to public inquiry. The wider public loves to take a stance on how much you enjoy your job— from fevered fans to "porn kills love" types, from the browsers of *Cosmo* magazine to the AIDS Healthcare Foundation. Building an illusion of blanket positivity about your job is not only about being a good porn star, it's about building armor against a society that wants you to be damaged.

I tried with the reporter to explain what the limitations were for women looking to speak out about assault in the industry. We talked about how Stoya, as a white woman with an independent company and a huge fanbase, could still feel pressured, as she said in Grant's article in the *Guardian*, to wait "months and months and months . . . over a year of months to be able to be able to call it what it was—which was rape." Even with the status and relative privilege she has, speaking out against Deen meant not only coming to terms with sexual assault from an intimate partner but also knowing that it would affect her career. Knowing that people would continue to watch videos of her and Deen with a new obtrusive lens; knowing that some porn studios would decide working with her was a liability; and knowing that since she, like many sex workers, has not chosen as of yet to go forth with a criminal case, that she could be subject to a defamation suit—although at this point Deen has stated that he will not be pursuing that option.

Which leads us to what Deen has said. Many people I know have chosen not to read the interview he did with Aurora Snow at the *Daily Beast*. The interview is exhausting to read. Snow asks him about each accusation and he discredits them one by one, suggesting that the survivors are jealous, vengefully lying exes; bandwagon jumpers in it for money and attention; or—perhaps the worst accusation of all—they are poor professionals who later regretted their work. He invites the audience to watch the scenes in which he allegedly raped Kora Peters and Amber Rayne for themselves. For who among us does not want the world invited to watch their assault, edited and marketed, so that people can decide for themselves what really went down? His tone is cavalier. Apology is so far from his mind that he defends his right to tell racist, rape, and dead baby jokes as just "dark humor." His interview responses create a world in which his reality is the norm, in which the women who have come out against him are just not cut out for the environment of porn.

I found this difficult to believe. When I started doing scenes with men from the crossover mainstream porn industry, I didn't expect the certain type of graciousness that I encountered, especially considering that these were people for whom working with trans men was a curiosity they were encountering for the first time. I've always felt that the environment of porn encourages you to be careful about your scene partner's comfort. In all the shoots I've been present for as a producer or an actor, there seemed to be an unspoken agreement that the actors will flirt and create real chemistry with each other, but that this chemistry is mutable. My fellow performers have always maintained a respectful distance, even as their tongue is in my mouth or their fist is inside me. I've felt safe during porn in a way that I have felt nowhere else.

I asked straight porn star Owen Gray, who worked with Deen for shoots on Kink.com, what he thought of his coworker's attitude. His response was:

> In our culture where cis(gender) het(erosexual) men have the privilege of not being sexualized by strangers constantly, they can often lack the awareness of appropriate boundaries, especially in a sexual atmosphere like working in porn. I personally approach all of my scenes with the assumption that the person I am working with is not genuinely interested in being sexual with me, they are there to perform a job, not to comfort my ego or give me sexual favors.

James Deen's betrayal is not just the betrayal of a man who rapes but also the betrayal of a fellow sex worker who is supposed to get the game. He's supposed to be able to put his hands around your throat while fucking your ass one minute, and respectfully sit next to you making small talk, waiting for the camera crew to fix lighting the next. Sex workers are supposed to have this shit down, because we know where the line between fantasy and reality is. Despite the protestations of those who claim that if you shoot aggressive porn eventually you will start abusing women, it feels to me that if you shoot aggressive porn, then you should be highly aware of when to turn energy on and off and be equipped with a commitment to always respect those boundaries. Sex work is a job, and one of the job requirements is your ability to negotiate consent. If you won't honor people's boundaries, you don't belong anywhere near another human being, much less on a porn set.

The questions this story brings up for sex workers remain. Can this call forth a new culture wherein porn performers do have an awareness of "appropriate boundaries"? Will systems be created that provide an opportunity for workers to report sexual violence in their workplaces without fear of reprisal? Moreover, does the relatively dignified national conversation about James Deen's assaults mean anything for other sex workers who are assaulted? Does the furor about Deen extend also to the thirteen Black women, many of whom were sex workers, who were sexually assaulted by police officer Daniel Holtzclaw? Or does the public only feel solidarity with sex workers who have hundreds of thousands of Twitter followers?

I hope this signals a tidal change. A moment where a sex worker calls out her assaulter and is not immediately, aggressively minimized is a blessing. When she is joined by others who say that they believe her, it is a blessing. When her story being amplified provides room for others to tell theirs, it is a blessing. Thank you to all those who spoke out, who will speak out, who told their stories even if no one listened, and who tell their stories to themselves to remember that it was not their fault.

*Originally published on* Tits and Sass *on December 11, 2015.*

# Red Flags

### LAUREN KILEY

I met Ashley* at a benefit concert for SlutWalk LA. It was in 2012 and several years before Amber Rose was involved, so it made sense that the benefit was a punk rock concert in a converted warehouse in Silver Lake. I hosted a table for Sex Workers Outreach Project (SWOP), handing out pamphlets, selling buttons, and collecting emails for our newsletter. This work also includes listening to everyone in the room tell you their opinion about sex work. Even in a relatively receptive environment, meeting a fellow adult performer felt like a breath of fresh air.

My experiences with both activism and sex work have been fluid. I've had a variety of names and roles. I've been in leadership and secretarial positions. I have worked for a variety of community and social justice causes and in several different niches of the sex industries. I've become burned out and dramatically retired from whoring and organizing, only to come back months later in new capacities. Like many millennials, I've had to work several jobs at a time and cobble together paying gigs here and there to put together a precarious livable income. For me, that's mostly included various forms of sex work and vanilla jobs. I have lived off full-time sex work earnings and I have had months where I didn't meet the minimum earnings payout on any platform. Picking up an extra

---

*Ashley is neither her real name nor her porn name.

shoot in a month could be a bonus luxury or the difference between making rent and overdrafting my bank account. This is true for a whole class of part-time sex workers who dip in and out of different aspects of the sex industries. This is especially true for a lot of sex workers when first starting out.

Ashley was a full-time porn star with several years of experience both performing and directing for her own site and well-known studios. Just about everyone I knew who worked in queer or lesbian porn was familiar with her and she had about ten times more social media followers than I did. She walked up to the table and promptly told me she didn't identify as a sex worker, but preferred the specificity of "porn star."

"I don't mean, like, any offense to prostitutes or anything," she added.

That probably should have been my first red flag. But I could see her point. I like to distinguish between filming fetish porn and mainstream porn for similar reasons. It's just a very different job and the industry operates in some pretty different ways, even while recognizing and respecting the obvious overlaps. She wasn't the first or the last porn star to say that to me at a SWOP table anyway. And some of them come around.

Ashley proceeded to drunkenly yell at some asshole who made some whorephobic comment. She was brash and unapologetic and I liked her a lot for it. She reminded me of one of my exes. They had the same hairstyle. We kept in touch via Twitter.

A few months later, she booked a photography shoot with me. She had shot with a few of my friends, so I asked what she was like. "Rough," they said. And that she "liked to push limits." But everyone assured me that they thought I could handle it. These were people I was particularly close with who knew my work and limits very well. I felt little bursts of pride and confidence in my own toughness and modeling capabilities.

And we were all correct. That first shoot was fun and hot.

A photographer rented out a room in a BDSM dungeon and it

was one of those scenarios we don't talk about very often, somewhere between a shoot and a session—but part of the point was something of a live, intimate kink show. It was closer to enacting the fantasy of a photoshoot than prioritizing the images themselves. A big part of why the photographer hired us was for the experience of spending an afternoon with beautiful women playing together in a dungeon. Ashley and I worked well together beyond having good physical and personal chemistry. It's hard to explain what that's like—intuitively leading a client through a couple hours when he doesn't necessarily have the language to ask for what he wants. I mentally promoted Ashley to a higher level of trust.

The photographer sent me a greeting card after the session, and he continued to send them on occasion for several years after. He sent a gift as well: a makeup bag with a shot of my body printed on it, strapped naked to a table, straining against the bonds while Ashley stood over me in a catsuit. I finally threw it out a couple months ago.

After the shoot, Ashley and I agreed to keep in touch and to work together again. I was excited to make my fetish work a little sexier and she said she was interested in making her lesbian porn a little kinkier. But she mostly shot content that involved fucking and I didn't, so we rarely had an overlap of work.

UNTIL WE DID. Ashley called to say she had an opportunity to book a fetish shoot, and I eagerly agreed. I had been shooting fetish porn for a little over two years at that point, and exclusively fetish clips. The vast majority of my porn is me talking about fetishes to a camera. I am an independent, part-time producer. I have perpetual ambitions of doing more and growing more successful, but I still work on a pretty small scale. I am not famous or well known within or outside of the industry. This was even more true back then.

Every other video shoot I had ever done was at someone's house. Even the fancy professionals who had rooms dedicated to shoot spaces or different sets were still operating out of their living spaces. It was a very different thing to go to a warehouse in downtown LA with an office in the front, a messy changing room, and the casual air of people who may or may not have been involved with the production milling around. It was less personal. Maybe that's more professional, but it was already a major difference. I didn't even realize we were filming for a real porn studio until I got there. I was going to be on a DVD and everything!

I showed up and they were running late and still filming a hardcore sex scene. I was a creep. I took some pictures. I was casually acquainted with one of the performers and thought she might like some hot behind-the-scenes photos. Regardless of my amiable intentions, this was a shitty move on my part. I didn't ask permission. No one stopped me. And I didn't see that giant red flag waving.

In my scene with Ashley, I was strapped to a bed while she used a vibrator on me. It's typically referred to as forced or coerced orgasms. We shot it in phases with an interview, a section of lighter play, and then a section of higher intensity. Somewhere in there a photographer shot still images. We didn't specify what we meant by "higher intensity" and this meant I had not explicitly consented to every action she performed. I remember the pain when she slapped me. I remember the surprise and humiliation when the camera got a close-up of her spitting on me. She didn't technically violate any of the boundaries we had set. This was "higher intensity." But.

I have filmed countless versions of the same scene, before and since, with a variety of people and a variety of fantasy scenarios. None of them have been like that.

The feeling that bondage elicits depends on the scenario. For instance, I respond differently to bondage for work and bondage for personal pleasure. But in any case, there are psychological and physiological effects. There is a feeling of helplessness, and adrenaline, and fear. And that's kind of the point most of the time, on camera or off. But this time it wasn't the dreamy euphoric version of subspace I had felt before. The loss of control was not comforting.

I know that I could have stopped the scene at any time, but I don't actually know that I could have stopped the scene at any time.

I was in something of a daze after we stopped shooting. My muscles were numb but my skin was vibrating. Ashley promised to edit the footage for me because I wasn't familiar with multi-camera editing. I'm still not very good at it. I never got any of the content. I never got paid. That scene was released (on DVD!) and is still being sold by the studio. As far as I can tell my name isn't even on it. Under any other circumstances I'd be pretty pissed if work I did was uncredited. But in this case I'm just grateful. I don't like thinking about people watching that scene. My stomach knots up and I can feel the blood draining from my face. There are other clips I'm not proud of. There is other content I cringe at the thought of people masturbating to. I know what it is to feel regret and embarrassment for porn I have performed in. This is a different sense of violation.

I SPENT A long time thinking that I had fucked up that shoot. And in some ways I did.

I should have been up-front about the fact that I was nervous and not entirely comfortable with the situation. We should have discussed the choreography beforehand. If we had, the scene wouldn't have changed by much but I would have felt completely differently about it happening.

I should have either left with the content or payment. We should have had the agreement about that in writing before we started shooting.

But I was not the only responsible party. Besides my erstwhile costar, there were the two directors, both of whom I understood to have stellar reputations and decades of experience within the kink porn community. They were active in similar activist groups I had been involved in. We had some mutual acquaintances. They had no business even agreeing to a content trade with me. It should have been a paid shoot. The idea and value of content trade rests on the premise that the partners are coming from relatively equal footing. This was blatantly not the case. Did the other people on set technically have a responsibility for my well-being? I guess not. Ashley had coordinated most of the shoot and they had no reason to assume things weren't going as planned. But when I am working with somebody new, I make sure to go over every detail as thoroughly as I can and err on the side of less intensity. Sometimes it takes more time than necessary and is annoying. It doesn't matter.

I don't think anyone should have to learn these lessons the hard way. We don't have a welcoming committee or training certification. We have whisper networks, friends, and internet forums. And those are limited in scope. Those are exclusive based on class, race, accessibility, and the sheer privilege of knowing where to look and having time to find them. Of course, those systems fail us; but I still fight to protect them because it's better than not having them. I have turned down shoots where references didn't check out. I have walked out of rooms where something just didn't feel right. And I know I have avoided some bad situations by listening and trusting my colleagues and community.

I didn't accept what happened and I still have trouble defining it as an assault. At the time, I just glossed over the parts that hurt because I didn't want to believe that the queer kinky porn community I was so invested in would hurt me like that. It was easier to make myself and everyone else believe that everything was fine.

ASHLEY WAS BLACKLISTED from the industry for #MeToo reasons a few years after our shoot.

The field of waving red flags began to fill gradually. There was some internet drama at first. Accusations of racism and transphobia. I defended her in some instances. I stayed quiet in others. It helped that a lot of the criticism was being launched by people I didn't particularly like. Then one of my best friends and closest sex work colleagues told me Ashley had been accused of groping another performer at a convention. Then more rumors started going around. The first stories I heard suggested that she had gotten drunk and handsy and sexually aggressive. I didn't know what to think. And after all, Ron Jeremy was also at these conventions. He wasn't banned until 2018.

Then more explicit allegations of rape and assault started reaching me. More and more stories and they started to echo each other like a bad *Law & Order* episode. The same best friend told me she had been afraid to tell me about the rest of the rumors because she knew Ashley and I were friends. I was gutted. Part of me was insulted. Didn't my friends know that I am a Very Good Activist? That I Believe Survivors? That I would have Done Something? But then I thought about the times I had spoken up in Ashley's defense. And how terribly painful it had been when I saw other Very Good Activists take the side of the accused rapist. And so I didn't blame my friend for not telling me. She probably did the right thing for both of us.

And I thought about that shoot I had with Ashley.

One of the rapes was on the same set, for the same studio, with the same directors. When that allegation became (moderately) public, they fired Ashley as a performer and director. The last update I heard about Ashley was that she had divorced her wife and left the country. It doesn't escape my attention that Ashley was effectively driven out of the industry while many other people with reputations for rape have not been. This isn't a happy ending without shades of homophobia and misogyny.

The directors I worked with that day are still producing porn, even working with well-known sex work activists. They are still getting nominated for AVN awards. This is not surprising. One of the glaring misconceptions about #MeToo is that there have been significant consequences for the people who make the most money. I don't know what the community accountability should be for the negligence that leads to rape on a producer's set, but I definitely think it should be more than a blip of embarrassment from a couple of public Twitter fights about it.

Whenever I hear a #MeToo story shared, one of the first questions that comes up is "why didn't you tell anyone?" I am in a very different position now than I was at the time of that shoot. But I still don't feel like I have the credibility to call out a major studio for a relatively minor incident that happened over five years ago. And who would I have told? And what would I have told them? That Ashley was rougher with me than I agreed to and pushed my limits so far that she was working around them rather than respecting them?

I told my friends. They weren't surprised.

Was I supposed to tell the directors the day of the shoot? It was the same day I had met them. They were good friends with Ashley and clearly financially invested in her. Was I supposed to tell my story on the internet? I have seen the results of performers who publicly complain about set conditions. I have seen the way rape victims are treated. I have seen the way big stars are treated. The most optimistic view I have of that option is that I'm not well-known enough to attract that much negative attention. But what would be the payoff?

I don't think the point of sharing our stories is limited to the consequences for perpetrators. Otherwise we've already lost. We have to shift most of the point to healing and supporting each other. Not because I don't believe in consequences, but because they aren't happening and they wouldn't be enough anyway.

The first time I told this story in full was to a group of sex workers. One of the first reactions was from someone else in the group who had also worked with Ashley. It had been when they were young and new to the industry and new to the Los Angeles queer scene. It had been a much worse experience than mine.

MY PHILOSOPHY OF activism for the past decade or so has essentially been to get a bunch of sex workers in the same room. It's community building at its most literal. I see sex workers taking care of each other. I see us opening our doors in the middle of the night to offer a safe place to sleep. I see us keeping mental databases of houses where a partner doesn't know what legal name to look for. I see us driving across the city to pick up a stranger because an unofficial network was activated in a group text thread. I see us cyclically giving money to each other's online crisis funds.

And I see us making spaces in the industry where the rules are different. I see the increasing accessibility of video cameras and editing capability letting porn stars create their own content and control their own sets. I see us sharing resources and getting each other work. I hear my friend talking about how she was letting another model come live with her for as long as she needed. And she explained to me very simply that in the BBW model community, "that's what we do."

I see us building a new economy. I see us pouring our sex work dollars back into supporting other sex workers. We buy each other's art, pay each other for services, and find ways to make us all more money. We aren't making up most of these systems. We are learning and borrowing from our elders and previous movements. We use social organization tactics from church groups, navigate health-care resources that grew out of the AIDS crisis, and apprentice in BDSM traditions that stretch back generations.

That's the "we" I want to build. My focus as an activist is no longer to convince anyone that sex workers are people too. I did that for years and, frankly, it was exhausting. I don't have the time or energy to convince anyone that it matters if we are raped, killed, or beaten. My time and energy are devoted to building this "we" and making it better.

## Demystifying Porn, for Pornographers

LINA BEMBE

### "PASSION IS MANDATORY"

"True passion and conviction are vital." I found this sentence neatly written in a beautiful notebook with a bright green cover and cosmic black-and-white details on the back, the thick ivory pages where I wrote reflections on my newly chosen porn career. The indie porn scene in Western Europe—especially in Berlin—has a DIY atmosphere, full of talented, creative people from diverse backgrounds who are uncompromising about their art and politics. People who often divide their work between shoots for the money and shoots to express radical ideas about politics, feminism, and how marginalized folks like to fuck. This atmosphere nurtured the idealism that marked my early years in the industry, when I wrote that "true passion and conviction are vital."

Idealism had to be the motivating factor. I'm a person of color, yet cis presenting, young looking, thin, conventionally attractive, and able-bodied. Even with all these privileges, the opportunity to make good money shooting commercial "ethical" or "feminist" porn was never really high. But what the scene lacks in commercial success, it compensates for with creativity. I remember having pizza with an American performer, their first time in Berlin, and talking about the European indie scene. They mentioned that people in this part of the world seemed to do porn out of "passion." I agreed with them, while thinking to myself: *As opposed to cookie-cutter films, just for the wank, just for the money?* To me, during that time, passion and artistic value were the most natural motivations for doing porn.

The political relevance of porn, revolving around bodily autonomy and the possibility of claiming sexual agency, felt very close to a path I was already exploring in my personal life, although not as consciously before choosing porn. I had finally found a way to express myself that seemed fulfilling to me and that others could enjoy. All these findings were summarized in that notebook, full of notes about the senses of safety, empathy, healing, and self-love I felt during my first years in the industry.

A few years after my initial notebook musings, I still think that in porn I found my true vocation. I'm still convinced of my ability to express through porn aspects of myself that I would have been otherwise unable to show, like how vulnerability can actually embody strength and power. However, there were other facets of porn work that I didn't consider as thoroughly at the time. Questions of safety practices or acceptable working standards, for which visible information and guidance are rather lacking. Regardless of how fulfilling I found my new path in porn, I also had to face a number of tough lessons about what it really means to do indie porn in Western Europe in our contemporary moment.

## UNDER THE GUISE OF AESTHETICS AND INDEPENDENCE: THE ABUSE

During my first months in the industry, I wanted to work in films usually catalogued as "feminist porn." I did my research and followed the work of fellow performers I admired. Following the path of admiration, I met the director who now I call my abuser. In interviews he talked about the importance of proper remuneration on porn sets, how he would never take advantage of his power position as a director, and about not crossing performer's sexual boundaries. Impressed by his emphasis on ethics in porn, I contacted him and proposed to meet. We planned to shoot a couple of videos under a "content share" format—per his suggestion—a term quite new to me at that time, but that means that we would create the films together and be able to use them for economic gain through our individual channels. At the time I didn't have any platform to sell my own content, but thought it wouldn't hurt, in case I decided to sell my own stuff in the future.

We met for beers on the night before the shoot. We talked about how my journey within the industry had been, how work was going for him, our challenges and aspirations. We exchanged plenty of laughs. He was respectful, and he gave me advice. I felt I could trust him. The next morning, I showed up at his place ready to shoot. We started with a coffee. I had plenty of time to do my hair and makeup, and prepare my outfits. The atmosphere was relaxed: he and I were the only ones there, and I didn't feel nervous about performing with him. The films we planned were to have natural lighting, a minimalist atmosphere, and a focus on me and my reactions. They would center on receiving oral sex, masturbation, and soft fetishes—all of which made me feel safe and reassured, more so than if we had gone for intercourse or sexual acts that, to me, demanded more intimacy.

By the time we finished shooting, I was satisfied with this new collaboration that seemed fruitful. In the midst of my satisfaction, he suggested we shoot an extra video. An extra video in which we would perform together.

I agreed. It wouldn't hurt to shoot another. Everything had gone so well, and I didn't know when would I be back in town. It would be another simple premise, both of us performing non-penetrative sex, with the focus mostly on me, in the same room where we shot the previous films. However, this time was slightly different. Half my body was tied up, the natural light was gone, and there was no extra lighting to compensate for it. He seemed more aroused. I noticed those changes at the time, but they didn't seem overly lascivious, not enough to question his behavior or stop the scene altogether. Now I realize that the degree to which I remember these details is an indication that something was off, and I knew it at the time.

Many months later, despite our "content share" agreement, this director never delivered that last film. Every time I asked for it, I got a different lie. In short, my abuser deceived me into having sex with him under the guise that we were creating work that would bring us both profit. I had no concrete plans for setting up a plat-form to sell my own content, so I was in no rush to get the films we shot together. Eventually, he confirmed that the video was not only missing but irreversibly "lost."

It took me a while to realize that his behavior was abuse. For years he tricked me into seeing him as a colleague: he offered advice and expressed himself as an ally, as someone committed to changing the things that are wrong within the industry—the pay gaps, sexual harassment, and inconsistent STI testing standards in Europe. He got invited to panels and hosted talks about ethics and pornography. Since we lived in different cities, I was out of contact with fellow performers who could perhaps have warned me about him or given me any sort of information regarding his abusive behavior. I only realized I had been tricked when other performers started to make public their appalling experiences with this person, some of them quite similar to what I went through.

I decided to share my experience on social media, as did oth-ers, the stories piling one on top of another. For me, making my abuse public was one of the few feasible measures to seek relief and heal the intense feelings of shame and rage I was processing upon realizing what had happened to me. I wanted to warn other people and see doors close to my abuser. Doing this as part of a col-lective effort made all the difference: my community validated my experience and I felt supported. The general audience beyond the porn industry had mixed reactions: many people wrote messages of support, but every now and then I received messages from people who blamed me for my situation, implying that abuse is a natural outcome of this profession. Not that I cared too much about those reactions, but the reminder of the pervasive, tired clichés about the industry was ever present.

## FEMINISM IS A PRACTICE, NOT A GENRE

Slapping the "feminist" label on porn doesn't mean the performers are safe from the most elemental problems of the industry. Feminism is sometimes embedded in porn as if it were an aesthetic choice, not an ethical one. On occasion it is used as a branding strategy to mark a fictitious difference from "bad" mainstream porn and profit from it. If "feminist" porn ignores the working conditions of its performers and producers, it is not "ethical" porn, no matter its aesthetics. Calling porn "feminist" without applying those values on set can potentially allow for abuse.

When we get fixated on the idea of feminism or ethics as a genre—a means of market differentiation—we end up buying into the fantasy that this niche is where the "good" people in the industry work, implying that there can be no abusers in our ranks. I fell into this trap at the beginning of my career, when I was writing about my true passion for porn in that beautiful green notebook. I was excited about the novelty of doing work that looked different from the porn I watched in my early years, which I found mostly dry, formulaic, too white. I was eager to make the "good" kind of porn, and I see now that the idea of making "good" porn out of passion turned against me. Not only did it prevent me from detecting abuse at an earlier stage, it added an extra layer of shame when sharing my bad experience: *If you're the "good" people, why didn't you detect the unethical behavior earlier?*

In my experience, working with a self-marketed ethical and feminist company has demanded unconditional endorsement: "We can only continue working together if you're fully over the ways in which you feel wronged by us." These were the words of a self-proclaimed feminist and ethical director who paid me less than my white, cis male costar and who sneakily omitted information about testing reimbursements. According to them, if I wanted to continue working, it was entirely up to me to get over the ways in which they admittedly wronged me. A classic manipulative move. Their "feminist" agenda had no room for actual processes of mediation, accountability, or reparations.

When I've defended myself against these self-proclaimed feminist and ethical companies and directors, they have reacted as if their unethical behavior was an unthinkable possibility. I've often doubted myself—had second thoughts about the price of speaking up being worth the effort. There's usually plenty at stake: privilege dynamics that could affect the work or the economic, legal, emotional, or mental stability of performers. In the case of sex workers, denouncing any form of wrongdoing inevitably becomes a form of overexposure. Whoever suffers abuse also has to struggle with legitimizing their claims, with being seen like a person worthy of reparations. When I have spoken to journalists about mistreatment in the industry, I have asked for various rounds of fact-checking because I fear any inaccuracy may bring controversy. I run the risk of being labeled a troublemaker, potentially affecting my ability to get work, as well as my emotional well-being.

On the consumer side, "feminist" porn as genre provides audiences with relief from the shame of porn consumption, an alternative that seems softer, "higher class" on many occasions, less loaded with the usual stereotypes about the mainstream industry. "Feminist" porn as a genre has capitalized on this layer of guilt. It has often spread the illusion that glossy aesthetics and pop feminism are all that is needed to "change" the industry, often forgetting that "change" should also happen behind cameras.

Feminism in porn should be a set of actual practices put to work in all stages of the production process, reflected in the final product. It's important to be clear about how our feminist ideals can take shape on sets and to continuously reexamine them for potential biases, hierarchies, and unchecked privileges. It is also important to recognize that even in the most ethically conscious, well-meant scenarios, things can go wrong. Still, there are actions we can take to prevent abuse, such as protocols or the guarantee of accountability processes in case problems happen.

As performers, we can demand more transparency at an early stage of the production process, ask for references within the industry before accepting work, be inquisitive and demanding about key work procedures such as contracts and delivery deadlines. On a collective level, it's important to share more information and resources, organize ourselves, and advocate for fair working standards—whether that means unionizing or forming any other visible organization that best serves our needs. These are feminist practices because they keep workers safe and hold those with the most authority accountable.

In order to gain validation and acceptance—and definitely to avoid losing work—many people offer up a happy face and claim fantasy working conditions, which blurs the very elemental fact that regardless of the porn genre, sex work is fundamentally work. We do not have to seek "empowerment" by claiming our work always makes us happy. We should defend our right to have bad days, to admit that feminism is a multifaceted, complex practice, not just a label directors can use to feel good about themselves and sell products without putting in the work.

I have performed in DIY productions with powerful political messages for the sake of the art. I've paid my rent from working on mainstream productions. I've made ends meet working in glossy "feminist" films that don't live up to those ideals. I've shot intensely pleasurable films. I have directed films of my own, collaborating with people I respect under clear rules about compensation for their work. I've educated myself on the value of independent, "clip store" content: how it can offer far more diversity than a lot of porn companies (feminist included) and help many performers stay financially independent and afloat. Over the years, my limits have gotten more firm and clear. I have also understood that doing porn with artistic aspirations entails a certain amount of privilege, enabled by a set of relative advantages. Passion is a privilege for those who can afford it. But porn is a job that needs to be handled for what it is: sex *work*.

*From Victim to Activist: The Road to Ethical Porn*

HELLO ROOSTER

I never pictured I would be in this position: that I would be a victim of sexual assault, much less an assault that happened on a feminist porn set. Especially not on Erika Lust's "feminist" porn set. Lust is the pornographer who was "making consent sexy," at least according to a 2018 *Rolling Stone* article praising her production company for creating the kind of porn that feminists wanted to see. The overwhelmingly positive media coverage of Erika Lust Films praises her performers for modeling real-world pursuits of affirmative and enthusiastic consent by asking their partners if they want to use condoms on-screen. Performers discuss their feminist politics on-screen, as well as their sexual limits and desires. In a world in which many feminists worry that the only access young people have to sexual education is through pornography, *Rolling Stone* tells us that Lust is here to save the day: Lust "believes her work can help the rest of us find our way toward a better sexual future, where explicit consent is a matter of course."

And so when I was sexually assaulted on the set of Erika Lust Films, it was the last thing I thought would happen.

BACKGROUND

Standard protocol: producers or directors introduce performers to their scene partners at least a day prior to shooting. Mandatory protocol: on the day of the shoot, everyone has a conversation about consent and sexual boundaries—sexual acts each performer is happy to perform, other acts that are *an absolute no*, and those that might be considered *a maybe*. Increasing industry standards: in order to circumvent and prevent "he said, she said" cases of sexual assault or misconduct, a list of those agreed-upon sexual boundaries would be written into a contractual document.

In my case, nothing happened according to protocol or industry standards. My scene partner and I established consent a month prior to filming our scene. She invited me to practice, train, and rehearse for the scene a month before the shoot, and so we practiced, trained, and rehearsed—in full—all the sexual activity we would perform on camera. Being a relatively new performer, I didn't question the nature of this proposition. I later came to understand this wasn't standard industry protocol, but my scene partner and coperformer, Olympe de G—who was also my director and my employer for two other scenes—let me believe it was. This was purely for the director's sexual gratification. An abuse of her position, textbook quid pro quo sexual harassment.

Despite practicing, training, and rehearsing for the scene, and despite clarifying my sexual boundaries on the day of the shoot, my scene partner violated my consent and the boundaries on set, sexually assaulting me in the process of shooting "ethical porn." By searching for Erika Lust Films online, I can still access and view my boundary violations, as can any other viewers of the film. This is an aspect of sexual assault on set that is particular to porn production: performers can reexperience their assaults time and again, on any screen. My sexual assault is being advertised and sold for profit as "ethical porn."

## INSPIRED BY SURVIVOR STORIES AND FACING STIGMA HEAD-ON

I am a Black, queer, nonbinary, masculine-presenting performer of color. My race and gender are not reflected in most of the stories our culture tells about sexual assault. Sex workers are also invisible in those stories. Privilege plays a role in whose story gets a platform. Sex workers, trans and nonbinary folk, women of color and other marginalized folks need our more privileged feminist sisters to stand together and help fight for our voices to be heard. Destigmatizing sex work is necessary to uplifting sex worker voices. Stigma affects whether or not victims of violence will come forward—whether their voices will be heard at all.

Despite the stigma, I came forward. I made my coperformer, employer, and director—Olympe de G—acknowledge and listen to the ways in which she had harmed me. This proved to be extremely difficult. Navigating the power dynamics that existed between us was challenging. I was alone in addressing these issues, with Erika Lust Films having few existing structures in place to address issues like these. If you label and regard yourself an ethical, feminist company, you assume you won't need them.

After trying and failing to address these issues in private with Olympe de G, I went to the CEOs of the company: Erika Lust herself and her business partner and husband Pablo Dobner. What I learned was that a similar incident had happened with the same director in question on a production called *The Bitchhiker* a year prior to my experience. This example was used not to validate, but to brush aside and minimize my experience. They placed me in a position of danger by having me perform with a known boundary-violator. They tried to wash their hands of all responsibility, placing the onus of responsibility and blame on me. "Forget about it and move on," was their response. Considering I was in no position of power to challenge this, I took their suggestion to heart and decided it was in my best interest to move on. This occurred in September of 2017, a month before the explosion of the #MeToo movement on social media. Without #MeToo, I would have buried the whole ordeal deep within my psyche, left it unhealed and unaddressed like so many marginalized victims of sexual violence have done before me.

It's not in the best interest of "ethical" and "feminist" porn companies to warn their performers about violations that have occurred on their sets. "Erika Lust: The Feminist Pornographer" is a brand. It's what distinguishes them from their competition. It's an image they are desperate to protect.

Confronting my sexual assault made me realize how much the harm disrupts our work: we often force our bodies to continue to work onward, past the trauma, in order to survive. If we stop and recuperate, sex workers have little to no benefits or insurance to financially support ourselves. Athletes have insurance policies and guarantees when others injure them. They still have a basic income to survive. Why aren't there methods in place that help to support sex workers in "our" places of work? I needed to address these failures and issues.

Performers and filmmakers were asked to attend film festivals and openly discuss their experiences, and so I did. Introspection and critical analysis were welcomed: this was the one place I found that this could happen. But what also comes with these festival screenings is seeing your abuse on-screen, in public, being played time and time again to an audience that might not know how sexual assault can look different for sex workers and performers. Example: a scene may be visually stunning, but ethically questionable in its production. "Feminist" producers tend to use *aesthetics* to demonize "mainstream porn." But aesthetically pleasing films are not always the result of ethical production. Ethical porn is a labor rights issue first and foremost.

I had these difficult conversations time and time again, at festivals all over Europe and North America. I made sure to keep an air of nonaccusatory poise, since the director wasn't there to defend herself and her actions, saying things like "consent can be tricky, especially for those who aren't well versed in it." I did this because I never wanted to vilify anyone without giving them a chance to defend themselves. I learned that the same courtesy wouldn't be extended to me.

## THE FAILURE OF A "FEMINIST" ICON

Erika Lust's response to me carefully talking about my experience—tiptoeing around the details, ensuring I didn't upset anyone—was much different from their response six months earlier, before the explosion of the hashtag. It seemed the #MeToo conversation had changed their response to dealing with sexual misconduct and violence. They weren't as dismissive as they were before. They sent me an email with the subject line "SINCERE APOLOGIES / We are improving our qty controls." However, a sincere apology was nowhere in sight; instead they wanted me to work with them on a document to ensure the safety of future performers. I did, but I would never be credited as a coauthor for my labor and time.

After being "called in" for mediation, Olympe de G escalated the issue to the public domain. Erika Lust CEOs, friends, colleagues, and I myself all discouraged taking the issue to social media, but she did, writing an open letter that accused me of being a jilted lover—scorned, not victimized. I had various correspondences that proved otherwise, but the accusation was shocking nonetheless. I pleaded with Erika Lust Films to take a public position regarding this, but they refused to act. They claimed they would do the hard work of being an "active ally," by supporting survivors, but that wasn't the case when it concerned their own company and workers.

## AESTHETICS VS. ETHICS

Once the incident became public, everything changed. The private support I had been getting from the CEOs evaporated. I was characterized as a Black brute—a common stereotype used to discredit and incite unease and agitation about Black men—and a stalker, engaged in the online harassment of a white woman. I scrambled to present the private emails of support Lust and Dobner had previously sent me, but in the end, depictions of Black men as aggressors in incidents of their own abuse have historically been used to silence us.

Because I spoke out, I was blacklisted: my peers were warned against associating, defending, or collaborating with me. If they did, they faced being blacklisted as well. In a *Huck* magazine interview a few months before, Erika Lust made this statement: "The media needs to report on sex workers' stories of assault, not only because they are at more risk but because they are often unable to report their abusers for fear of punishment. The effects of sex work stigma are active in society and a huge majority of media is complicit in further entrenching and normalizing it."

## GUIDELINES FOR CREATING "ETHICAL PORN"

Before Olympe's smear campaign, I had begun work with Erika Lust Films to create better ethical standards for their company. This work took the form of two documents: a "Guideline for Guest Directors" and a "Model Bill of Rights." I wanted others to understand the trauma and harm that had happened to me and others, and the vulnerability that performers endure when performing for their cameras. Through the creation of these documents, I transformed from victim to activist.

The fourteen-page document meant to guide guest directors includes sections on casting, fees, sexual health testing, how to interact with performers before, during, and after sex scenes, as well as how to interact with them on social media. Guest directors must consult a checklist of objectives to make sure that performers are in the best care, and the document states that "it is important in creating ethical porn that we try to balance the power between directors and performers, and create a safe space where performers can express their concerns openly." This philosophy and "code of conduct" was missing when I performed for Erika Lust Films, and I was proud to have been part of a team that had put it in place: indispensable safety measures for other performers going forward.

But, adding insult to injury, the company erased my labor and contribution to these ethical standards. This erasure coming after that of my sexual assault made me wonder: as a victim of color, was my humanity even seen and acknowledged? Even as I write this, I wonder: Why does the onus lie on us, the marginalized, to make change? Marginalized victims are often looked toward to find the solutions to end rape culture and violence, when in fact porn production companies and people in positions of power should hold themselves accountable. Helping to find solutions was something I deeply cared about, but having my contribution erased was a retraumatizing experience.

## THE ROAD TO ETHICAL PORN

The creation of truly ethical (and feminist) porn is an ongoing project, requiring ongoing conversations. One document can't fix the problem of rape culture and sexual violence. Sex workers and performers must come together: organize, unionize, and build a safe(r) community. No one should feel they must be silent. No one should fear being blacklisted in order to keep the peace, to be treated fairly and have reasonable working conditions. The road to building ethical porn starts and ends with prioritizing the voices and labor rights of sex workers and porn performers. We must give performers the tools they need when seeking justice for sexual misconduct and sexual assault on set. Sexual assault can't be brushed aside and excused with a simple apology and the statement that is used far too often: "Let's continue shooting." By prioritizing *apologies*, producers, directors, and company owners say they are building a model of *restorative justice*. There is nothing reparative about this approach; it enables rape culture. The choice of how to proceed after sexual assault, including steps for repair, should be given to the victim. Sexual assault is an everyday risk and hazard of sex work, and the tools for mitigating those risks must *always* belong to us.

## What I Have to Do

femi babylon
(formerly known as suprihmbé)

"I don't gotta do anything but stay Black and die!" was one of my mother's most commonly uttered phrases during my childhood. "Stay Black" is a common Black phrase. Stay true.

Mami is a first generation, Gen X college graduate, but I sometimes can't tell if my gramma is as proud of her as she was of my uncle, her favorite child. My grandmother is a boomer and worked the same job as long as I knew her, until she was forced to retire early. By the time I was in high school, she was living off social security and my mother was sending her money. Mami never taught me about money or how to manage it. She had the phone bill in my name for a few years, but I didn't learn about credit until I maxed out a Chase Bank credit card. She had a closet full of clothes and shoes that she rarely or never wore. Mami was a high school Spanish teacher, then a principal, and she was queen of the side hustle before white people got their hands on it. She braided hair, sold Avon, made her own candles. We were a wavering working-class family. "Pink collar." After the divorce my two sisters and I became latchkey kids and I walked to and from school at age seven. When I was eight or nine, the whitelady neighbor next door called child services on my mother. I can't imagine what for. We were mostly quiet, tiptoeing in and out of the back door, laying blankets on the stairs and sliding down into a pile of soft bed things. When the social worker came, we dutifully lied, claiming our Auntie was meeting us at home and just stayed inside.

Mami said the whitelady also asked, during one of their former over-the-fence conversations, why she didn't ask for alimony during the divorce proceedings. My stepfather was abusive. I'm not sure why my mother declined alimony but as I got older I heard her say, "I didn't need it." Black women are supposed to take pride in our ability to overcome.

As a young girl I never thought about work, or marriage. I thought about writing comics and growing my hair out. I thought about traveling. I thought about freedom from my mother, who was also abusive, mostly verbally and psychologically, but occasionally physically. It took years of growth and self-defining adventures for me to scrub my mother's words from my mind. Unlike most other kids my age—including my siblings—I didn't work in high school. I wasn't allowed. I didn't get an allowance. Every once in a while my grandmother gave me pocket money, but Mami took money from our piggy banks whenever she felt like it and dared us silently to ask for it back. Because I was barely passing in high school after being a high-achieving straight-A student in elementary school, my mother stopped investing in me. I had lost my value. Even though I wasn't a troublemaker, I wasn't a child she could brag on anymore, and I reflected badly on her as a parent. I was anxious and deeply depressed. I sat in the basement at my grandmother's and played goddess in *The Sims 2* until the wee hours of the morning and barely passed my classes. Since I wasn't growing anymore, my mother stopped regularly buying me new shoes and clothes. So when I was finally in college, free from her clutches, one of the first things I wanted to do was get a job so I could have money of my own to buy these things for myself.

Before I got my first vanilla job, I was propositioned by a young man.

I was "exploring my sexuality" at the time and my favorite movie was *The Players Club*. I saw the movie when I was too young to be seeing it. It has a number of quotables. My favorite: "Run me my money." Most of the time when we talk about it, we only mention Diamond's hot pink, gauzy dance scene to R. Kelly's "It Seems Like You're Ready," the infamous "Dollar Bill" speech delivered to Diana a.k.a. Diamond's cousin Ebony, and "Use what you got to get what you want."

When I was around fifteen or sixteen a cousin of mine had made a passing comment, probably as an insult, that I could be a stripper. But I took the idea seriously, turned it over in my mind for months and months. I had always been obsessed with lounge singers, brothels, whores. Women who were, by my definition, free.

Of course, these women also couldn't "have it all." If they were loose or promiscuous or liberated in one way, they were always doomed in another way. Like Ethel, from Diane McKinney-Whetstone's novel *Tumbling*, who saved herself by fucking and releasing men, but had no loyal girlfriends or support system and ended up secretly giving away both her children to the dignified, but scarred, churchwoman Noon. Still, Ethel was the kind of liberated I thought I might be. She had her own moral code and it set her apart from the other women. She was danger, she was other, she was a hussy. And even at seventeen I thought I'd rather be a hussy than constrained by societal norms. So when a young man said, "I can give you a little money if you—" I set my mouth to do it.

Hard easy money.

I wasn't good at it at first, but it didn't matter because I was young and inexperienced. Boys have been taught to appreciate that, and as men they learn to prey. Though I have always preferred girls and women, I was much more tolerant of boys and men at that age because I leaned toward obedience. I hadn't yet found myself and though I stood for certain things, I hadn't yet fully fleshed out my values. I was newly seventeen in college and men's eyes lit up when I told them my age and hit the knees. There was a space of ambiguity here, as there always has been. Was I working? Was this "sex work"? To me it was a hustle. I needed the money, the need was urgent. Yet sometimes I was fucking for my own pleasure; to learn how to have sex *skillfully* was my goal. There was also the allure of men who were, and are, a clear and present danger. I was assaulted or coerced into certain acts. It was not simply the danger of being a "sex worker," but of being a woman in this world. There was a high chance I might be assaulted, and I decided to take the risk.

This is the problem with terms like "sex work," a term that wasn't necessarily created for women like me, yet nonetheless has a certain amount of utility. The women—most sex workers are women so that's where my focus is—who embrace "sex work" want their erotic labor to be considered "real work." I understand this. On a fundamental level, many sex workers want to be accepted as "regular workers." Yet arguments around labor and decriminalization betray a certain libertarian politic that is highly embedded in current and past sex work rhetoric: to be recognized as a freely acting agent, and also to have our (erotic) labor exceptionalized. On both a personal and political level I find it frustrating.

I eventually got bored and found a minimum wage vanilla job at one of the restaurants on campus. I hated it. Was this work? Showing up to the same place every day, even when I didn't want to, just so I could buy food and shoes? Having to take home Sun Chips and provolone cheese for dinner to avoid spending my meager wages? Why was that work? I felt like six to seven dollars per hour just wasn't enough for me to take it seriously, even if I'd had nothing before. I would rather have nothing.

I sensed I was about to get let go, so I found another vanilla job, this time at a Chick-Fil-A in a cafeteria on another part of the campus for eight dollars per hour. An improvement. I was wary of one of my coworkers. He was nice to me, and his kids were older than me and also worked in different areas in the cafeteria. But he was too nice. Handsy. I have always been standoffish and intimidating, despite my lack of size. He never bothered me, but I found out months after I quit that he had been accused of sexually assaulting one or more of his coworkers. Go figure.

The college stuck me with a $3,000 bill at the end of the school year and that was the end of that. I half-heartedly attempted to raise some money via a yard sale over the summer to pay down the debt, but my mother confiscated (stole) the money. I never accused her, but the money was in the drawer and then it was gone, and I knew my sisters hadn't touched it.

By the end of the summer my mother was asking me to look for an apartment, another thing I had never done and never been taught to do. She seemed determined for me to leave. I scoured the internet for places to live but I didn't know what I was looking for. When I would show my mother listings she would give me half-assed answers or brush me off. She rarely spoke to me directly at that point. I made a list of three places and we drove down there, an hour south of Indianapolis, to look. She cosigned on the first apartment we looked at, without asking about the quality of the neighborhood or looking into the company. I ended up with a one-bedroom row apartment in the hood of Bloomington. The plan was for me to go back to school, but I knew that wasn't happening. Three thousand dollars seemed like an insurmountable amount of money, and I knew I was at the bottom of my mother's list of priorities because she told me so. She had two other kids to worry about.

Plus I had rent to pay. Originally the plan was for my mother to pay the rent until I found a decent job. I had no idea how hard that would be. The rent was $415 a month and when I moved into the apartment I had around $550 in my bank account. The prospect of paying rent gnawed at me like a mouse on closet panties.

They say one of the four core principles of human agency is forethought. Well my brain was telling me that if I didn't do something quick I would end up homeless. After weeks of unsuccessful job hunting I quickly deduced that I wasn't gonna be able to find a job as quickly as my mother had claimed. Students were coming back to town and I was one young Black woman in a town with one strip club, the bulk of whose economy depended on the public university.

Like a good girl is supposed to, I explored almost every other option until none of those options manifested anything for me. I told my friend, "I think I'm gonna have to go strip because I don't know what to do." I had been wanting to try stripping for a long time but I still did my due diligence of looking for a vanilla job.

I had wondered if it would be hard to be naked. I rode my bike the few miles to the strip club with a pair of wedge heels (my first pair of heels) and a lingerie set tucked in my backpack. By the end of the day I was back in my barely furnished apartment, employed and preparing for my day shift, and surprised at how easy it was to get naked and how hard it was to dance gracefully in heels. Luckily it was a hole-in-the-wall white/mixed strip club and many of the girls lacked both color and rhythm. I didn't learn any pole tricks there. But I taught myself a lot of floor work and I learned how to talk to adults without looking at the ground or gazing off to the side. I learned how to stand my ground and set boundaries. I learned how to save money.

I considered my labor to be work because it was providing for me, though I had never heard the phrase "sex work is work." Later, when I began riding in cars with strangers, I started to consider my work to be the opposite of work, an opposition to "regular" work. Anti-work.

When I was stripping I worked a double shift at least five days a week. A double shift was about from noon to midnight. When my new pussy smell wore off I began to work all day to save for a futon to sleep on and money to move. As the club began to get drier and drier, I started paying attention to what the Black girls said about Indianapolis. Misogynoir—racialized misogyny directed at Black girls and women—dictated that I would have to "change my look" to compete up there, but what was my other option? Macy's hadn't hired me on full time like I thought they would, and I had grown weary of vanilla jobs.

My goal was to work less and make more money. I openly spoke to my regulars about earning money to move. One of them was a businessman who had been trying to get me to leave the club with him for a while. I took him up on his offer and suddenly I was a prostitute.

With that shift into trading sex, I was able to secure a cheaper apartment and plan a move to Indianapolis, where hopefully my future would be brighter. Another regular of mine owned his own vending machine company and gave me his phone number and job information so that I could claim I worked for him in order to secure a lease. And thus, at eighteen years old, I embodied two more core principles of human agency: intentionality and self-reactiveness. I figured out how to reserve a moving truck and conned two guys from the club into helping me move my shit. A month before I turned nineteen, I bounced out. I arrived in Indianapolis with twenty dollars in my pocket, on a mission to turn things around.

It wasn't as easy to find work as I thought. Although Indianapolis is a bigger city than where I came from, I was only able to find work at a Black club. I wear my hair natural, and it was difficult to get past auditions, even when I wore braids, and even though I'm slender. My skin and hair deterred me. The Black club was equally difficult in a different way. I was much more reserved around Black men because they expressed an overfamiliarity related to their feelings of ownership of Black women. I was able to wear my hair the way I wanted but I made very little money and it was often attributed to my hair not being straight. The only other women who wore their hair unrelaxed wore buzz cuts and were extraordinarily beautiful. I struggled to fit in. My politics have always been "left" of my peers, and I found it hard to balance my values with my need to make money to survive. I fell into street prostitution at first, then pursued it. I worked alone. I didn't know how to screen clients or what that even was at the time. I didn't have many friends and I was struggling with an infection contracted via an eczema scab. I got into strange cars with men. My cell phone was often off. I had no internet access once I moved away from Bloomington, and I often felt hopeless and isolated. I took men and women home constantly to abate these feelings with casual sex romps. Still, I struggled to make ends meet, even though the studio apartment I'd moved to was fifty dollars cheaper than my previous one. I borrowed $400 for rent from the club owner, desperate.

Older men who saw I was struggling wanted me. They offered me covert sips of their drinks. Extras seemed to be an unspoken rule in this club, because all the women were Black, and all of us were poor. Drugs were common in all the clubs I ever worked at. In Bloomington it was pills, coke, alcohol, and heroin. In Indianapolis it was weed, alcohol, and coke. The day shift DJ had his eye on me. He was forty-three years old. I cluelessly maneuvered around his advances, unaware of what I was doing until another dancer pulled me aside and told me to be careful. "Men often think you're leading them on when you act like you do. I know you're just a kid but he has a history of dating the younger dancers so you need to stop messing with him. You don't see how he looks at you, but we do." I hadn't thought a grown man like him would be interested in me. I was recklessly playful with him, and I would hang out in his booth sometimes before my shift or I would pop in when business was slow. He always played my song requests. Until one day when I slept with a patron he knew. Suddenly he started requesting a tip for every song I requested. I hadn't any idea that I was "supposed" to tip him. I didn't make enough money to do so, and he knew that. I was upset that it took me so long to learn what many men are like. Because I wasn't giving him what he wanted (pussy) he treated me differently. I stayed away from the DJ booth during his shift after that.

The night shift DJ was my favorite person at the club, though. He was kind, and he had a daughter who was my age. He was impressed by my taste in music, and he invited me over to his house to hang out with him and a girlfriend. He treated me like the woman-child I was, and it was off-putting. But I latched onto him. The three of us spent the night listening to music, talking about our lives, and drinking box wine. They didn't offer me the wine, I was allowed to make my own decision, and they snickered at me feeling the need to sneak it at first. I had never drunk more than a sip before. I sang the woman a song because it was her birthday and I delighted at her response. At the end of the night, I fell asleep at the foot of the bed. It is moments like these that I cherish. The strange sense of safety among strangers. A loose compilation of misfits and transient family.

I wasn't making enough money to pay rent, so I called up my "aunt," my former babysitter, who was seven years older than me. She secured a spot for me at the club she was working at in Green Bay, Wisconsin. Many of the women I know who ventured into erotic labor had been "initiated" or introduced to it by a friend or family member. I remember my mother making sly comments to my young aunt about her lesbianism and her stripping. I know that a lot of women who consider erotic labor a further exploitation of women's bodies wonder: How does it all fit? Particularly for a Black woman who is already doubly or multiply exploited? Stripping down for the male gaze for profit, allowing their eyes and hands to travel our bodies as we milk it for all its worth. Is this power? White sex workers have embraced this as a form of empowerment. They cite pussy as power, a cissexist move to claim a place of dominance under capitalism. "We are winning capitalism," I heard one wealthy white sex worker say proudly. But are we? Am I?

Traveling didn't bring me any closer to winning capitalism. I learned how to handle money but what is that skill worth when you live in a constant state of economic lack and financial panic? We grasp on to these individual empowering moments like a ring in a garbage disposal; the panic that at any moment the blades will cut us is always lingering, even when the disposal isn't on.

I feel loss, but not in the sense that anti-porn and anti-trafficking proponents would hungrily grab onto and exploit. The loss is in the fact that I do not fit here. I am losing against capitalism, not as an erotic laborer, but as a Black woman mired in poverty, in racism. I am disempowered, not by my profession or side hustle, but as a victim of structural oppression. To prove that I "love" my (sex) work under these conditions is a pressure I simply cannot, and will not bow to. I found stripping and prostitution liberating. I own my trauma. I consider the fact that I could find so much joy in the face of danger a triumph. I enjoy being a fantasy just as much as I enjoy being real. But the perils of being Black and woman and poor weigh on me. I have been a sex worker throughout my young adulthood and into my late twenties, through motherhood and beyond, but it has never been sex work that drained me. Engaging in erotic labor presented me with options I never would have known I had. I became myself. I defined myself.

Ebony's vicious rape near the end of *The Player's Club* is often left as a footnote, or a lesson learned because she fucked Diana's man. We gloss right over Ronnie's oral violation of Diana—she fucked Diana while she was blackout drunk in front of a group of white men at a private gathering, without Diana's consent. Diana graduated from school but the strip club was presented as a place of danger and degeneracy. Ebony left the game and started working a minimum wage job at the same shoe store her cousin used to work at. The adage at the end of the movie rings clear and true to those of us who might reap the rewards of surviving capitalism: "Make that money. Don't let it make you."

# FAMILY

## Florida Water

REBELLE CUNT

His skin smelled like menthol cigarettes and chlorine. I was motionless, eyes fixated on the assortment of colognes decorating his dresser top. "You knew what this was," he grunted before finishing. The creaking mattress quieted beneath us. We lay there in silence, rain dropping occasionally, tapping at the bedroom window. I hoped that he would still give me a ride to work.

He pulled his swim trunks up from his ankles and tossed me the clothing I was wearing when I arrived. "We gotta make a stop on the way to the club but I got you." I rushed to gather my things, fighting back tears. *Do NOT break in front of him, there are dressing rooms for that.*

Very few words passed between us on the ride back to the club, where we had met. He didn't look at me until we arrived at an elementary school, and I didn't ask why we were there. We waited in a moving line of cars until we reached a stop sign. The crossing guard grabbed a small girl's hand, walked her over to the passenger side, opened the back door and helped the little one in.

"Hey Ty," the guard said, familiarly. "I believe Alena had fun today on her field trip."

Ty looked back at his daughter, smiling from ear to ear.

"Yeah, she loves nature and animals and all that, don't you Alena?" The child nodded.

Everyone said their goodbyes while I sat quietly, body in pain and mind blown. I couldn't believe I was witnessing this paternal act after leaving that house.

"Daddy, who's this?" Alena asked.

"She's just a friend, baby," Ty assured the child.

Her eyes lit up at the word "friend." She was ready to ask more questions, when I'm sure his comment was meant to keep her quiet. My heart started to beat faster.

"Did you play in the pool?" Alena looked at Ty and asked. Ty glanced down at his damp swim trunks. I could still feel his hands holding me down, pushing my legs apart. I could still feel the water from his hair falling onto my face, like the rain that came when he finished. "A little bit, sweet pea. Daddy was teaching his new friend how to swim."

Alena looked puzzled and let out a giggle. "That's silly. All big kids should know how to swim." She offered to teach me. I managed to smile.

We arrived at Emperor's quickly. It was a straight shot down Adamo Drive. The parking lot was pretty empty.

"Here's a little something for cleaning up." Ty handed me forty dollars. We had agreed on a hundred for the kitchen, living room, and laundry. Before responding in anger, I looked in the backseat. Alena was asleep. I said nothing and instead got out and closed the door behind me. Ty sped out of the lot, gravel and dust covering his tracks.

THERE WAS HALF an hour left before the club actually opened. No customers. No dancers, minus myself. I was grateful, since this gave me space and a little time to pull it together. I washed up in the restroom sink, caught a glimpse of my reflection. I scrubbed away the chlorine, the menthol, his sweat. I found myself missing clubs with showers.

*You can break now.* I started to cry.

The night felt like a string of conversations and interactions for which I was barely present. I couldn't focus, but I managed to make enough to afford a stay in a nearby hotel for the next few days. Considering the many nights I'd spent off the alley behind Brocato's, this was a win.

I checked into a spot just up the highway and continued working at Emperor's for another month. Most nights afforded me food and extended my stay. I kept paying to stay, but there were moments I just wanted to go back home to the Midwest. I wasn't increasing my earnings and I hadn't come up with a plan, so I was living exactly the same down in Florida as I had been up there.

I called my mother. We hadn't spoken in almost two years.

The phone rang. I looked at the time and hung up. A few minutes went by before she called back. Shocked to hear from me, she immediately asked, "Are you okay?"

"No. I don't think so."

She didn't bother with any more questions. "I'm gonna get you home, baby."

Within days my mother and a family friend had thrown their resources together and paid for my trip back north. I said goodbye to the waters I'd grown to love. The ocean, the hotel pools, the heavy Florida rain. I wished I had learned how to swim. I thought of Alena and her offer to teach me, unaware of what her father had done to me right before we picked her up from school. Unaware of the monsters that lurk night and day.

When I arrived at her house, years since we had last laid eyes on one another, my mom welcomed me with open arms. We just stood there in our embrace, each unwilling to let the other go. I could feel her tears hot on the side of my neck, and her body rocked mine the way elders do at church.

"You hungry?" She broke the embrace with her most familiar question.

"Hell yeah." I exhaled, and smiled for the first time in what felt like weeks.

We made our way inside and I took my bags to the extra bedroom. The smell of chicken and cabbage filled the air. "Just gotta throw on this rice and gravy," Mom called out from the kitchen. I had missed my mother's cooking. She was happy to see me, to cook for me, to nourish me. Our years of bickering seemed so small in this moment.

The rice steamed in its bowl and the gravy got thick. Mom's hands were covered in flour. She turned off the stove, fixed our plates, and sat them at the dining room table. I leaned in and took a deep breath. Something wasn't right. Something about the gravy. I stood up and rushed to the bathroom. This wasn't road sickness or nerves. I cursed into the toilet and wiped my face with a washcloth. Mom stood in the doorway. She knew what it was before I did. "I'll call down to the Women's Center and set up and appointment." I nodded, avoiding eye contact.

The signs were clear before my return, but I hadn't admitted it to myself. For weeks I had been nauseous in the mornings and craved snack food more than usual. Sleep had become my preferred hobby and my body was changing. But I was in denial. At the clinic, a very happy nurse congratulated me and reality finally set in. I was eight weeks pregnant.

"We like to stick by our new parents every step of the way. You have access to counseling here—pampers, formula, and classes are all free of charge." The nurse handed me a gift bag full of pamphlets, future check-up information, and chocolates. At the very bottom of the bag was a book for children. I thanked the nurse for her help and saw myself out. Once I was back at my mother's house, I called and set up an appointment with Planned Parenthood.

"HAVE YOU EVER had a procedure like this before?" the Planned Parenthood receptionist asked.

"Yes. When I was twenty-four or twenty-five?"

We set a date for early September, just a month before my thirtieth birthday. I had a few weeks until then to hustle up the money I needed. Every day I logged onto the cam modeling site I worked for and put in as many hours as possible. I met up with a few former clients in the area for dates. I earned enough to handle the costs of the abortion by late August. I also saved up enough to start looking into housing options. If I was going to heal and move forward, I would need a place to call my own.

THE NIGHT BEFORE my appointment, I received a phone call from Ty. "I've been feeling really bad about what happened. Even prayed about it. I should have just let you clean up the place like we agreed." He added, "Ya know, I'm a God-fearing man."

I knew this tone and that story all too well. Ty spoke of what had happened that day in Tampa as if I were a temptress sent from the underworld to test him. It was clear that he didn't "feel really bad" about the pain he'd caused me, but because he'd failed whatever test he thought I represented. He "felt really bad" about keeping company with a whore and he called me to absolve him of his sins. Strange, how memory works. I recalled begging him to stop. He recalled me begging him to keep going.

I didn't absolve Ty. Instead, I told him that I was pregnant. He interrupted—"You don't actually expect me to fall for *that*, do you?"—before I even got to mention next morning's appointment.

"I hope you figure out who the actual father is and—" CLICK! I hung up the phone.

I woke up at six a.m., hopped into the shower, and waited on my ride to the clinic. When we pulled into the parking lot, we were met with a small group of protesters. I turned away from them, looked in the opposite direction until we reached the entrance. The lobby was cold and already crowded. I waited near a small television. Mom sent me a text message from work. I knew she wanted to be there, but it was nice to hear it from her. I also knew she couldn't afford to miss a day's work.

Just as I started to drift off to sleep, a miracle in the uncomfortable waiting room, the front desk called my name. An older woman with a clipboard in hand motioned me to follow her. We walked down a long hallway until we reached a smaller waiting room.

This one was much cozier. There were snacks, blankets, juice, and recliners. Two women were seated, waiting for their turn. I got in line, choosing a recliner close to the restroom. There was a pattern: two to three seats between each of us. Near to one another, but far enough away at the same time. One by one we were called to the back, our chairs refilled with new bodies.

I lay there on my back, eyes glued to the ceiling, legs spread, and feet in stirrups. The doctor spoke with me as the medication started to kick in. Tears streamed down my cheeks, and I counted backward from one hundred in hopes of falling quickly asleep.

When I came to and was released, Mom was parked, waiting outside the exit. We spent most of our car ride in silence, but she held my hand tightly, and looked over at me when she stopped at stop signs and red lights. She didn't know what to say, and for some reason, I found comfort in that. She didn't *need* to say anything, and she wasn't going to force it. I stared out the window, attempting to block out the memory of that Florida water rushing back. I wondered, *Will I be able to keep my head above the surface?*

We pulled up to the apartment, neither of us rushing to get out.

"Hey you. Whatcha thinkin'?" Mom poked me affectionately.

I wiped my face and looked into hers. "Swimming."

# A Letter to My Love

MILCAH HALILI and APRIL FLORES

My Love,
It was the first day we were together when you carved your initials into my back. I had planned for the carving, but not your initials. Not at first. We were scheduled to shoot an experimental adult movie for a smutty art film festival, and we were prepared for you to cut me. But that day, you marked me forever.

With that carving, we reclaimed the meaning of sexualized violence like queer people took back the word "queer." We wore it like a badge. An emblem of our love, proof that we fell in love under the moonlight.

Well, at least that's what you said, that we fell in love under the moonlight. But when I told you it was actually the streetlight you laughed. I was grateful that your sense of humor matched mine.

We didn't predict how beautiful the natural light would be in the studio apartment that we filmed our scene in. Just like the happy coincidence of that natural light, our love was unexpected. We didn't have three-point lighting, but we lit up the whole room.

Sexualized violence was a part of my birth, as a baby and as an adult. When I was conceived, it was the honeymoon period, when everything was still sweet. Before my father's hands ever pinned down my mother's wrists. Fools rushing into the darkness their children would carry until death. Like a ritual, my mother and father would start yelling, and they would hide in the bedroom.

The door was usually ajar and, like clockwork, I would peer into the daily scene of my parents fighting. I always knew how the fight would end, with my mother crying, staring at the ceiling, while my father held her down and forced his lips on her neck. Every fight I watched felt like a little death.

The first time a femme fisted me, I was conceived again. She was a sex worker, a practitioner in the San Francisco BDSM scene. It was the first time I had ever been broken open.

Being fisted for the first time felt so familiar, similar to how I felt in my church as a little kid. I loved Sabbath school. I'd listen to the parables my teachers would tell us, and try to make sense of the lessons in each teaching. My mind would spin for hours, trying to decipher the meanings of each parable's metaphors. I loved our choir too. The sounds of a community harmonizing to praise blessings and make sweet music.

Initially, the melody of my moans as I felt the pleasure of a fist pounding my insides was foreign to me. I never knew this life could hold so much physical and mental ecstasy, especially since most of my life was struggle and misery. I felt powerful and vulnerable, and it was so gratifying to make my dominant happy.

When you fist me, I get lost in the waves of the sensations of your curved fingers hitting my cervix. One of my favorite moments in the first scene we filmed was when the entrance of my pussy grabbed your wrist. You punched your hand further as I sucked you deeper into me. When you fist me, all my memories of pain float into oblivion.

Queer hos, women who take shit from no one, and men who are gentle and sweet, they raised me into the man I am today. Men who could have taught my father about consent, and women who could have taught my mother to fight back. Our sex worker community is everything my parents lack.

Our BDSM community taught me the meaning of pain as baptism and serenity. Before kink, my only relationship with pain was negative. It was something I needed to disassociate from, just like the little kid who would watch their father sexually assault their mother. Although I chose to watch my parents fight—perhaps because it was better to know what was happening than to imagine worse outcomes—I never consented to the hurt I felt from that trauma. When dominants hurt me, I'm asking for it, and the control I have in those moments mixed with the adrenaline I feel from each hit transforms itself. It feels so good to know that my body can manifest what's supposed to hurt into a feeling worth desiring.

The kink community is the personification of the mother I wished I'd had. One who could have kicked my father's ass. A family that could have loved me unconditionally.

You, my love, you are my family. You're my community. You've shaped me into the person I am today. When I feel the keloid on my back and the raised lines that make up your initials, I'm reminded of how you've taken me and how you will always be a part of me.

I'm so proud of you, how you've grown as a person and how you're redefining the way you want to take up space in sex work moving forward. As we navigate the sex work industry together in new ways, you as an entrepreneur, and I as a web developer, I'm positive that we can help the generations of sex workers who come after us.

Like the hos who came before me, I aspire to be a role model for those whose mothers and fathers may not ever understand sex workers or why we do what we do. Our love and what we create out of our love will outlive our lifetimes, glitters of hope on the horizon. You and I, we'll be immortalized through our art.

Love,
Milcah

My Love,
When you and I met, I was buried deep in the grief that followed the death of Carlos Batts, my first husband, partner, collaborator, lover, everything. I was trying to exist and build a new

life without my best friend. The one who I had made plans with. The one who I had built dreams and made art with. I struggle to remember who I was back then, when pain was so fresh and every part of my life was suddenly foreign. The new me felt like a stranger. I have learned that pain has left my memory with many holes in it. You and I both laugh about this, because sometimes our memories fail us as a coping mechanism.

When we met, I was spending all my time distracting myself, forcing myself to be social when I really wanted to shrivel up and disappear. I was drinking to numb my loneliness and pain. I was drinking because being brave and strong was exhausting. I was drinking to give me strength to perform happiness and maintain the friendships I had cultivated with Carlos. Straight vodka burned my lips and throat as it fooled me into believing that I was doing what I wanted to be doing. I was always on the go, trying to outpace my grief, but just like my shadow, grief was always there, attached to me, encompassing me in the dark.

My home was full of old memories, so I never went there. It was a sad apartment that was always either too hot or too cold. An unfinished mess of unpacked boxes, packed-up dreams and plans, physical reminders of my loss. I could feel the walls closing in on me. I only used my bathroom and a sliver of my bedroom. I only went into the living room to entertain my various lovers. We'd get drunk and high and then fuck on the gray sectional I held onto because of my attachment to the past. My love, I know you hated that couch because of those very reasons and were happy when I finally agreed to get rid of it. It took all of our strength, but together we lifted and carefully angled it through the front door and down the stairs. I felt your relief as I kicked the cum- and lube-stained cushions. I watched them silently bounce down the dilapidated burgundy stairs.

When we met, I was proud of the stable of men I had curated to appease my physical needs. Sex had become a way to escape from reality, my form of meditation. Whenever others would suggest meditation—always without me asking—I would swat their words away. Sex was my escape. Drinking was my escape.

I first encountered sex work like most people in my generation: watching *Pretty Woman*. I was about fourteen years old when my best friend Sabrina and I watched it for the first time. A few years later, I saw porn stars on late-night TV talk shows like Jerry Springer. I admired them when I was supposed to pity them. They seemed to exude sexual freedom and autonomy, even when the audience was trying to shame them.

It was the early nineties, and Madonna's *Erotica* album was in heavy rotation on our family CD player. My sister and I would dance wildly in the living room and sing along to the album that defined the spring of my sixteenth year. I was still a virgin, and I felt like Madonna's lyrics gave me a hint into the excitement, self-expression, and enjoyment that was awaiting me, once I found the right guy to lose my highly guarded virginity to.

It wasn't long until I unlocked the mystery of why I was always fascinated by sex workers. My sister and I learned that my paternal grandmother had been a sex worker in Ecuador in the early sixties. One hot summer day in a park near my father's place, where a group of Ecuadorians met up on the weekends to sell food and congregate, I asked my dad about his biological mother. He told me that she was a brothel sex worker, and that he found out from one of his teachers. "I followed her one day after school to see if she really went there," he said.

Without shame, he confirmed that she did indeed work in a brothel; and in that moment I realized that I had a family connection to sex work and my fascination made sense. We called her *May* at her request, never calling her *Abuelita* as I wished I could. She had given him up when he was a baby and they were sporadically in contact throughout their lives. My grandmother was single her whole life and had a strained relationship with her only child. I came to believe that sex workers were solitary beings, but that was before I met Carlos.

When I met Carlos in the summer of 2000, I had never modeled for a professional photographer before. "He's going to put naked pictures of you all over the internet!" my mother warned. I went to his apartment and shot with him anyway. Our romantic and artistic relationship grew, and soon we were married and constantly working on creative projects that blended art and sex. Our work moved from still images to film. I was offered a part in a scene, and found what seemed to be my calling: I loved being in front of the camera and was now exploring my sexuality with my husband by my side. My work was well received. I was happy and lucky to be able to use my body to empower other fat women to feel worthy of sex and challenge the norms of what is seen as beautiful.

"At least you experienced great love." When someone endures a loss, people are well-meaning, but they often say some stupid shit. Many people reminded me that some never get to find their soul mate. "At least you had thirteen years with yours." These words stung the most. How was someone else's lack of love supposed to make me feel better about the death of mine? Despite the sting, I started to believe them.

I wanted to love again. I oscillated between believing that I was only allowed one great love and believing that I could have a deep connection with another. I'd tell my other single friends, "I hope there's someone else out there for me." My intuition told me that there was someone out there, living their life, and having the experiences that would eventually lead us to each other. "I'd like to believe that each day that passes us is bringing us closer to each other."

I could feel the invisible-but-strong energetic string that tied my path to yours.

I was in a rush the first time we met, so the memory of our encounter is faded. We were both taking part in a photo shoot at *Penthouse* for some political thing. You were on your way out when I was on my way in.

"I'm Milcah Halili and I'll be on your show tomorrow." My

producer had booked you for my radio show, *Voluptuous Life*, the very next day.

"Cool. What are you into sexually these days that you'd like to discuss tomorrow?" I asked. You told me that you were really into role-play, and I gave you my number.

When you got to the studio, you were a cheerful, engaging, and fun guest, sharing your love of role-play with me and my listeners. We bonded over both being size queens, our love of travel, and laughed together while we got the callers off. We promised to hang out when you moved to LA.

I entered the adult entertainment industry with Carlos, and I never fully considered what it might be like to be in it without him. Once I was widowed, telling prospective dates about my work was something I needed to learn. I believed that no one would fully accept me because of my sex work. I started to believe the narrative that I had been hearing my whole life: that sex workers are unlovable and the work we do can never be accepted by a loving and supportive partner. Sex workers are solitary. I would be solitary.

I went on dates with men who had different relationships to and understandings of sex work. I wanted to find some connection, any connection. I went out with a fellow performer who I had done a scene with, but immediately knew it was wrong when he couldn't hold a conversation with me. Besides, his messy eating grossed me out. I went out with a few super hot fans who were just happy to be in my presence, eager to please me. Those connections fizzled out quickly, once the novelty wore off and their flaws became evident. I went out with fellow artists who I thought would understand my medium and support my growth. I was disappointed to realize that just because you are both artists doesn't automatically mean you have a connection. I went on Tinder dates full of hope and possibility, but I often wondered if the people on the other side of the table secretly knew my work. Some men I saw withdrew from the pressure of dating a widow and said, "I don't want to date you because I will always come second to Carlos."

I believed that no one would want a sex worker. I believed that no one would want a widow. I made peace with that, and resolved to do my best at a life on my own.

When we met, you saw me because you were a sex worker too, but I wasn't sure how long we would last. I remember an uncomfortable text exchange we had when I was visiting New York. It was cold and late, and I was making my way through the East Village drunk and high on coke. "It will be easier if we just stay casual," I texted you, because deep down I felt unlovable.

Porn and sex work gave me so many unexpected gifts. I have made some great friends, have had a platform to empower people across the world, and I had unexpectedly become part of a strong community. Conventions and award shows feel more like family reunions. You pass each other on your way to signings, share a quick minute in the elevator catching up on projects, and lament the fast-paced days of networking while waiting for a table at the nearest restaurant. I had actually never felt the porn community as strongly as I did in the time after losing Carlos. I was surprised and comforted when they showed up and surrounded me with words, donations, and supportive energy.

We in the sex work community have shared experiences, similar struggles, and face the same stigmas. There is a level of familiarity and comfort I feel when I am around other sex workers. It's a bond that is hard to explain. I felt this connection with you immediately.

Once you and I started hanging out more frequently, I was drawn to your mind. Your way with words attracted me like a magnet. Your outlook on the world was refreshing. I felt comfortable with you. We were communicating constantly.

Our sexual chemistry was like nothing I had experienced before. We were having sex day and night, never taking breaks for food or sleep. Once we realized this, we started scheduling time for our other basic needs. Two months into our courtship you said, "I want to go on a real actual date you. One where we're not at a bar or in bed."

It was a beautiful fall day and I drove you to the Natural History Museum. I was awkward while we admired the gemstone collection and shy as we casually strolled the cavernous rooms that house real dinosaur bones. In the rose garden, the fear of getting caught smoking a joint made me just as nervous as taking your hand and putting my arm around your waist. We had been fucking all the time, but these small acts of affection felt so monumental and taboo. I had learned to detach my feelings from sex. One of the dirtiest things I could do is actually share affection with another.

Our romance moved very quickly. I was scared of how willing and open and clear you were about wanting a serious committed relationship with me. I wasn't used to anyone being so upfront about their desires. It was uncomfortable. Society told me that my status as a widow made me undesirable and that moving on wasn't the true way to respect the memory of my lost one. I frustrated you when my words contradicted my actions. I broke your heart a little each time you could feel me being sexual with another, even if it was all the way across the country. It took me a few months to allow myself to open up to the idea that this dynamic new person was so willing and eager to be in a relationship with me.

"Omg I need to vent to you!" I texted one weekend early into our relationship when we were both working away from LA. You were always there for the venting. Healing our trauma is one way we have connected. It challenges us when we are triggered, and in those moments we go back to acting like scared children. I haven't known another person so invested in working through their past. I was relieved that I didn't have to explain the sex work part of my life to you. I was grateful when you listened to me vent, and that you recognized the frustration I had with the emotional labor that demanding clients require.

You have helped me acknowledge old pain and realize that it is important to try and take care of myself. You remind me that life has happiness and beauty and that there is hope, even if it's a just a tiny glimmer inside sometimes. No one has loved me as gently as you do. From death came my rebirth. You have been a vital part of this rebirth because with you, I've stopped running from reality. You gave me safety to slow down and move through the uncomfortable murkiness of loss. Since meeting you, I have come out of darkness.

More than anything, our connection has been pure. Our sense of humor and inside jokes delight me every day. I am your Fat Spoon, you are my Fancy Spoon. Our temperaments are similar, and from the beginning, we shared the same goals of wanting to be married and start a family. "I want a puggy and a frenchie and two babies!" is what you've told me since we first met. My time with you has motivated me to grow and heal in unexpected ways. I never thought I would find joy in getting eight hours of sleep, drinking plenty of water, and saving money. Finding joy in these simple everyday acts makes me certain that I want you by my side for the rest of my time here. I'm so grateful that our days lead us to each other, and sex work was the avenue on which our paths would align.

You are my soul's mirror. You are my best friend.

Love,
April

# A Family Affair

DIA DYNASTY

"GRANDMOTHER!!!" I wailed as I tried to push outward one more time, squeezing my eyes tightly from the mounting pressure and pain. I had a hard turd stuck in my tiny butthole, without enough abdominal strength in my little body to push it out. Terrible tearing pain. My grandmother came rushing into the bathroom. "It hurts," tears streaming down my face. She disappeared and reappeared with my youngest aunt, my newly acquired uncle from a different aunt, and a large metal spoon. The young aunt grabbed my wrists and this stranger, an uncle by marriage, grabbed me by the ankles, and they hoisted me off the can. Hanging in the middle like a wet hammock, I was already in a state of shock as my grandmother came at me with the spoon and have no recollection of what was done with that spoon, but I can make an educated guess.

Nobody talked about this incident with me afterward. We all pretended it didn't happen.

THE FIRST TIME we met, Gregory walked into my BDSM studio in a porkpie hat with bright blue eyes. A white, military-trained, cisgender man, mostly bald and in his midsixties, he seemed familiar with the basic protocols of coming into a FemDom space: showing respect by calling us "Ma'am" and not getting too comfortable. My play space is aptly named La Maison du Rouge, a studio apartment

183

furnished with a metal cage and a spanking bench and large mirrors covering two walls, other walls dressed in deep, womb-like reds and lush black velvets. After disrobing, Gregory fit in there, standing in his pallid milky flesh suit. There was a slight tremor to his hands and his face intensified with earnestness whenever he spoke. He was particularly clear in his desire to serve women and to be held in heavy, immobilizing bondage. Our first session was in November, so Lucy and I basted him in our urine and then mummified him in saran wrap—a juicy Thanksgiving turkey. My partner in crime and constant source of bad bitch inspiration, Lucy was hired at a boutique all-Asian dungeon a year after I started working there. I showed her some basic BDSM techniques, like tying rope and wielding a whip, and we quickly cultivated a psychic connection in our deviousness. As we did time at the dungeon, we started to commiserate about the misogynistic male owner's tantrums, the woes of tampon strings, and the office politics involving red lipstick, body shaming, and the dungeon's tyranny over social media representation, which was unavailable to us.

The second session with Gregory earned him his name: Big Baby G. Outfitted in a white tutu and soft leather bondage boots with spikes inside, he was resplendent in our attention. He was careful to set his soft leather boots down tenderly on the ground, not daring to stand or walk unless instructed. Adorned in padded leather mitts that were tethered to his sensitive nipples through the pulley of the D-rings on his collar, we made him reach for a teddy bear. His cries were that exactly of a big baby. We shoved a giant crying baby mask on his head and thus he was christened Big Baby G. Despite the torment, his eagerness to please us was beyond that of what many clients exhibit, and I was genuinely cry-laughing from beginning to end. I enjoy power exchange in its many forms, especially when it has a sense of ridiculousness and playfulness around it.

Generally, clients come with a list of interests and limits which sets up the parameters of play in a session. BBG had very few parameters, so with blanket consent from him, Lucy and I had free reign. Which in turn allows a dynamic where the client becomes our toy and it's just Lucy and I playing together in our own twisted universe, two feral children goading each other on. She and I have a compatibility in our deviousness where one administers the torment and the other comforts and soothes the person so they can sustain more. We are the good cop, bad cop; the angel and devil; and it forms a complete circle of laughter and terror.

A few more sessions in, and BBG presented us with his desire to be chaste, for us to hold the keys to the tiny padlock that would fasten his metal chastity device. A joint ownership of a shared slave seemed like a fun idea in theory, but this was a new dynamic and I was unsure of how much work it would entail. I'd taken on "slaves" before—in FemDom speak, a Mistress/slave relationship is an exclusive one, where the Domme becomes the "owner" of a client, who is then trained to be her servant, her maid, her pet, her gopher, and her personal assistant—but I had never shared one. Lucy was quick to agree, but I felt like a reluctant parent adopting this adult baby and assuming a perverted sense of responsibility for him, starting with his dick cage. Apparently, a woman's work is never done when it comes to men's dicks.

Some clients have a distinct fantasy of being "owned" by a dominant woman who holds the key to a literal cage containing his "troublesome" penis. The fantasy revolves around the loss of control to a woman and her whims of merciless torment, oscillating between good behavior and punishment. There's usually very little room in the fantasy for real-life logistics or the desires of the "key-holder"—it's an asymmetrical sexual dynamic. In the grand scheme of Domme-client relationships, key-holding can cement the power exchange, and create a sense of financial security. It does so because the Dominant must be connected and accountable for the client's sexual health, and be accessible in the event of an emergency that requires removal of the chastity cage. But BBG agreed that he would take guidance and direction from us in this slave training, as well as provide supplies for our play space. So what could go wrong with a big baby?

I welcome clients who are looking for a deeper sense of submission and devotion to start slave training. This is a nebulous curriculum based on the client's kinks, personality, and privilege, but is an opportunity to mold the client into the best version of themselves. In turn, I learn more about myself as a reflection of them, and vice versa. Cultivating familial relationships that grow and deepen was never something I sought to do with my given family, as I always felt like an outsider around them. Hearing BBG's desire to, essentially, be cared for, I saw an opportunity to embrace, explore, and apply the maternal feelings I usually reserve for my cat to a man. I wondered how I could eroticize this maternal feeling, as BBG was partially dependent on me for sexual release. All of it seemed like a challenge, but one I was willing to take because I believe personal transformation can be achieved through the practice of BDSM, not just for the submissive, but also for the Dominant.

Lucy, BBG, and I charted our progress after each session at our family meals. I vaguely recall a time in my life when I ate dinner with my mother and stepfather, but the most memorable things about those meals were how I had to keep my mouth shut as my stepfather repeated his thoughts on tartar sauce. But these family meals were different: joyous times for casual conversation about anything and everything. Lucy and I decided what BBG would eat so he could input the carbohydrate calorie count into his glucose monitor. BBG had taken to calling Lucy "Daddy."

"BBG, how did you perceive your mother?" I asked him.

"She was a goddess who could do no wrong."

Uh oh. I could see where this road was leading: into Mommytown. I have been making a series of deliberate life decisions to thwart this progression.

It was time for a family outing at the "world's oldest BDSM training chateau" and my friend was the Headmistress. This quaint, woodsy, upstate property is a sort of kinky bed and breakfast staffed with collared and scantily-clad slaves of all body types and ages, structured in old-guard, high-protocol ways. A sense of formality kept the "slaves" in their positions—trained with strict limits and directives of behavior aimed at serving their respective Dominant. Only the Dominants were allowed to mingle casually and sit in the chairs—the slaves had to sit and dine on the floor. Individuals who seek to learn about BDSM come here for workshops and play parties, as well as more committed training curriculums that yield a fuller understanding of lifestyle BDSM.

Our family outing included me and Lucy, her personal slave Pain Puppy, and of course our BBG.

The main house was a bright, open space with a sofa, a divan, and a set of two Victorian balloon chairs, all facing each other in an open square, filled by a soft, plushy Moroccan rug. Downstairs, the expansive basement was filled with everything you could ever imagine a space called a "dungeon" would house. Red carpeting, chains swinging from the ceiling, a "medical" area behind a hospital partition, medieval torture contraptions, rows and rows of striking implements, and shelves lined with sinister spiky objects.

For me, the chateau was an energy vortex, imbued with over twenty-five years of high-protocol power exchange crystallized in its very foundation. I loved petite and spritely Headmistress, with her playful, intuitive approach to domination. But being in that space, I felt tense with performance anxiety about the idea of constantly playing "Dominatrix" as opposed to simply being casually dominant all swirling and pulling inside my head.

Lucy and I were scheduled to lead a workshop in playful humiliation. Pups was a veteran of humiliation—from light and playful to deeply degrading—but BBG was a relative novice at engaging in this form of play. They both were told that they would become our demonstration bottoms and both agreed, Pups eagerly wagging his tail and BBG with a knot of lines and brows on his forehead, but a willful determination to please his owners.

I observed that BBG would often take on more than he could physically handle because his will to please overshadowed his bodily limitations. It took him a long time to do simple tasks and the fumbles were thoroughly exasperating to me. Such is the state of motherhood. BBG dropped things on the floor, picked them back up, and dropped them all over again. I regarded him as a problem child, one that had to be carefully monitored and constantly pumped full of positive assertions and clear, bullet-pointed directives. As a part of the slave training curriculum, I'd instructed BBG to learn to meditate. Despite his meditation practice, he reported stress was causing his glucose levels to rollercoaster and the little monitor he wore would beep insistently. It started to feel more and more like a baby monitor. My proverbial teats were sore.

Boundaries were never modeled for me growing up. I'd never seen my single mother enforce her own boundaries and I grew up isolated, without the opportunity to put down roots, much less walls. The poop spoon. An inability to defend my human borders. No words were ever offered. After being sexually assaulted when I was around eight years old by a kid whose parents were babysitting me, I told my mom and nothing happened. Physical boundaries for my body were never discussed, nor enforced. Emotional boundaries were even more abstract. Add all of this to the cultural tendency of Asian families to avoid talking about our emotions, and we have a void. A dark, vacuous void of language, modeling, and agency when it comes to creating boundaries.

But here I was, in the boundary-sensitive world of BDSM, running a playful humiliation workshop. Lucy and I spoke on the basic principles of this subjective and vulnerable form of play. The audience joined in the dialogue about how differently each person experiences humiliation triggers and that one thing that may humiliate one person may not affect another person at all. We began with our demo bottoms—Pups, BBG, and Sadley (a long-time submissive client and devotee)—adorned with animal face masks. A pig, a chicken, and a puppy all crawled around sniffing each other's butts.

The pig humped the puppy and the chicken clucked at the sight. There was a "stripper pole dance contest" as well as "wedgie musical chairs" and the audience had laughs and lighthearted pokes at our demo bottoms. Some find humiliation erotic because of the focused attention given to exploiting a submissive's embarrassment at being "less than"; a rush of hot blood to the face and the quickening of the thumps in the chest can exhilarate.

As the workshop was concluding, refillable enema bags came out, one for each bottom. The excessive amount of liquid used to fill up each bottom was sure to cause some kind of poopy mess, which is usually a surefire path to embarrassment. I was a bit concerned about BBG, a novice to humiliation doing such an intense public act, but against my better judgment, I fed the tube into his back door and diapered him. I did the same with Sadley while Lucy gave Pups a double dose of enema water. Each of them filled to the brim, we instructed them to stand on wee-wee pads, the kind you pick up at your local pet supply store. The first submissive who needed to evacuate was ordered to declare, "I NEED TO SOIL MY DIAPER NOW!" Sadley closed his eyes and embraced his inner zen. Pups shimmied a little dance as Lucy tickled him. BBG stood stoic and unmoving.

"This is the end of the workshop, I think you can figure out the rest if you don't want to stay for it," I told the audience. A courtesy to the squeamish. But the audience sat still, transfixed.

BBG was the first to announce his degradation. As he began slowly filling up the diaper, that familiar smell wafted toward all of our noses. These were adult diapers made for adult-sized loads. BBG's diaper swelled and drooped. BBG rained so much poo that we scurried to add a few more wee-wee pads to his pile. A low rumbly, bubbling noise muffled out of his diaper as it distended out slowly. The audience vanished.

Poop is an occupational hazard for a sex worker who plays intimately with other peoples' bodies, often when they are giving up control; dealing with someone else's poop is completely normal to me. I have accepted this as a part of life and am usually not the least bit bothered by it.

BBG didn't have the same comfort level. "I'm sorry, Goddess. I've been backed up for two days," he confessed.

Oh yes, that was very clear. In the chaos of this emotionally distressing moment, I was calm like an emergency room nurse.

Despite this being a workshop for "playful humiliation"—which to me meant light and fun and erotic—it had devolved into this fecal tsunami. I doubt the audience anticipated this intense, odoriferous conclusion to the workshop. But I had no time to think about the audience because BBG was definitely going through something that needed my attention.

"I feel like I have caused my owners embarrassment and humiliated myself and failed as a slave to be a good boy," BBG announced. Of course that poo-nami in the dungeon made him feel this way! The dungeon diaper fiasco escalated beyond what was expected for any of us and must've been mortifying to expel. Despite the audience's kindness in assuaging BBG's woes afterward, he still needed comfort from his owners. If my poop spoon incident was an experience deliberately created to humiliate me as a child, BBG's feelings probably were not that far off. Sometimes we don't know our limits until they have been breached, thus boundaries are often learned through experience.

"BBG, you won the degradation contest as the first one to soil your diaper. You were brave and did exactly what we wanted you to do, goodboy," I explained. The tangle of knots on his brow lifted.

"Then I am very glad it happened and that I was able to do what you wanted me to do," he managed. A small choke in his delivery indicated his intense emotions welling up, ready to spill over the brim.

The poop spoon. There was nobody to hold space for the myriad emotions I felt at having my grandmother do this caring but humiliating thing to me in front of my family. There was nobody to talk to about the violation of my body that seemed like no big deal to anyone else. I wasn't going to let that happen to BBG. I met a part of myself that I'd never met before: the protector. No big baby of mine was going to go through this experience without a hand to hold. Often, we talk about boundaries as that which keep things out. But boundaries can also hold space for what must be discussed in the confusing emotional landscape of newly felt feelings.

Sex work has helped me define and enforce so many new boundaries I have set up for myself: physical, sexual, emotional, and mental. I did not have these facilities when I was younger, but as I began working as a Domme, I saw that these boundaries were vital to this industry. Even in the realm of fantasy, so much of what we do feels real to our clients. And oftentimes, it feels real to us, too, even when we know that it is happening in a small compartment of fantasy. Even if that small compartment is on display to a consenting audience witnessing a full-on shit storm inside of adult diapers.

I am caretaker to Big Baby G. Perhaps not in the traditional senses of caretaking or nursing, but I know that my presence in his life has allowed him to open up to new possibilities. I know he feels loved and grateful because I tell and show him care and kindness, even if it doesn't take the form that we recognize most clearly in our culture. In return, he is a version of the obedient and loving goodboy, the baby I never chose to have.

# "Are You Safe?"

### REESE PIPER

I woke up to the sound of my phone ringing. Half-awake, I rummaged through the blankets and clothes on my bed. After a moment, I found it nestled under my eyeliner-stained pillow. "Hello," I answered, groggily. My sister's voice echoed through the phone. "I've been trying to call you. Are you okay?" I threw the covers off my twin bed. I was staying in a hostel dormitory in Austin, Texas. I walked into the shared kitchen. "Yeah, I'm fine," I mumbled. A pause. Trying to sound more upbeat, I added, "Everything has been good. How are you?"

Head pounding, I poured myself a glass of water and gulped it down. My sister chatted about the politics at her office job, how a male colleague kept invading her personal space. I was only half listening: the previous night's champagne had settled in harshly. The morning light filtered into the kitchen and dappled my face. I closed my eyes to alleviate my headache. "That's awful. Can you talk to HR?" I asked without much emotional inflection.

She discussed her options for a few more minutes and then moved on to me. I stood up and paced around the kitchen, picking at my acrylic stiletto nails. She asked about the hostel I was staying at, about my travels, but mostly about the strip club. She was eager to know how work was going.

"Did you find a club to work at?"

I bit off the nail from my index finger, drawing blood. The night before, I auditioned at two different strip clubs. At the first, I walked into the foyer with an eager smile and asked if they were hiring dancers. A beefy manager dressed in a gaudy gold suit looked at me with indifference. He asked me to undress in front of him. "H-here?" I stammered. He shot me a frustrated glance. I stripped down into my bra and underwear as gawking customers walked past. "You have to take off your top," he said. I unhooked my bra, exposing my tiny breasts. He stared for a second. "Okay, you'll do."

I made a quick excuse to go back to my car and darted out of there. I had been working in clubs for a little under two years and that was the first time I had been asked to strip down in a waiting area. In the past, some managers have asked me to audition on stage, others have hired me on the spot. I expected a bit of callousness during the audition process, but examining me with such an air of indifference left a sour taste in my mouth. But I brushed aside my annoyance and took out of my bag a list of strip clubs that I'd culled from the internet. I drove to the next place on my list.

I pulled into a parking lot of a quaint building with a flashing neon light hanging overhead. It was smaller and less crowded than the other club but the manager greeted me with a smile and immediately showed me to the dressing room. "Whenever you're done getting dressed, come find me and I'll show you around the club," he said, exiting the dressing room.

"I FOUND A little club to work at. I liked the manager a lot," I said to my sister.

I pulled a piece of bread from the toaster and slathered butter on it. My stomach heaved as I brought it to my lips. I threw it away and reached for a glass of water instead. "How were the customers?" she asked, her voice dropping. I walked out to the balcony and lit a cigarette, my hands shaking.

AFTER CHANGING INTO my lace teddy and platform heels, the manager showed me the stage, the communal lap dance room, the private rooms. I quickly got to work, approaching customers, selling dances, pushing rooms, excitement flowing through me. It felt good to make money. At around midnight, I sold a half-hour room to a middle-aged man with silver hair and a wide grin. I led him into the room, closing the red curtain behind us. As I settled on his lap, he reached into his pocket and shoved a key of cocaine into my nose. I pushed back with surprise. "You don't want it?" he asked, slightly annoyed. I took a deep breath in and smiled. I didn't want to lose the sale. "No, no, I do. Can I have another bump?" He smiled and we took bump for bump for the remainder of our time together.

The rest of the night was less clear. I remembered taking multiple shots, sipping various mixed drinks, selling another half-hour room to a man who wanted to snuggle, but memories flashed across my mind like flipping through pages in a comic book. I took a drag from my pink Capri cigarette and sat down on a tattered lawn chair as the end of the night surfaced into a clearer picture.

At around three a.m., I took two young men back into the champagne room for the last hour, my body draped across them as I enjoyed their four hands caressing me. We laughed and joked and drank but they grew restless. The younger of the pair kept inching his hand near my vagina. I swatted it away a few times until he forced his fingers in me. I stiffened. I tried to maintain a mischievous grin when I told him that I would get in trouble while I wiggled his hand out. I looked up at the cameras, wondering if the manager would come in and scold them, and realized that there weren't any.

"THEY WERE EASY! I met two guys at the end who just wanted to hang out and drink," I said.

"I wish I had your job!"

I mumbled a few "uh-huhs," eager to get off the phone.

"Are you sure you're okay?" she asked.

"I'm just really tired. Can I call you when I get to New Orleans?"

She agreed but then hesitated, her voice dropping. "Are you safe?"

"Yes, of course. I'm always safe."

AFTER WE HUNG up, I packed up my things and checked out of the hostel. I took a taxi to the bus station, looking out at the dark clouds rolling in while sipping a jug of water, and boarded a Greyhound bound for New Orleans, bright-eyed and enthusiastic. Although I was hungover, I was proud to be traveling on my own, thrilled to be earning more than a livable wage. As the bus turned onto a highway and headed east, I willed myself to forget about the man's fingers and pushed away any uncomfortable thoughts. With each mile, my energy surged and little by little the images from the night before ebbed away until they unwove from my memory.

Later on in the evening, a tornado ripped through the Louisiana countryside. Rain pelted the windows. The bus passed an overturned truck and I cried out, my hands shaking in fear. "Don't worry child," an older woman next to me cooed, wrapping my hands in hers. I thought of calling my sister to tell her that I loved her. But I didn't want to worry her. I gripped the woman's hand.

My older sister is the only one in my family who knows about my job. When I first started dancing, I crawled into her plush king bed one morning. I took a deep breath, almost balking. "I have to tell you about my new job," I said. She stiffened. "What?" she demanded. When I told her I had been working at the strip club she refused to meet my eye, her body turned away from me. She stood up and ran her fingers through her brown bob. "It's surprisingly a great job," I said, growing panicked. She shifted uneasily. "Most of the customers just want to talk," I continued. She turned her body toward me, her face softening.

"Is it safe?" she asked.

"Very."

She was silent for a moment and then asked, "What happens if a guy gets too pushy?"

"There are cameras everywhere," I said with confidence.

She smiled and climbed back into bed with me. "Wait, where did you learn to dance?" she asked in a lighter tone. We giggled over my childhood clumsiness and incoordination and I let out a sigh of relief. I knew that in order to gain her acceptance and support I had to make stripping palatable; present it as a job free of any hardships. She would be happy for me to be a sex worker as long as I was happy to do it.

For a while, I slept on her couch and worked at a nearby club in Manhattan. After each night of work, I tiptoed carefully into her apartment, trying to make as little noise as possible. I didn't want her to wake up and see how drunk and exhausted I was. I didn't want questions. When we both awoke, I relayed stories of amusing customers with their vanilla demands. I never lied but I never told the whole truth, painting only the shiny top layer of the industry, like oil on the top of salad dressing. The less she knew the better.

We interacted this way until I stumbled through her door one evening and fell on the hardwood floor. I stood up and darted into the living room. "You okay?" she asked, walking toward me. She saw my pupils, enlarged from a night of cocaine. "Yeah, I'm fine," I slurred. I slumped on the couch. She went into the kitchen and brought me a glass of water.

"How was work?" she asked

I looked up at her. "Terrible."

I sat up and gulped the water. "This fucking guy kept pushing me for a blow job," I said, my voice rising in anger. I ignored her shocked face and continued to tell her how he threw a tantrum like a toddler when I refused to do more than a dance; how he undid his pants, yanked my hand, and placed it on his dick. Even in my drunken state, my thoughts became clearer, the weight of my silence lifting. It felt good to unload. "I hate when customers enjoy the pull and tug on my boundaries."

My sister looked horrified. "Why didn't the bouncers come in?"

"They don't always watch the cameras."

She tried to speak but kept stumbling on her words. Eventually, she said, "You know you don't have to be there."

I sighed, lay back down, and turned away.

"It was just one bad night."

The next afternoon a silence lingered between us. I beat myself up for opening up to her and she struggled with how to address me. She asked if I wanted to watch television together. I suggested something easy like *Friends*, and we watched without laughing. I picked at the edges of my fake nails.

"Are you heading to the nail salon later?" she finally asked.

Relieved, I saw her bait and took it. I looked down at my hands, the acrylic chewed down into jagged mountains, and held them up for her to see. "I have to—I can't go to work like this." We laughed and the tension between us broke.

Feeling more emboldened to speak, my sister asked tentatively, "Is what happened yesterday normal?"

I hesitated. I could defend myself by bringing up her grievances at work. A few weeks before, her male colleague stalked her outside of her office, demanding changes to the roster. Since it wasn't the first time it had happened, she went to HR but they seemed wary about taking appropriate action. We stayed up late and brainstormed ways to handle the situation without causing a spat, or worse. *No*, I thought, *that's not a good idea*—she might use that against me. I could hear her retort: *That's not the same.* I thought maybe I should just be honest but if I admitted that customers sometimes pushed and violated my boundaries, then I risked feeding into her newfound wariness about my job. Everything she had been taught about strip clubs was negative, and I tried to challenge those lessons with my positive stories, but we grew up thinking clubs were dark pits of exploitation, hard and dangerous places for women to work in. From the media, we believed strippers were dirty people, beneath us. I had begun to unravel that stereotype, so if I admitted anything that verified her initial viewpoint, then I risked confirming it forever.

But my sister was my best friend, my confidant. If I kept a huge part of my life from her, I risked ruining our relationship, isolating myself.

"It's not common."

She looked relieved.

"Promise me if it ever becomes common then you'll look for another job?

"I promise."

I moved out of her apartment a few weeks later.

THE BUS ROLLED into New Orleans in one piece. I thanked the woman who held my hand through the storm and headed to a nearby hostel. I dumped my things on the floor next to my small bed and passed out for a few hours. When I woke up I got ready for work, using the cracked mirror in the dormitory to curl my hair and paint my face.

The air felt heavy and tense when I hopped on the tram and walked to the club my friend had suggested, a tiny dilapidated house with flashing neon lights nestled in the middle of Bourbon Street. The bouncer looked at my ID as the sky broke. Water dripped from the ceiling in the club. Lightning flashed. Within an hour or so, I discovered the rooms didn't have cameras, or if they did, they weren't being watched. The first private room I went into, the customer immediately tugged at my thong. "I'll get in trouble," I whispered. "No, you won't." He slipped his finger inside me. I pulled away and tried to wiggle his hand out of me, but he locked it inside like a claw. "I'll get fired," I repeated, my voice firmer this time. He pulled away. He grabbed his things and stormed off. "What am I paying for?"

I laughed at him and brushed his words off. Nothing a drink wouldn't ease. I walked downstairs and told myself to stick to the communal dance room. But as I headed to the bar, I slipped on the floor, falling flat on my butt. I approached the DJ booth.

"I just fell. Do you think you can put a bucket down or get someone to clean up the floor?" I asked, sounding more annoyed than I'd intended.

He ignored me.

"What's your name?" he asked, his eyes narrowing at me.

"Piper."

"We already have a Piper; you can't be Piper."

"Well, she's not here now. I'll change it when she gets here."

He laughed at me. "I'm telling you, you can't be Piper. This isn't a discussion."

I laughed back at him. "All right fine, it's just a name," I said, walking away. "I'll be Reese."

He played "Bohemian Rhapsody" every time I went on stage in retaliation. I sighed in annoyance and drank heavily into the night. After work, I slumped against the side of a cathedral in the French Quarter, watching the sky lighten, waiting for my anger to cool. I was tired of putting up with people clawing at my vagina, and even more tired of management's disregard for my safety. I didn't want to just forget it happened. I wanted it to change. A sob caught in my throat.

I called my sister, knowing she'd be getting up for work.

"It's so early. Are you okay?"

For a quick second, I was furious that I couldn't just tell her about my night. Why did she get to complain about work and I didn't? How come her complaints were met with solutions and the only solution to mine was to quit? But my annoyance quickly drained into sadness. I broke down, feeling the weight of my unspoken experiences. I hadn't realized until then that without the outlet to speak, I had deprived myself of the space to feel.

"I had a really bad night," I said.

I didn't have the energy to hide, but I also didn't have the energy to bridge the gap between us. I knew she wouldn't have words to offer solutions to my concerns, partly because I had hidden the reality of my job from her for two years, but also partly because solutions to sexual harassment and neglect on the job are not offered to sex workers. Stripping is viewed through the lens of sexuality, not work, and, thus, trauma is seen as more grave and glaring. Even if stripping is just a job to me, even if I have no intention of quitting, the only answer to neglect and trauma is to walk away.

"What happened?"

*Anything you say will incriminate you.*

"I just struggled to make money."

"I'm sure tomorrow will be better. You always turn your bad nights around."

"You're right."

"Are you sure you're okay? Are you safe?"

I touched the pavement underneath me, listening to the muffled bustle of the dwindling night. A few people scurried across the Quarter. I looked warily at my bag with my night's wages tucked in the pocket. I should have called a taxi but I wanted to walk back to the hostel to blow off steam.

"Yes, I'm always safe."

## Good Faith

### TINA HORN

In the mid-1970s, the man who would later become my father joined the Unification Church. He had moved to a commune in Northern California after finishing college and wanted to share his newfound devotion with his parents back in Brooklyn. So, he took them to see his guru, the Reverend Sun Myung Moon, at a Madison Square Garden rally.

That night, Moon spoke through a translator to a crowd of twenty thousand people. He proselytized that all of human history was culminating, that the third world war was going to happen within the next three years. He preached his sexual philosophy, which has since been quoted as, "Woman was born to connect in love with man's sexual organ. Man and woman's sexual organs are the place of the true love palace."

And then Moon declared that Jews were responsible for the death of Jesus.

An enraged word pierced the hush of the reverent crowd. In front of thousands of my father's fellow acolytes, my grandmother stood up and screamed at the top of her lungs:

"*LIAR!*"

Her son was humiliated. But this moment of shameless dissent would become an iconic one for me. I keep the story close to my heart the way other people wear heirloom lockets. Still, if I met you while tipping red wine into mugs at a house party and the subject of cults came up—as I find the subject tends to in our anxious times—this isn't the story I would tell you.

Here's the one I would: Unification Church members like my father were to remain celibate before they were deemed worthy of participating in mass weddings officiated by Moon. After these weddings, they would become the True Children of Moon and his second wife Hak Ja Han, known as the True Father and True Mother. My dad, a communications major, was known even then for his persuasive charisma, and so he was sent on road trips to collect acolytes. On one such trip, the church sent as his companion a schoolteacher in her late twenties who had moved west following a Lutheran upbringing in Iowa. She was *not* persuasively charismatic, and was in fact skeptical of Moon's teachings. During that road trip, they spread the good word all right, but they apparently didn't take their vow of abstinence very seriously. On one drive, a group leader noticed my mom leaning over to put a stick of gum in my dad's mouth. Subsequently, yours truly was born in sexual rebellion.

That's the tale I would tell you, and some of it is even true. My parents were definitely Moonies, but we never talked about it growing up. In fact, my younger sister and I weren't raised with any faith whatsoever. I *might* occasionally fudge the years to construct a salacious punchline about my conception being *the reason* they left the church. This makes great bar talk, a very sensational origin story for a long-time Dominatrix and queer pornographer. If every artist's work centers on a single obsession, mine is sexual power.

FROM A YOUNG age, my attraction to power exchange and pain play was as innate as my multivalent gender orientation. It was more than a single fetish that held my fascination. I was aggressive and restless in my early conventional relationships, like a perverted lab animal that was growing too big for its cage. Unlike many religious people whose proclivities develop from a need for new rituals, I had an organically agnostic approach to my erotic life. I was curious about everything and subscribed to nothing. Which gave me a very good disposition for sex work.

It wasn't until my twenties, when I discovered forums for experimenting with sex professionally, that BDSM became a proud part of my identity. I discovered an informal commercial dungeon in the Bay Area where I worked collectively with other Dominatrices. We had monthly staff meetings, negotiated the rules of engagement for our paid sessions, and cleaned up our own lubey dildos. To clients, we were goddesses in thigh-high leather boots; in the basement locker room changing back into street clothes, we were colleagues and friends. We called one another "Mistress" (as in "Mistress, your bicycle almost fell on the latex drying rack so I moved it!") with a confirmed ironic wink. The owner of the business was our boss, and there were shift managers, but the Master/slave element of BDSM stayed strictly in the session room.

After a few years of exchanging cash for working with men on their illicit desires, I more aggressively pursued my own. I enmeshed myself in Leather subcultures centered around values like exchanging comprehensive education, fighting social oppression, and creating mutual care. And sex. Lots of weird, hot, cathartic sex!

Leather was never fundamentalist: it was open-source, which made it the ideal erotic philosophy for my adult life. Power was to be played with in order to be understood, and that required rituals of communication performed in good faith. Pleasure was not to be pursued at the expense of someone's agency. Intimacy and ecstasy happened when everyone opted in. Vulnerability was a gift we exchanged with those who deserved it. The more I opened my body and heart freely to my friends, the easier it was to see nonconsensual power trips coming a mile away.

Queer Leather community has offered me a middle path between pleasure and pain, healing and suffering, structure and anarchy. I feel very clear about the appeal of BDSM: for me, it has always provided a space to confront and undermine authority, including the emotional control my parents try to hold over me.

I HAD ALWAYS been content not knowing much about my parents' lives before I was born; they rarely offered and I rarely asked. When I was thirteen, they separated and are both still single and discontent. I actually didn't know anything about my celibacy-breaking conception story until I was twenty-five and in therapy with my dad. We were attempting to reconcile after our first period of estrangement. I told him I was working happily as a pro-Domme. He told me that he and my mom had met in a cult.

In the years since, when I've asked my dad, typically a notorious overexplainer, what drew him to Unification, he never can seem to give me a satisfying answer. He usually just shrugs, saying, "Well, honey, it was the Age of Aquarius."

In forty years since leaving that group, my dad has continued to explode outward seeking purpose, while my mom continues to apathetically implode, seeking only oblivion. I wonder how their early adulthood attempts to find a True Family together led them to very distinct but equally lonely twilight years.

I am now the age my mom was when she gave birth to my younger sister. Like many grown children, I do not want to repeat my parents' mistakes. Since my love, my friendships, and my work all center around explorations of intimate power through the cultures of kink and the politics of sex work, I find myself considering the questions: What is the meaningful difference between identifying as a Leather queer and participating in a cult? How do you know whether you're in a kinky polyamorous family or part of an abusive scam? And has settling into a comfortable role within Leather communities helped me to heal from generational trauma that my parents never seemed to have resolved for themselves?

Plenty of my polyamorous kinky friends have intimate lives which, frankly, might appear to outsiders to be indistinguishable from a cult: chosen Leather families in which adult queers instate consensual hierarchies dictating anything from domestic chores to erotic play. I'm constantly surrounded by limbs bearing whipping bruises, murmured boot-cleaning protocols, echoes of "Yes

Ma'am" and "Please Sir" and "I'll just send my sub out to grab us more coffee." It has become urgently important to me that I'm able to differentiate consensual Domination/submission from the exploitation of cults; not only to separate my own tastes and impulses from those of my parents but also to be able to tell if a BDSM relationship has gone from being consensual to coercive.

SINCE MY FATHER wouldn't tell me much about his time as a Moonie, I went looking for answers elsewhere. I reached Dr. Janja Lalich on the phone from her house in Butte County, California, not far from where I grew up. Lalich is a professor of sociology at Chico State, and the author of several books on charismatic relationships, political and social movements, ideology, social control, and issues of gender and sexuality, including *Cults in Our Midst* with Margaret Singer.

"You should be allowed to say no," Dr. Lalich said when I asked her how to tell if you're in a healthy group relationship. "To question anyone in the hierarchy including the Dominant. You should be allowed to leave when you want, without any rebuke or shunning. You shouldn't be made to believe that this is the only way to live. You should be able to untie the bonds!"

The more I learn about my parents' lives before me, the more I wonder why I had accepted origin stories with so many plot holes. But guardians can raise you with more than faith: they can also discourage curiosity. Maybe I had been raised with a familial version of "bounded choice"—the term for the internal logic of cult followers which Lalich prefers to "brainwashed." This logic is often inscrutable to those outside the belief system. When you're on the inside, you find it normal, since someone else is shaping your world. I guess my parents raised me to be inquisitive about everything in the world *besides* their past lives, to think it was perfectly normal that I didn't really know anything about them. I guess a lot of authority figures do that.

Lalich spoke about the experience of being in a cult, filling in some of the blanks left by my parents. One particular detail made my blood run cold. She explained that most cults assign a "buddy" to new members.

"That person is supposedly guiding you," Lalich continued. "What they're really doing is monitoring your growth and reporting back to leadership."

Of course, this false pretense was the basis of my parents' relationship. My dad, though six years younger than my mom, was her "discipler" in Unification. As Lalich described the "closed reality" that disciplers create on behalf of the leader, I wondered for the first time if my parents ever restored their compromised capacity for listening to their own intuitions. And I thought about how much more I trust my own gut since playing with erotic power alongside my adult friends and partners.

My need for assurance that I'm not being indoctrinated borders on the neurotic. BDSM soothes that neurosis with a sometimes comical amount of built-in processing. Scene negotiation and safe words and consent check-ins can feel invigorating even if they're also tedious at times. Ultimately, they offer an infrastructure of individual agency and subcultural accountability: the *opposite* of discipling. Speaking with Dr. Lalich reassured me that my sexual experimentations have given me the tools to resist abuse rather than make me more vulnerable to seduction. My parents and their cult background gave me a counter-model, a way *not* to be.

My ass has been beaten black and blue while I'm adrift on waves of euphoria. I've given and taken orders, administered and yielded to deserved punishment. My leather pants have been shined with saliva in view of hundreds of casual observers. I've fisted men in the leather slings I helped install into warehouse ceilings. I've guzzled the piss of strangers in bathroom stalls. I've called female partners "Daddy" with a tone that in no way invokes my male genetic predecessor. I've done it for cash and I've done it for fun and I've done it for love; no one has ever persuaded me to pledge my allegiance to anyone or anything. And in all of my years of experience with sexual countercultures, I've only met one group that set off all my internal silent alarms, one that I now feel meets Dr. Lalich's criteria of a cult.

"HELLO, MISTRESS," says the tall, tense white man at the bus stop. He looks to be about fifty, someone who has seen little excitement. "I'm slave brain. That's *brain*, not Brian. Most people ask me that so I figure I should clarify."

I hoist up my black rolling suitcase. slave brain reaches out to grab it, then hesitates, confused. I've seen this look on slaves before. He is wondering how this little woman in Chaco sandals, black jeans, and a tank top could be a "Mistress." This is how I always give myself away. I've known plenty of Dommes who expect male submissives to literally throw their coats down in puddles for them. But my domination style has always had a camp wink and piggish urge to rut around in filth. For me, being a sex worker doesn't mean I'm a formal Dominatrix 24/7. I'm all for patriarchal restitution, but dominating someone I've just met—who isn't paying for the privilege—actually feels to me like extra emotional labor. A slap in the face is still attention.

I'm headed to a rural East Coast town, on the recommendation of a new friend, Michelle, who I've met through mutual colleagues in the feminist porn scene. Michelle is a captivatingly stern pale goth queen, busty and heavily tattooed, the kind of pro-Domme who capitalizes "Me" and "My" in her emails.

In one such recent email, Michelle has invited me to take sessions at the "kinky inn" she's involved with. I'll call it the Space. I've recently moved to New York from the Bay Area, and I'm still getting used to the different cultures of BDSM and sex work on opposite coasts. I've always been a professional "switch," meaning I'm comfortable performing the role of both dominant and submissive, sometimes in the same sessions. My expectation is that the Space will be like the dungeon I've worked for in Oakland, or some of the other professional studios I've rented in my travels to Toronto and

LA. Apparently, the Space hosts play parties and couples retreats, and also welcomes guest professionals to take sessions. According to Michelle, they have enough of an existing clientele that I don't even have to take out an ad online. And they're especially excited to learn I'm an experienced sub.

The website of the Space boasts about its own kinky reputation in self-aggrandizing terms. I have to admit, I've totally fallen for this marketing, probably because I want to believe such subcultural places are real. Their social media presence is vague enough to inspire me to fill in my own fantasy, and I'm expecting something old and grand like the house in the Bette Davis movie *Watcher in the Woods*; or, more to the point, the deviant isolated manors of Pauline Réage's *Story of O* or Laura Antoniou's *The Marketplace*.

I follow slave brain across the parking lot, a vast sprawl of mostly deserted asphalt. I get into the Jeep Cherokee of this strange man because that's what I came here to do. I trust him because Michelle told me a slave was coming to get me. I trust Michelle because she's a fellow kinky punk sex worker, a reckless principle that has nevertheless gotten me in surprisingly little hot water so far. I guess I'm in it for the curiosity almost as much as the money.

"So, what's the Space like?" I ask brain as he drives us into the woods.

"Oh, Master M changed my life," he says, his eyes on the road but suddenly dreamy. "You're *so* lucky. And the new headmistress is wonderful, too." I ask what her name is.

"Quinn." He blinks. "Mistress Quinn."

"So, why do they call you brain?" I ask.

"Well, Master M gives everyone a slave name. My name is Brian."

"So, your name *is* Brian!"

"Yes, but Master M says I *think* too much. So, my slave name is brain to remind me not to think." A contented grin spreads across his face, as if he is reflecting on a great blessing.

The Jeep pulls onto a rural road, bouncing down a sloped gravel driveway, where my provincial mansion fantasies are given a rude awakening.

The Space is actually just a squat, gray, one-story house. It's not the modesty that catches me off guard, but the dissonance between the grand fantasy it's selling and the reality I'm now seeing. I let slave brain take my bags this time. After holding open the screen door, he moves aside for me to meet Master M and Mistress Quinn, who are standing expectantly in a small country living room.

Master M looks like he is pushing seventy, sinewy and rough-skinned, with a stringy gray ponytail and black beady eyes. Quinn can't be older than twenty-five. Her considerable breasts pour over a leather corset, which she wears casually under black cotton leggings and a hoodie. She has a round, open, girl-next-door face and long shiny brown hair. She does not shake my hand.

Michelle is there, too. She seems irritated with M and Quinn for reasons no one bothers to explain to me. The three of them seem distracted and standoffish, neither friendly nor particularly professional. They show me to a comfortable bedroom with its own bathroom and inform me that dinner is in an hour. slave brain is dismissed and Michelle follows him up the road in her car. I'm alone at the Space with Master M and Mistress Quinn.

They inform me that I have a client booked for tonight. The thought of cash soothes my discomfort as we sit down to a home-made dinner at a large wooden table. Master M serves venison stew and congee. They offer me red wine and a joint, asking questions about my experience "in the scene." Trying to find some common ground, I explain that my professional BDSM practice has a different dynamic than it does in my personal life, but that I really love my work and exploring power and . . .

"She takes a long time to answer, doesn't she?" M says to Quinn, and they both laugh at some joke I'm apparently not going to be let in on. The way they touch each other makes it pretty clear to me that they fuck. I'm unnerved by the creeping sense that I'm being appraised.

I've met eccentric dungeon owners before, but the worst they've been is impersonal while giving me an orientation: *Here's how you buzz your client in, here's the MadaCide, here's the binder of dusty old Portishead CDs, I'll be in the other room smoking menthols.* The Space is making me feel *dis*-oriented.

I ask my host some reasonable questions. "So how do you screen clients?" and "Where do we negotiate our scenes?" and "Should I collect my money before or after session?" All my queries are met dismissively. "We'll discuss it later," or "You don't need to worry about that."

So far, I'm not able to discern a concrete reason to feel in danger; but they aren't giving me any cause to trust them either.

After dinner, I change into a sheer pink and black polka-dot teddy and robe, pulling on opaque black stockings and a garter belt because I'm still not sure how East Coast clients will react to hairy legs. I'm instructed to wait in the guest bedroom listening as my client, Steve, arrives.

M calls me out to the living room. I'm surprised to discover that Quinn has already led Steve downstairs to show him the basement dungeon. Every place I've worked has had its own particular style of theatrics. But I'm used to a clear differentiation between the role you play in session and the person you *are*, the person being hired. Back in Oakland, the worker always greeted the client at the door fully dressed and negotiated the scene for herself.

Here, M instructs me to kneel in front of him on the thick, musty carpet. Getting on my knees in an ordinary living room, next to couches and a coffee table and an acoustic guitar, feels much less comfortable than crawling around on a dungeon floor. It's dawning on me that M and Quinn see me as the same class as slave brain.

Several voices, deep inside my body, wage a war that lasts an instant. My female-socialized subconscious coos, *You probably just missed something. It'll be over faster if you just go along with what he wants.* My insolent self-preservation screams, *Call the whole thing off! Don't kneel to this man! Michelle will come pick you up!* And some punkass part of my nature, the part that always prevails, wants to see what M thinks he can do to me, and how much I can resist while placating him at the same time. So, I do as he says.

"Our slaves always stand with their eyes down, to show humility, and their chins up, to show pride in subservience," M explains as he begins to stalk slowly around me. *Does he want me to feel beneath him because he's hiring me?* I think to myself. It's also possible that he believes the money that Steve is paying me and the cut I'll owe the Space is beside the point. If part of the fantasy of this place is for clients to interact with "trained house slaves," I might have agreed ahead of time to play that part. But the client is downstairs, and Master M is not *my* master. So, who is meant to benefit from this pageantry?

M leans forward and begins to stroke my ear. "This is your clit," he whispers, as if saying it would transubstantiate one collection of nerve endings to another. I don't feel anything in my clit. But drops of sweat pour down my side from my underarms. I stay still and quiet.

M pulls his fingers back and continues to stalk around me. I sense a wave of smugness. That unwelcome appraisal feeling again. *Does he think I am enchanted by this?*

"It's time for you to go to the dungeon," M intones. I stand shakily and walk to the basement door, avoiding eye contact.

As my eyes adjust to the dim light, I see Quinn and Steve in the far corner, standing expectantly next to a leather sling. Quinn has removed the casual part of her outfit, and now cuts an impressive figure of a tightly corseted girly dominatrix. Steve is a very conventional-looking, middle-aged white client, bursting out of his skin with anticipation at the sight of me wobbling on kitten heels down the wooden stairs. The dungeon is fully and uniquely stocked with horn-handled crops, matching alligator skin floggers, and hand-built bondage furniture, but the walls are covered in trash bags. It feels like I'm in the haunted garage a family makes every year for Halloween.

"Steve likes to tickle!" Quinn explains. I'm comfortable with tickling fetishism: the top is looking for an involuntary and unstaged response. But I don't understand why Quinn is telling me this instead of Steve. I'm used to having my own negotiation with a client, especially one who will be dominating me.

Together, they guide me into the sling, wrapping leather cuffs around my wrists and ankles so I'm laying back, spread-eagle and fully restrained. Any moment now I am expected Quinn to leave me alone with my client. It's unsettling to have her there observing me. I would have understood if she or M had explained they would stand by for safety reasons or because I'm new to the house, but that's not what's happening. My dynamic with my client is completely thrown by her deliberate presence—imagine a therapist being nonconsensually monitored by the person whose office she is renting.

Steve approaches me slowly. Then he dives in. He doesn't caress or stroke. He just goes directly for my ribs and jabs mercilessly.

This kind of fetish torture usually makes me feel euphoric and strong. But I'm also used to clients with finesse, who work with me in real time to build a sort of movement narrative incorporating ebb and flow. Steve is just relentlessly attacking. His face is shocked and delighted. Ordinarily, I would "top from the bottom," teaching a new client how I like to be teased, but Quinn's creepy presence has me all out of whack. I laugh. I shriek. I curse excessively and loudly—"*ohholyfuckingjesuschristshitaaafuckingaaaauuuufhh!*" If I'm going to be in this weird isolated dungeon in the woods, I figure the least I can get out of it is the catharsis of screaming vulgar bloody murder, something I can rarely justify in a thin-walled city building.

My squirming and giggling and chain-rattling is amplified by the tension of this entire fucking situation. Ordinarily, even if I'm enduring something challenging, I can ground myself to the presence of the other workers in the house. They know who I really am when I'm out of character. Here, there is no anchor. I'm learning that they expect me to *be* the character.

Every so often Quinn approaches and joins in on the tickling. I could use a safe word, or call the scene off, or tell her to *fuck* off, but I'm worried that this will be seen as insolence, a reason not to pay me. I choose to let Quinn touch my body, but the choice is bound to the disorientation of my situation.

Finally, Quinn tells Steve his allotted hour is up. They unlatch me, and I'm quite shaky getting up the stairs, where M is waiting for us. Quinn, Steve, and I stand in front of an expectant M, who again instructs me to kneel in "slave position."

"I'm very disappointed in you that you would use such language in my house," he says, referring to my litany of cursing screams.

I have no idea what to say. I'm embarrassed and furiously insulted being spoken to like this in front of my client. I thought I had done a very professional job making this tickling fetishist very happy. No one has ever questioned the way I process pain and sensation. Cursing is my style, and my style is the experience a client is paying for. Steve genuinely didn't seem to mind my language, so why should M? The Space seems more concerned about maintaining manipulative hierarchies than doing good business, which is antithetical to everything BDSM actually means to me.

After Steve is sent on his way, I collect my cash with relief, retreating wordlessly to my room. I draw a scalding bath, pouring excessive milks and salts into the tub, seething with indignity and confusion. I realize the boundaries between personal and professional are very blurred here, in a way I'm not used to, in a way that disturbs me.

I open the linen closet in my room and notice the labels: maroon towels are for slaves, black towels are for guests. So which towel is for me?

In the morning, I leave the house in my exercise clothes without seeing anyone. I run up the gravel driveway and turn left on the dirt road. I don't encounter any cars or people or other houses. Just trees and birds and clean mountain air for miles. This is a rare treat, to be able to run and let my mind go, even close my eyes, with no surprises and no traffic. I try to breathe the fresh air as deeply as I can. As I run, it occurs to me that if I had to leave, this would be how I would have to do it.

I stay at that house for two more days. During that time, I see a different client, a regular to the Space, who single-tail whips me mercilessly with no warm up. He makes me walk naked through the surrounding forest carrying a wooden cross, explaining that I'm a "goddess taking on the suffering of the world." As an atheist I find this extremely ridiculous, but I do take some pride in enduring outrageous scenarios for the satisfaction of paying customers.

I hit my limit, though, when he attaches me to the cross by suspension cuffs and raises it, by hydraulics, up the side of a tree. I look down at M, Quinn, and the client, all visibly amused. For the very first time in ten years of stomping and spitting and cursing and cumming for money, I instinctively imagine my best friend—who has been unconditionally supportive through some truly weird sexual shit I've done—feeling concerned about the position I'm in. So, I use my safe word.

M clucks in disapproval, and I live through an excruciating pause. A safe word is supposed to be a ripcord. You're not supposed to have to negotiate with the parachute once you've pulled the ripcord. All of the times I'd used yellow for *slow down* or red for *stop everything*, the client had checked in and dropped whatever roles we were playing. No one has ever seriously shamed me for invoking these consent tools. No one has ever questioned my professionalism or devotion to my craft or value as a sadomasochist as a result. Until now.

But they do let me down off the cross. And the session is over. And I do get paid. And I do decide it's time to call Michelle.

As I roll my suitcase out the door, Master M tells me scornfully, "It would be good for you to come back. We would love to have you, since you can *barely* take the pace of one of our kindest Masters."

Staring out the window of Michelle's station wagon, I feel the dread of a horror movie third act. We head back to her place and spend a few days together. I don't really tell her about my experience. I roll my money into a sock and zip it into a compartment of my bag. We take her dogs for a walk and swim under a waterfall. We cook vegan dinner with her best friend, a short, dark-haired guy with huge ear gauges who owns a local tattoo parlor. He makes fun of my ten-dollar, pink smokeshop belly-button ring, just visible under my loose tie-dye shirt, and I snap at him that not everyone can afford fancy things.

The next day, he walks into Michelle's apartment and drops to his knees in front of me. Pulling latex gloves from the pouch of his red and black hoodie, he starts unscrewing my belly-button ring. He produces a new piece with aquamarine gemstones that sparkles so much brighter than the cheap one I've worn for ages. Slipping the new silver through my piercing hole, he threads the shining ball in place, muttering; "I just don't like to see good people with bad jewelry."

We head to a dive bar where Michelle introduces me to the local motorcycle gang, not just guys in leather jackets, but a real gang, with initiations and hierarchies and birthrights. There's karaoke. I sing "Sympathy for the Devil," slithering flamboyantly as my beer foams out of its bottle. Broad men with scratchy-looking beards buy me drinks because they claim they have never seen a woman sing like that before, which as always I find difficult to believe.

Michelle takes me to the parking lot to catch the bus back to Manhattan. I never ask her further about her relationship to the Space and frankly I can't explain that choice.

Maybe I was ashamed that there was some expectation I had misunderstood. Or maybe I was just happy to have survived with several bills stuffed in my boot, on my way home to the city. Maybe I didn't want to push my luck.

Every so often, I meet someone who has trained at the Space, even close friends whose approach to sex work I respect and BDSM lifestyle I trust. Though I'm typically notoriously overinquisitive, I find myself biting my tongue instead of asking them to explain the Masters and Mistresses and slaves and clients out there in the woods. I realize now that I don't really want to know more. All I care about is staying as far away from that house as possible.

My personal philosophies of kink and sex work did become clearer to me after that weekend. I'm not looking for new authority figures. I'm not looking to recycle the suffering of old gods. I'm looking to make something new.

Sometimes, when I look down at the shimmering blue of my belly-button ring, it reminds me of that moment of kindness, of a man willingly getting on his knees in front of me to give me a gift, expecting nothing in return. It reminds me of pulling out of that gravel driveway, and of everything people everywhere have endured to make their rent.

When I meet the Master Ms of this world, the people who try to take advantage of their perceived power over me, I try to invoke the spirit of my grandmother, screaming "LIAR!" at the top of her lungs in front of hundreds of acolytes at Madison Square Garden.

If a family is a cult, then I'm in a perpetual state of trying to walk away from the influence of my own. Even though the healthy consensual BDSM situations I've been in have put me in many positions of literal subservience—down on my knees, withstanding torture—nothing has made me feel freer. Because when you surrender from a place of recognized strength, you learn to see false prophets for what they are: people who expect filial piety when they haven't earned the privilege.

*Originally published on* Hazlitt *on July 8, 2019. Special thanks to Haley Cullingham.*

# SURVIVAL

# The Alchemy of Pain: Honoring the Victim-Whore

ANONYMOUS

I am writing this for me; and also for you, dear victim. And, you, alleged ally. I write as a full-time slut who moonlights as a sex worker (or "whore," as I prefer), and has lived most of her life as a victim of sexual assault.

The first time someone touched my pussy I was around eight years old. It was a relative and it has haunted me. And it feels like a generational curse. My mom survived sexual assault and harassment growing up, too. I imagine my family as a network of authoritative failures, of misdirected affection, of violence confused with tenderness. I was raised by some mistuned and kinky-ass motherfuckers, goddess help them all. And, as a bunch of middle-class white folks, this kind of rampant fuckery gets to happen without the overbearing state surveillance that typically impacts low-income families or families of color. There were no visits from DHS workers, no reports made, no one brought to trial—and thank goddess, because there is no justice nor peace in that mess.

I am writing this because some people have this cute number of people they have slept with that they get to sheepishly disclose at doctor appointments and I can't. I don't. Just like I can't even count the number of times I was molested or raped. This is because from early on I had no idea what was sex and what was assault. This boldface line was fucked up for me when my body did disturbing things like respond with desire to the touches of others that repulsed my head, my heart, and my soul. It was also fucked up by all of y'all—by a society that glorifies rape-trial melodrama: you know, the ones where the victim is put on trial for the actions of their own perpetrator, their own audacity to exist, and the absurdity of the ass-backward criminal justice system.

I am writing this to ask you not to use the term "survivor" or "thriver" around me ever the fuck again. This neoliberal bullshit wherein I am left to clean up someone else's mess and to make y'all feel better about it.

I am writing primarily though, about a trope, an archetype, a joke that won't die, a goddamn law in this society: that victims of child sexual assault become sluts and sex workers—especially sex workers. While such arguments have been smartly tackled by queens like Maggie McNeil and Charlotte Shane, I am writing to argue: OF COURSE WE DO.

Of course we swing from poles, mimicking the playgrounds of our deranged childhoods.

Of course we cloak ourselves in synthetic cheetah skins, like some postindustrial selkie our own skin stolen from us.

Of course we dress like schoolgirls, attempting to reclaim a precious time of growth that was so rudely interrupted.

Of course we literally fuck authority—rich men who make this world turn (to shit): bankers, CEOs, lawyers and judges. What other relationship with them could we expect to have?

Of course we are vulnerable to trafficking and exploitation, because we don't know who the fuck to trust in this world, and have been failed by those who were meant to keep us safe.

Of course we become creators and curators of playtime, of elaborate scenes and fantasies. Playtime was stolen from us when we were young, so we understand it best.

Of course we are going to mercantilize this shit in a capitalist system.

Of course we learn to mistrust cops and FBI agents and social workers and drug counselors and nurses and doctors, agents of the prison industrial complex, and the even larger shadow it casts: the nonprofit industrial complex. You have been taking our kids, sending us to jail "for our own good," and leaving us there to die for years. Such failures happened before we met these agents of the state—though this is often quite young in our lives—when we learned the devastation inherent in legitimized forms of unearned power.

Of course we position ourselves as close as we can to queens. The strange industry of sex (an industry that is as strange as any other in late-stage capitalism) is, of course, not entirely made of victims of sexual assault. In it you will find masters of the mysterious energy of sex. We needed to be close to those who turn that which hurt us into something magnificent and dazzling.

Of course there will be those hustlers willing to extend the alchemy of this hustle to the furthest logical point, whores like Rachel Moran and Gloria Steinem, who are making millions off their own suffering—and mine. While my blood burns at your twisted logic of prohibition (that which they call "abolition"), my heart breaks because your healing has become a handmaiden to the very systems seeking to destroy our lives.

To all the queen-goddesses out there: you sluts, you whores—I hope that I can someday unlearn this pain to walk among you with such glitter and grace. Thank you for your guidance.

To myself, and my fellow victim-whores: we can stop apologizing for these systems which rendered us their prey. That shit ain't on us. We do not owe anyone apologies for what was done to us as we heal from it—especially when we as victims are given so few options for doing so.

To those prohibitionists posturing as allies: Why must my life be a data point to justify your liberation? What are you going to do to ensure mine, too?

*Originally published on* Slutist *on August 29, 2016.*

# When She Says Women, She Does Not Mean Me

## LORELEI LEE

All the buses stopped at Old Town. We didn't have cars or tele-phones, so we waited there and watched. We sat on the cement medians in close circles, smoking. We wandered off to fish for change and tequila, to beg for wax cups from the snack bar. We were fourteen and fifteen and sixteen. Liam had his ankle monitor on. His hair glued up high. The cops were watching, and we felt their eyes on us—a stiffening in our backs, a tamp on our laughter. The buses unloaded and we stood to see if one of us was getting off. A slow exodus of grown-ups working day shifts at the Old Town restaurants that just left baskets of chips or bread on the outdoor tables, their bright plastic grease cloths beckoning, but we could never swipe the leftover food there. We were not surreptitious.

We'd spent so much time invisible, so we'd made ourselves impossible to ignore. Our hair was purple and our pants were ripped. We wore necklaces of beer tabs strung on twine, we draped chains around our necks and waists. We rattled when we walked. We had armor, but no stealth. Because of this, we could see each other coming. We could keep track of each other.

I kept count. I counted us all day and night, no matter how stoned I was. Our crew was eight girls. Eight of us meant safety. If there were seven, we had to go searching.

WHEN I WAS nineteen, I paid my way to San Francisco with

pornography. I answered an ad for the cheapest room I could find, and when the girl who lived there asked me, I lied and said I was straight. I didn't know anyone. Men or boys asked me to go places, and I went. At a party in the fall, I wore tight red pants and no bra. I drank what was handed to me. I fell asleep on a bed and woke up and this boy was fucking me. His smell and skin and my teeth grinding and I was drunk or high, I don't know which, and I couldn't move. I could not make him stop. I passed out again and woke up and his body was there on the bed and I inched away and it was so gray, San Francisco was always so gray, always so predawn, and I did not want to jostle anything, gathered my limbs, my fragile center, slipped out to the gray street and the shivering bus and stepped gently on the stairs up into my rented room and washed myself with hot water and drank hot coffee to burn the inside of me and began the work of pretending it had not happened.

THAT SAME YEAR, my boss at the coffee shop left me five messages in three days:

"Hey, just wanted to see if you want to go to that show on Friday at Great American Music Hall."

"Hey you haven't called me back so just checking in again to see if you want to go, or maybe get a drink."

"Hey you know it's pretty rude of you to just smile at me like that and then not even call me back."

"You can't just be nice to people and then act like it doesn't mean anything."

"You think you're so special but you're not. You should be more careful."

At work, he did not mention the phone calls. He watched me. I laughed at something a coworker said and he yelled, "less talking, more working." He started scheduling me so that I only worked alone. As I wiped down counters, he stood close to me, holding a clipboard, not looking at me, just keeping his big body next to mine.

IN OLD TOWN and in Ocean Beach the cops were always watching us. Were always stopping us in the street. Were always making us empty our pockets and backpacks. We felt them coming, we could see them from a block away and we stiffened, tried to duck around corners, tried to avert our faces. At night, they shone their flashlights into our eyes. Some nights they made us stand in a row. They held photos of missing children up beside our faces.

We were not missing.

THE BOY WHO raped me had paid to see my naked pictures on the internet. He'd done this with his friends, the group of them together at the computer with someone's brother's credit card. I knew this because one of them told me. They told me he wanted to fuck me. This was intended as a compliment. I have tried to imagine what they said to each other in that room, hovered over the screen. I can't hear them. I come up with nothing.

"YOU'RE STUCK IN your trauma."

At the Brown Jug, they always kept the lights on. The woman who tended bar leaned her chest onto the wood counter and didn't smile. The time never changed, and we put our quarters in the jukebox and peeled the labels off bottles of Pabst and pretended we were not hiding. I had met Adam in a writing class. He bought me a knife to carry and told me my stories were "good," were "almost there."

I was always almost there.

I was twenty-two, and for a year I had been meeting men at bus stops and train stations and getting into their cars and checking the locks and going where they took me and taking what they would pay me.

It was 2003, and in San Francisco, whores were organized. They had community meetings. They shared tax tips. I went to these meetings, and I tried to feel as though I knew my business. As though I were a business. I didn't know what I was. Sometimes

I thought that I was just not a good enough whore. I could not feel the confidence those other women seemed to feel, though I tried to pretend that I did. I needed the money too much. I believed it too much when people told me I was worthless, that being touched for money reduced me, subtracted piece by piece.

Adam played guitar and wrote stories and made farm wine and knew about art. He was twenty-seven and he had read a lot of books. He had a college degree and a girlfriend and an admittance to a university that would award him a master of fine arts. I wanted all of the things he had.

That entire year, I spent days when I was not making rent walking and walking and walking around the city. I bought Styrofoam cups of coffee and chewed the edges in parks. I walked miles at a time, the city so small I had to turn around at Fisherman's Wharf or the windy piers beside the ballpark and cross it again. Everywhere there were people passing me in a hurry, people who had places that they needed to be. I thought all of them—carrying their shopping bags and eating their salads at outdoor tables and talking seriously in high-buttoned coats—were connected to something, were inside of something I could not even see the edges of.

I thought that if Adam loved me, it would get me inside.

"You're stuck in your trauma," he said, "that's why you let men ejaculate on you for eight hundred dollars." We were sitting on bar stools, our beer wrappers shredded, he had put some slow song on, probably Steve Earle, *Someday I'm finally gonna let go*, and he pulled my legs over his lap and I knew he did not love me and still, I cried as though he did.

IN TRUTH, I had only made $800 once. I thought that man was just too stupid to know that I would have done it for much less. I feared that he would change his mind, and when he handed me the envelope, those eight thin bills felt as precious and unexpected as the jewelry boxes men gave to women in the movies. Later, I realized that $800, to him, simply wasn't very much.

SEX WORKERS, says Catharine MacKinnon, are "the property of men who buy and sell and rent them."[1] She says that to rape a sex worker means simply to not pay her.

WHEN MEN EJACULATED on me it did not feel like trauma, it felt like money. Like rent. It was not painful. It was not confusing. I did not hate them. I felt nothing about them. I knew what I was agreeing to. I knew what I would have when I walked away. I knew that I would walk away. I knew that I owned myself. That owning myself meant having a way to make my money and walk away. That the walking away, more than anything, was the thing that made this work different.

SEX WORK, tweeted Ashley Judd, is "body invasion." It commodifies "girls and women's orifices."

"Cash," she says, "is the proof of coercion."

ON MARCH 11, 2019, the New York City chapter of the National Organization for Women (NOW-NYC) held a protest on the steps of City Hall, demanding the continued criminalization of sex work. Decrim NY, a coalition of New York sex workers, had recently announced efforts to introduce a state bill to get rid of New York's "loitering for the purposes of prostitution" law, a law that overwhelmingly targets Black and brown trans women, who can be arrested for simply standing on a sidewalk, wearing "revealing clothing." Speakers at NOW's protest called the decriminalization bill the "Pimp Protection Act."

NOW-NYC's president said, "Yes, you've heard it right, the sex trade could be coming to a neighborhood near you." New York City, she said, could become the "Las Vegas of the Northeast." As though sex work were not also illegal in Las Vegas.

A small group of sex workers came to counterprotest. They held signs that said, "Sex Workers Against Sex Trafficking."

The anti-decriminalization protestors stepped in front of them to cover their signs. Speakers said that the sex workers were "ignorant of their own oppression."

ONE AFTERNOON IN Old Town, a man walked up behind me and I felt his hand suddenly grip my ass and run down between my legs. As he continued past me I realized there were actually three men together, all of them grown-ups. All of them laughing.

The cops were watching, like always. Something inside of me broke and I shouted.

"That man grabbed my ass!" I pointed at the three men receding across the parking lot.

"Which one?" said the cop.

"I don't know," I said.

The cop shrugged. "Maybe if you didn't dress like a homeless person, men wouldn't do those things to you."

I DID NOT tell anyone that I had been raped. I did not tell anyone and still they said, "What is wrong with you that you allow men to pay to touch you."

They said, "What happened to you that made you like this?"

I heard these things again and again.

I heard them so often that I feared that they were right, that I had only tricked myself into believing that there was a difference between the things I'd chosen and the things I hadn't.

In my bed, not sleeping, Adam's heavy arm over me, my body between him and the wall, I thought: I am broken.

I did not know what I was, and I did not know how to be anything else.

I knew that to become a person that men like Adam could love would mean making myself visibly weak. Would mean performing the kind of weakness that other people—people inside of the place with invisible edges—could find lovable. Would mean claiming ignorance so they could see me as worthy of being remade.

I knew that the weakness they wanted was nothing like the real weakness inside of me. The real weakness inside of me could only be healed if I trusted my own rules. If I did not give my pain away for other people's stories.

IT WAS IN a porn studio that I first began to feel as though my body was a thing I could love. I did not take the job in order to feel this. I did not even understand it as it was happening. It happened slowly and also all at once. I showed up to shoot and the man that I would be working with asked me, "What are your limits?"

I had no idea what he was talking about.

"What do you not want to do?" he asked. And on that day, I could not tell him. No one had ever asked me that question before.

"We'll try some things," he said, "and you just say 'red' if you want to stop."

So I tried things. Some of them I liked and some of them I didn't and some of them I didn't care about one way or another. Every day when I came to shoot, they asked me the same question: "What do you want to do today? What don't you want to do?"

Eventually, I could answer. I could make a list. This is what I want. This is what I don't want.

There was a day when I was tied up, suspended in rope in the middle of a warehouse in downtown San Francisco, and a man was hitting me all over my body with a deerskin flogger. I was in mid-air, ropes pressed into my hips and thighs and chest with measured tension, leather thudding rhythmically against my back and breasts and I felt a kind of elation, a swelling in my center. I felt strong. I felt myself getting stronger. The scene ended, and they lowered me to the ground and they untied the ropes and blood rushed back into my knees and elbows and I felt suddenly clean. I felt whole. More than whole, I felt unbreakable.

They handed me a check, and it did not feel like coercion, it felt like safety. It felt like I had taken something from them.

"IT IS IMPOSSIBLE," says Andrea Dworkin, "to use a human body in the way women's bodies are used in prostitution and to have a whole human being at the end of it, or in the middle of it, or close to the beginning of it. . . . And no woman gets whole again later, after."[2]

IN LOS ANGELES, the days were all the same but also they were all different. We were Moretti's girls and he gave us rules to follow. He told us when to be home and who we could or could not date and he took us to work and to the grocery store and to the Starbucks and to Malibu for fish tacos and to DiMaggio's for steaks and wine. We walked behind him in the restaurants and at parties and at go-sees at the Vivid and Wicked offices, a line of us in glitter and spandex and Pleasers and fishnet and lamé. I loved being one of his girls. I felt like I was inside. Not inside of the place that other people were in, but still, inside of something real.

I worked. All of us worked. We lived to work. We called it the "porn dorm" and we called it "porno boot camp" and we got up at five a.m. and worked until two the following morning. We worked two-a-days and we worked seven days a week and there was not a single day of the year when someone, somewhere, was not making pornography.

There were bad days.

I was booked for a solo and the director kept trying to fuck me and then finally just jerked off onto my leg even while I told him to stop. He laughed and put his dick away and then later he put me on the box cover. I was nominated for an AVN award for the scene.

I was booked for a double with my friend Annette and the director sent the photographer and makeup artist home so we'd be alone. He wheedled at us all day, trying to keep us there, trying to make us drink things from cups in his fridge, telling us he'd been watching all our films. Annette and I kept eyeing each other, trying to figure out where this was going, trying to figure out how to get our money and get out of there. Finally, he set up a tripod on his bedroom desk and sweated away on top of us like we were not even there. We didn't even pretend. I lay there limp and let him drip and groan on me. He put us on the box cover. I told Moretti not to make me work for him ever again.

One day on set, a male performer grabbed me suddenly by the throat and pinned me to the wall when no one else was looking. "You like it," he said, and laughed. On another day, in the bathroom of a hotel, he hit me so hard my face bled.

One day I worked with a man I was certain wanted me dead. We were in a basement, there were concrete stairs and he dragged me down them. He ground my head into the concrete floor and stepped on my face and I thought my skull would crack. I just held my breath and waited to see if I would live.

THERE WERE GOOD DAYS.

There were days when I got to work and suddenly, wordlessly, I connected with the other performer and the thing we made on those days was a kind of magic. I learned to feel exactly what the camera could see. I wore bandit's-mask makeup and knee-high athletic socks in a bathtub and squirted rainbow-colored water out of my asshole and we played in the water like it was a summer sprinkler and laughed until we could not laugh any more. I walked through the sunlit terrace of an abandoned mansion and turned my body perfectly to the light and became a museum statue. I filled my own eyes with spit and laid my head upside down over the back of a pool table and cried black bubbles and contorted my limbs so that every part of me was bent to the edges of bodily possibility. I pulled men's bodies into mine and watched their eyes change and knew for a few moments how I owned them, how I had taken away a kind of power they were so used to having that they'd forgotten how tired they were of having it. I stood on top of a mountain naked, draped in bits of fabric that flew in the wind but never covered my nakedness. I pissed in the dirt and screamed and bared my tits and came like rockets and gripped my own body like it would keep me from falling. I put entire fists inside of me and then the six-inch stilettos of my high heeled shoes. I was everything but pretty. I screamed and spit and grunted and moved in impossible ways and made the crew gasp. I'd made art or won a race, I wasn't sure what. On those days I felt as though my body were a sharp tool, as though my craft were unmatched. I felt utterly human, as though I had laid plain the thing I was made of.

"A SEX WORKER," says Dorchen Leidholdt, is a "de-individualized, dehumanized being . . . stranger after stranger use her body as a seminal spittoon."[3]

THE GOOD DAYS and the bad days were overwhelmed by days when everything went as expected. Days when I showed up and laid out my clothes and we chose something and I put my makeup on and took the stills and waited for male talent or waited for the light or waited for the dialogue and did six positions and a pop and took my check and went home. I felt bored more often than I felt anything else. I felt bored and I felt as though the thing I was inside of was invisible to everyone who was not inside of it.

When I was not working, I was exhausted. I was more exhausted than I had ever been. Some mornings, when it was time to get up to go to work, I cried.

"You cry now, but you'll cry when you have no money," Moretti said.

I cried and then I went to work.

The day would be good or it would be bad or it would be neither and I would collect my check and Moretti would come and pick us up and take us to Jerry's Deli and we would eat chicken soup and black and white cookies, and I loved him. I loved these women around me, each of them with their bodies like weapons. I felt as though I did not belong anywhere but there.

I'VE RARELY TALKED about my rape and I've rarely talked about violence I've experienced while doing sex work. I have not talked about these things because I am afraid. Because I know how stories like mine get told. Because I know exactly how good anti–sex work "feminists" are at carving out the pieces of our stories to make them mean something else, something less complicated and more easily sold. I know how good they are at flattening us, at excavating our experiences to make stories that are only an imitation of the things we've lived. I know how good they are at making us no longer human but symbols of this thing they call womanhood. This thing they've made that I do not see myself in.

I'm afraid, but also I'm angry. I'm angry that I could not talk about violence without fueling descriptions of me as an object, written by women claiming to be my allies. I have survived violence in sex work and also I have chosen again and again to do this work. I have performed sex and femininity and also I am not a symbol of anyone else's womanhood. I have been poor enough that sex work seemed like a gift, poor enough that sex work changed my power in the world by giving me the safety that money gives. To say that I needed the money is not the same as saying I could not choose, and to say that I chose is not the same as saying it was always good. I have been harmed in sex work and I have been healed in sex work and I should not have to explain either of those experiences in order to talk about my work as work.

"WOMEN MUST BE HEARD," says Ashley Judd. And I know that when she says women, she does not mean me.

## NOTES

1. Catharine MacKinnon, "Prostitution and Civil Rights," *Michigan Journal of Gender and Law* 1 (1993): 13–31.
2. Andrea Dworkin, "Prostitution and Male Supremacy," *Michigan Journal of Gender and Law* 1 (1993): 1–12.
3. Dorchen Leidholdt, "Prostitution: A Violation of Women's Human Rights," *Cardozo Women's Law Journal* 1 (1993): 138.

## The Invisibles

IGNACIO G. HUTÍA XEITI RIVERA

Something shook me that day in psychology class. Something shifted, was unhinged, or even shattered. I can't tell. I was in my early twenties, in community college, a newly out lesbian, and an independent mom. I had already been on my own for several years, since the day I left home as a teenager. The day that I stuffed two black garbage bags with my clothes, threw them out my fourth-floor balcony, grabbed my school bag, and walked out the house like every other morning. But this time, I didn't return.

I didn't leave because my childhood was horrible. It was a regular childhood for the most part—wonderful at times and shitty at others. I left because I was exhausted occupying the shadows of my older sister. Her mishaps, transgressions, and failures cast unearned doubt onto me. My mother was a bit freer with her—in the beginning. She allowed her to wear makeup at fourteen, reluctantly allowed her to have a boyfriend, gave her freedom, and she fucked it all up. For both of us. She became entangled with the wrong crowd, got mixed up in drugs, and caused our family a lot of heartache. My parents weren't about to make the same mistake with me. I lived under watchful eyes. I was told—it seems like daily—to learn from her mistakes. I never got the chance to learn because my mother eliminated the possibility. I wasn't allowed to join any extracurricular activities, have friends over, go to friends' houses, or go out to parties. It felt like my whole world revolved around my sister's wrongdoings. After she ran away, the goal to "protect" me became stronger. I was tired of her, and the room we once shared.

I grew up in a Boricua household. Youngest of three, I was raised in Brooklyn, New York. I've always been the weirdo of the family. I'm the queer one, the nonbinary one, the polyamorous one, the vegan one, the sober one, the one who recycles. When I was a little girl, I lived in my head a lot. I was an avid diary writer and would escape into books any chance I could get, I advocated for street animals in our neighborhood, and I had a very big secret. That secret made me feel the weirdest of all. From the time I was that little girl, up until I was the twenty-year-old lesbian sitting in psychology class, I carried that secret. Although I always had the sense of knowing that what happened throughout my childhood was wrong, I didn't have a name for it and I didn't realize the impact it would have on me.

That day in class, our professor prepared us to watch a short film about family reunification after sexual abuse. This eighties-style film showcased a family—mother, father, and two adolescent girls—in a therapy session addressing the father's sexual abuse of the eldest girl. I can't even remember what the therapist or the family said. I just remember feeling my body. I was trembling. My throat felt blocked. I wanted to scream, cry, and run. I could hear my heart and nothing else. I was so utterly confused. My father had never done anything to harm me, so why was I having such a strong reaction? I ran out of the classroom to the bathroom and fell into a puddle of tears and rage that I could not identify.

I tried desperately to control the downpour onto my flushed cheeks, taking long deep breaths to calm the anxiety. The face of the eldest daughter from the film was burnt into my brain. Her fear and discomfort were apparent. I was sad for her. I was angry for her. Why did she have to sit in front of him—the one who harmed her. I realized how similar we were. A mirror image of shame, fear, and confusion. I made several attempts at reentering the classroom, but each time I failed. The tears would not stop and the thoughts and feelings had just begun. All became clear. The thing that had no name, the secret, was (re)introduced to me—the manipulations, the unwanted touches and threats; I had been sexually abused. It wasn't my father who did these things to me, but it happened in the house I ran away from, in that room we shared, at my sister's hands.

WHEN I BEGAN working in a dungeon, I was not new to BDSM. I was an avid "player," and in those days I was navigating submission with joy. A friend of mine who worked at a Midtown dungeon told me about the job. When I accepted work there, I was told there would be a training, but we were merely informed of the house rules. I had to learn on the job. I began to appreciate what some called the "Bad Johns" list or the "Frequent Flyers" list, where the names and stories of the ones to look out for were told. We shared stories about those who had unique fetishes or bad hygiene, and also named the dangerous ones. There was "Mental Dental," who came equipped with his own needles, novocaine, and extractor forceps. Or "Pig Pen," the cuddler who didn't bathe. There was also the guy obsessed with muscular women. He'd love to watch our baby-oiled bodies flex and then try at every chance to force our hands to jerk him off. Then there was the guy who'd pay for submissives and tie them up to get forced blow jobs. There was also the "Dangerous Top." We were warned about his aggression, his need to push the boundaries of pain. The Dommes and other sex workers shared their warnings to watch out for manipulators, harm doers, and con artists. Yet, they couldn't help me dodge all bad situations.

The majority of my clients were interested in my Blackness and my Latinaness. Clients prepared themselves with fantasy-filled, jungle-fever role-play skits based on a Spanish-talking hot mama, a Black Goddess sentencing them to punishment for their whiteness, making them beg for mercy. I wanted to gain clients, not lose them, so I played along.

Most of the Dommes at the dungeon were small framed. I

wasn't, so I would often be picked to do wrestling scenes. There were two types of wrestling: competitive and fantasy. Fantasy was easy. There was really no muscle involved, just bodies rolling around while we grunted and moaned. But there wasn't as much money in fantasy wrestling as there was in competitive wrestling. The competitive sessions paid more because we definitely used muscle. There was this guy who came in several times to see me. Ahead of time, he would request that I wear a two-piece suit. While in session, we would wrestle intensely. He was very strong, broad, tall, muscular, and hairy. He would toy with me, let me get the upper hand at times, but put me in my place every time he got me on the mat. Pinned down, his hands would explore parts of my body that I had not consented to be touched. He would push aside my clothes to touch, rub, and lick as his sweaty body lay on mine.

I never complained and kept such instances of sexual violation to myself. I would go back and forth in my own head, telling myself that on the one hand, sexual violations came with the territory, and on the other hand, I knew that I deserved to be treated better. Sadly, I was too used to that type of aggressive behavior to formulate a reasonable frame of reference.

WHAT DOES ONE scene of abuse—my own experience of child sexual abuse—have to do with the other—repeated assaults by a sex work client? People often want to know if one type of trauma led to another, to explain the possibility of choosing sex work as a product of one's past. *Did something happen to you? Were you abused as a child? Do you have daddy issues? Were you raped?* As a sex worker, I've been asked all of these questions by people seeking revelations about why sex workers are sex workers. There must be a trauma or tragedy to bring someone to demean themselves as a sex worker. The fact that I was sexually abused as a child and now I am a sex worker who's experienced sexual abuse as an adult is a complexity I hold within myself. As much as sex work has given me a path to heal, I continue to be a work in progress.

MY SEX WORK was part of my journey to find my body, desire, curiosity, agency, and sexuality. When I had previously considered sex work to help supplement my income, the fear of losing my infant daughter had been too great. I was a "single," lesbian of color, "welfare mom" as it were, and too afraid to add another stigmatized descriptor. But my daughter grew older and I felt more connected to my body than ever. Years of learning about sex and bodies had empowered me to claim my own pleasure, and be excited and curious about the world of sex. Sex work was therapy for me. And I was getting paid for it. Most of the time my work made me feel electrified, but at others, I felt insignificant. I suppose a teacher, a mother, or a security guard could say the same. More than anything, when it came down to it, sex work happened to sit at the intersection of money, flexibility, and more time with my daughter. I was a survivor who chose sex work from a place of empowerment; however, not all sex workers come into work from empowerment, and not all sex workers have to grapple with survivorship complicating their work.

Sex workers are simultaneously the perfect victims and the wrong kind of victims. Well-meaning sympathizers who don't hold our "brokenness" against us make sure that it defines us. When we are sexually assaulted on the job, the victim paradox obscures the legitimacy of our grievances. On the one hand, sex workers are seen as the perfect victims because we are assumed to already be survivors. On the other hand, sex workers are the wrong kind of victim: we cannot experience sexual violence because of the nature of the work we do. I was a sex worker who happened to already be a survivor. However, I did not become a sex worker out of brokenness, barely glued together by self-loathing sex work. The types of sex work I have chosen to do are ones that come with power and privilege. I have worked as a naked prostate masseuse in a parlor with security, a nude dancer protected by glass walls, a pro-Domme in the comfort of a camera-filled dungeon, and an adult film actor on sex-positive queer feminist porn sets. Sex work for me is about harnessing my own power, pulling down the deadpan body hovering over powerless sex acts and claiming agency.

As a naked masseuse, my clients weren't allowed to touch me. I did all the touching and prodding. My naked body was but a prop. I wasn't touched when I danced. I loved being the girl behind the glass wall. I would do my dance and touch myself. I would listen to the heavy moans over the phones adorning either side of the glass. The men would explode while clenching the receiver, holding themselves with their other hand, pressed up against the slutty glass. I felt power in my ability to seduce. In my work within queer feminist porn, I love to be touched. I have agency in porn work—from who I do scenes with, to what we do, what items we use, and how we discuss and practice safer sex. I've felt most in my body there.

THE EXCLUSION OF sex work from the realm of work itself precludes any discussion around workplace protections for sex workers. The sex worker, the broken whore, is either deemed a survivor prior to entering this line of work, or assumed to become one after starting. Within this framework, there is no room for nuance or discussion that doesn't end with the abolishment of sex work itself. When sex work isn't work and sex workers are too broken for protection, where does the conversation about the sexual assault of sex workers belong?

Any work we do to end sexual violence should be led by those at the margins. Sexual violence does not discriminate according to identity or privilege, yet as survivors, we all have our unique struggles. We are in a tremendous moment that is redefining consent and taking a broader look at sexual harm. However, sexual violence cannot be fully addressed until we reckon with the epidemic of child sexual abuse. We cannot continue without understanding where sex workers fit in as "valid" targets of sexual harm. We must build a movement that is not just about white women. We must fight for the invisibles: the street worker, the little girl, the Black trans woman, and the go-go dancer. It's about shining light on the sprouts of deep buried secrets, making visible the incomprehensible, and proclaiming that our stories and our healing matters.

## Wounds and Ways Through:
## A Personal Chronology of December 17

### AUDACIA RAY

### DECEMBER 17, 2004

About a dozen people gathered in Washington Square Park in New York City. Someone handed out cheap red and white candles that had been on sale for Christmas. We held the candlesticks in our gloved hands. Our bodies, wrapped tightly in our winter coats, formed a half circle in the near-solstice darkness of the evening. I don't remember who spoke or what they said, but I do remember the piece of the vigil that would become standard at every December 17 event I would attend over the following decade: the reading of the names. Someone had done the painful work of collecting names from news reports about murdered sex workers, and we stood in the cold and listened to them read out loud. Name, age at death, location. Repeat. Many were name unknown, age unknown, and a location where the body was found. It was several minutes before they had all been read. After the reading of the names, the group dispersed pretty quickly. It was too cold to spend much time comforting each other or sharing thoughts. I was glad it was over quickly. I left in a bad mood, feeling like I'd wasted my time shivering in a cold park, thinking about the depressing and personally irrelevant topic of violence.

I attended my first International Day to End Violence Against Sex Workers event—the second ever annual event—out of a sense of obligation. I didn't want to go. It seemed like a serious bummer that didn't have anything to do with me or my experience. I had been a sex worker less than six months, and I had found it to be empowering. Nothing terrible had happened to me, and I didn't think anything terrible had happened to the handful of other sex workers I knew. I had made the leap from being slutty via Craigslist Casual Encounters to selling sex a few clicks over on the site's Erotic Services section, and I was obsessively documenting both in daily posts on my blog. I lived for the adventure of it all; I felt liberated and in control of my body and my income. My reductive understanding of empowerment would become deeply complicated in coming years.

As a twenty-four-year-old white, queer, cisgender woman living in Brooklyn and working toward my MA at Columbia University, I understood that sex work was socially and politically stigmatized. I had privilege to spare, so challenging the taboos around sex work—even just the idea of choosing sex work when I had other options—was exciting to me. Through the sex blog I started writing the summer before I began doing full-service sex work and porn, I crafted a version of my experiences that was analytical, but also titillating. I started the blog under a pseudonym and initially didn't post pictures, but quickly started to take the risk of increasing exposure and reducing privacy, first by doing porn and cross-posting some images to my blog as well as eventually by coming out to my family as a sex worker and legally changing my name to the name I chose for porn, activism, and sex blogging. The more I shared online, the more I was rewarded with writing gigs, speaking engagements, media hits, and awards. People wanted to know what I thought about subjects ranging from feminist porn to the best sex toys. My blog brought me in touch not just with an audience of curious onlookers, but also with other sex workers, and being an out and proud hooker made my opinions count.

As I built my social capital on a foundation of white privilege, youth, and conventional attractiveness, my star rose in sex blogging, porn, and sex worker activist circles. I connected with a group of women who were working to establish a magazine called *Spread*, making culture by, for, and about sex workers. Though we initially only talked about the magazine and not our personal experiences, the founding crew of $preadsters were all around my age, white, and child-free. I assumed that our experiences were very similar, though I would later learn otherwise.

They say sex work is dangerous, but I didn't see it. My clients were mostly kind, mostly not pushy, upper-middle-class, over-whelmingly white New Yorkers who liked the idea that I was a student and worked independently. I maintained this perspective through *Spread*'s collaboration with the more established sex work-ers' rights group Prostitutes of New York (PONY) to organize the 2004 vigil for December 17. The event had been conceived of in 2003 as a day of vigil after the conviction of a serial killer, Gary Ridgway, who confessed to killing at least seventy-one women in the Green River area between Seattle and Tacoma. In his presen-tencing statement, he declared that he chose sex workers because no one would miss them when they disappeared.

The vigil was important to the $preadsters, but I didn't think these murders had anything to do with me. The women who had been murdered were mostly street-based workers, many main-tained drug habits and supported families. Some folks were trans. Their lives looked nothing like mine. I understood violence as something extreme—unwanted and damaging physical pain that could be disfiguring or deadly. It didn't seem like a possibility that I would experience anything like that in my daytime encounters with married businessmen. I didn't think that any of the sex workers I'd been getting to know had already or would ever experience the threat of violence either.

For years, I would loudly proclaim that I had never experienced violence as a sex worker, even after that stopped being true. I was defensive about this claim. I wanted to protect my much-maligned profession and prove that it wasn't as bad as the press it got. Much later, I came to understand that the narrow definition of violence that I had at this moment was insufficient, that violence is not just physical but actually includes the use of power to control, manipulate, or harm. It is so common that to name and try to heal from every act would be overwhelming. And furthermore, violence is not just a thing that happens between two people; it can be enacted by institutions like the police and hospitals. It is not simply active harm, but blocking access to health and economic security. But I didn't understand any of that yet. All I knew is that on this appointed day, I would think about murder and feel bummed out. After my first December 17, I had planned to go out and see friends, but instead I went home. The party mood I had planned to be in was out of reach. My night was over.

## TRUST

After a year of sex work, I was learning to balance my relationships, my personal sex life, and the demands of clients and photographers. After starting out as a full-service sex worker, I made the choice to limit myself to modeling and massage sessions, establishing boundaries that I lacked during my first few months. I was living up to the sex-positive, ethical-slut ideals I was projecting into the world, surrounding myself with people who supported my choices as a sex worker. I started to expand my modeling repertoire and build friendships with a few photographers I liked. These relationships were collaborative and creative—sometimes we both got paid to produce something commercial, sometimes we'd just work on a weird idea we had.

One of these photographers had also made photos with a bunch of women I admired, and I wanted to show up in his portfolio alongside them. After we had shot some commercial stuff in studios together, he approached me with an idea for a personal project that would involve nudity. Most of the shoots I had been doing, both for fun and money, involved me getting naked. That piece of it felt normal to me; I liked being naked and it made me feel free. There wasn't any money in it for either of us: we'd share copyright and I'd get prints and digital files to keep. Instead of spending money renting studio space for the day, he suggested we meet and shoot at his apartment.

I arrived at his apartment building in Greenwich Village on a hot, late spring day, and walked up a few twisty flights of stairs to his apartment, getting sweaty under my loose clothing. The photographer was waiting on the landing outside his apartment when I made it up the stairs, and we hugged hello, his dark hair brushing my jawline when he got close. We drank tall glasses of water and sat on the floor in the middle of the biggest room in his railroad apartment, where he'd pushed most of the furniture into a corner to make space for his light kit setup. He pulled out a portfolio book and showed me images from the nude portrait series in which I was about to participate.

The portfolio featured pictures of the women I admired as I'd never seen them, nude and with minimal makeup. I was used to seeing them as glittering statues of womanhood, dressed in latex or elaborate feathered costumes, rhinestones dramatically adorning their cheekbones. But these photos were so different, intimate, close, a little raw and vulnerable. I wanted to know the women in this way, felt almost jealous that he had gotten this access to them, and honored that I got to see these images of them. The pictures weren't posted online, while many other pictures he'd taken of the same models were. He laughed as he showed me, saying, "Oh, they'd kill me if they knew I was showing anyone these pictures." In a few photos his hand reached into the frame, sometimes just at the edge, sometimes making contact with the model's skin.

I immediately wanted to be part of the project. A few of the models were dommes who I'd seen at parties and shoots. One was a model who I was starting to cultivate a friendship with, but felt a bit shy around. He was clearly proud of these images. I wanted him to be proud of the images we'd make together, too. His comment about the models not wanting other people to see the images didn't really register with me. These women seemed to trust him. They all continued to work with him and recommend him to others.

I unceremoniously stripped off my clothes as we gossiped about mutual acquaintances. I felt comfortable, relaxed. He invited me to lie down on my stomach on his bed. I felt the mattress sag as he knelt behind me, and the camera clicked away. His leg brushed against the outside of my thigh, and then I heard the distinct jingling of his belt buckle coming undone. I froze, confused. We were friends. He had always been easy to work with. I trusted him. We'd previously shot glam fetish photos, including a shoot with my girlfriend at the time, who was also a sex worker. After that shoot, the three of us had a meal together and my girlfriend teasingly said I should date him since we had a similar nerdy affect.

His voice switched into a hoarse whisper as he moved closer. Although I had been very up close and personal with photographers before, I realized that none of them had ever touched me; this was new territory. I had always been flippant about the stilted way many photographers gave me privacy to change clothes or take my clothes off, the way they tiptoed around boundaries they thought I should have. I usually dispensed with their nervous behavior by joking about how I was just going to be showing them my stuff in a few minutes anyway. This man whispered, "I like to share vulnerability with my models; I think the pictures are better that way, don't you agree?" The pictures he'd shown earlier me *were* intense, some of his best work. I kept thinking of his vast portfolio and the tacit approval of those other models. But I was uncomfortable. "Relax, relax, relax," he repeated over and over, nearly chanting, as he got closer and started to move his hand up my leg, all the while snapping photos.

I rolled over, not because I wanted to expose myself to him, but because I wanted to see what he was doing. His pants were open. He continued shooting, angling the camera, a digital one with some heft and a long lens, down at me as I moved. My vision felt fuzzy, my limbs heavy. He lay down next to me and pressed his now-hard dick against my leg. He set the camera beside us and rolled on top of me. I clamped my thighs together.

"Come on, relax. It's just me," he said, almost whining, seemingly offended that I had tensed up and gone cold. I said nothing, I could not respond. "I thought we had some chemistry. Sorry if I misread," he coaxed, faux-humbling himself, as he continued to try to press himself into me. He had his dick in his hand and was trying to push it inside me, even as he apologized. I kept my thighs clamped and rolled my hips so we were next to each other on the bed, and then I reached for his dick and quickly got him off with my hand. I felt nothing, thought nothing. Something in me took over and piloted my body to this action, which in the moment I understood as cooperation, an acknowledgment and assent to his need. Years later, in therapy, I would come to understand my decision as a protective act of harm reduction. I jerked him off to mitigate the violence, to put an end to this assault in a way that he would read as a concession, through an orgasm that I bet correctly would neutralize him.

He wordlessly got up, came back with a damp washcloth, and wiped my thigh clean. I looked everywhere in the apartment except his face. We made some small talk but didn't directly mention what had just happened. The space to address it closed up quickly.

What had happened made me uncomfortable, but I didn't give it a name. I didn't tell anyone about it. When I left and took the subway home, my body felt strange—subdued, cold despite the heat of the day. Although I often blogged about my experiences at photo shoots and in my sex life, I didn't blog about this day. I figured maybe I would post about it once I received the pictures. I liked to show my readers what went into doing a photo shoot: being naked in a cold room, arching my back until it ached.

The photographer never shared the images with me. Months went by; I didn't follow up with him, and he didn't invite me back.

I had agreed to go to a sex party later that night with a casual partner, who picked me up at my apartment and drove us into

Manhattan. The wind from the open car window traveled over my body as we drove across the Brooklyn Bridge. All night, there was something in me that felt different, colder, less responsive to touch and the enthusiasm of the other guests at the party. I squashed it down. I needed this party to ground me, make me feel present in my body, desired and desiring, acting on my desire. I dove into a pile of women I knew and a few men I didn't, kissing and groping, where some hands were gentle and others were more persistent. I drank a lot. In the early hours of the next morning I fell into bed, feeling like the fun, hot experiences I'd had at the party could not erase the grip the photographer had on my skin earlier in the afternoon.

## TORN

A few weeks later, a casual sex partner accidentally tore my labia. I had been encouraging him to fuck me vigorously with his hand, when he slipped and a too-long fingernail pierced my outer labia. There was so much blood that it was hard to see what exactly had happened or where the wound was located. He looked panicked, then started laughing and said, "It's a good thing I've seen so many horror movies!" He grabbed a roll of paper towels from his kitchen. I wasn't really in pain, just stunned by the flow of bright red. More than the injury, I felt disoriented by the quick turn from feeling good and wanting more to the surprise of injury. I shrunk into myself. I wadded up paper towels to apply pressure to my entire vulva, soaked through the first batch and grabbed a second. By the third bundle of towels the bleeding had slowed considerably. I held them in place while I waddled to the bathroom to rinse off and see if I could find the site of the wound. My date stood awkwardly to the side, offering no help. After I rinsed the blood off, I didn't have the courage to look at the wound. When I walked back into the bedroom, he was dressed. He said, "Well, I guess that means our date is over." We stood for an awkward moment until I realized that he was done with me, didn't want me to stay, and wasn't going to offer any additional support.

I wouldn't even consider going to the hospital. If this man to whom I'd trusted my body wouldn't come near me, I could not imagine walking into the emergency room alone and showing this wound to a bevy of nurses and doctors. I wadded up a fresh batch of paper towels and carefully put my underwear and then my pants back on, and walked slowly through the busy evening streets of Manhattan to the subway. I stared into space as I rode home.

When I got back to my apartment, I called a sex educator friend with whom I had shared many group sex adventures. She was supportive, unflappable, and solutions-oriented. She came right over to my apartment, let herself in, and found me curled up in bed. "Come on, let's get you cleaned up," she said, supporting me as I walked slowly to the bathroom and undressed. She got the shower hot enough for me and sat on the toilet while I stood under its stream. As I pressed my back against the shower wall and slid down into a sitting position in the bathtub, it was clear to her that I was in shock, even if I remained oblivious. She turned off the shower and climbed into the tub with me.

Always ready to show people their vulvas under better circumstances, my friend brought a large hand mirror with her. She asked, very gently, if I could show her where I was hurt. I spread my legs for her and she gently opened the folds of my labia to see an angry, crescent-shaped wound on my right inner labia. "Do you want to see it?" she asked, and I nodded my consent. She handed me the mirror and kept a hand reassuringly on my leg. What I saw was a tiny hole in my labia. Confirming its actual size made me feel better—I had been imagining a disfiguring wound—but I became dizzy with the recognition that my body had been changed by what happened earlier. We agreed that it didn't look like it needed stitches, but that I would make an appointment with my doctor first thing in the morning to get it checked out. We slept curled together, with her as my big spoon.

When I saw my doctor the next day she confirmed that I didn't need stitches, but she also admonished me for not going to the emergency room. The doctor spoke to me with a focus on the wound to my flesh, not acknowledging the wound to my psyche. The sex was consensual, and yet I felt violated and going to the hospital would have deepened that feeling. I didn't feel like the violation was intentional, but an abstract, passive voice told me that a bad thing had happened, an injury had been incurred. This wound was, in a sense, deepened by the emotional violence my friend had done to me by his joking and dismissiveness: "I guess that means our date is over." Both my injured body and my emotional reaction were burdens to him, inconveniences.

After seeing my doctor, I tucked a panty liner into my underwear and went to see my afternoon massage client. My friend encouraged me to cancel, but I did not want to acknowledge that something heavy and difficult had happened; I wanted my life to be normal and good.

That night, I went home and blogged about the incident. I started the post like I started many of my writings about my sex life, describing the action in a mix of documentary and erotica styles, leading up to the abrupt moment of the injury and its aftermath. I wanted my readers to be shocked by this moment of injury, as I had been. I ended the piece with, "It will get better—I know I'll heal and my cunt won't be broken forever, but I just feel awful today: shaken, sore, and achy. Worse than the physical pain, I feel like the happiness and security of my cunt is a thousand miles away, floating on a plane of dull, achy, and marred flesh."

I had not allowed myself to feel much about the assault I'd experienced weeks prior, and would not call it by that word for years; but I allowed myself to fully feel betrayal and rage about the accident. My friend had not hurt me on purpose, while the photographer clearly had every intent to violate me. After both incidents, I rushed into trying to recalibrate and establish normalcy. I did not want to be changed by them. The accident brought concrete, physical injury, so I was less able to move past it unchanged. And I had more language for what had happened—it was an accident, random and unfortunate, even if it did feel like violence. I had a physical wound: a tender part of me to take care of and heal. After the incident with the photographer, I didn't know what I was left with, what part of me to attend to, so I buried my shame and confusion. And since I had participated by getting him off, I didn't think I could claim it as violence. I was committed to maintaining the narrative that the sex industry was not as terrible or dangerous as everyone said.

Channeling my anger through my blog post about the injury and inviting my readers into these feelings with me felt cathartic. My date was a part of my sex blogging social universe, and many of my readers and blogging peers were also people who went to the same sex parties, people with whom I had had sex, as had he. He apologized profusely in the comments, but I can't remember if he reached out to me privately. "I broke our Dacia!" he wrote, "I'm so sorry." I felt irritated that he, or the community, was staking a possessive claim to me with that "our." In this moment, I belonged to no one.

In a follow-up post after I wrote about the details of the night and the injury, I hung onto my anger. I was angry that the rest of my friends could go off to a sex party soon after my injury when my enjoyment had come to a screeching halt.

I would continue to say publicly that I had never experienced violence.


TAUGHT

There was no one moment of epiphany in which I began to understand the broad umbrella of what violence is: how it manifests in my life and the lives of sex workers who are and are not like me. It was cumulative: it took time to realize I had refused to look deeply at hard things, and at times perpetuated violence myself. I definitely owe that learning process to Black and Brown sex workers—especially trans women of color—as well as women in the international sex workers' rights movement and collaborators who showed me what I was initially unwilling to see.

Violence can be great or small acts, and many acts in between. It can be a violent man posing as a client, hitting and choking and threatening workers. It can be deceptive managers who traffic would-be workers into situations they would never agree to on their own. It can be police coercing massage workers into trading sex in exchange for their freedom from arrest and detention. It manifests as whorephobia from judgmental doctors, and the information sex workers withhold from health-care workers for fear of stigma. Violence exists in the structural barriers that prevent workers who have prostitution arrests on their records from moving forward with their lives.

Violence exists in the ways our brains fold in on themselves, convincing us that what happened isn't that bad, that it is easier to push forward without naming the thing that happened as violence. It exists in the ways sex workers create and uphold a hierarchy within the larger industry and have disdain for people that do kinds of work they'd never do (or might do only if the rent was past due). Violence exists in the ways that white sex workers uphold white supremacy both in workplaces and in activist spaces. Violence exists in the maintenance of "empowerment" and "choice" narratives that exclude sex workers who have ambivalent or negative feelings about their work.

## DECEMBER 17, 2018

Over more than a decade, the annual December 17 events have marked the ways my reckoning with violence has changed. One year, a fellow activist spilled red paint over white sheets in the shape of bodies on the steps outside Judson Memorial Church. I started emceeing the event at some point, usually breaking down in tears in front of the crowd. We moved from outside the church and into the warmer sanctuary space, where ministers to queer youth welcomed us. One year, the event immediately followed the discovery of the bodies of four sex workers on a beach in Long Island. Their deaths were declared the doing of an active serial killer who, as of this writing, remains at large. One year, I got called out for making December 17 a space for white feelings while the reality is that Black and Brown sex workers, especially trans women, are often the most vulnerable to state and interpersonal violence. That year, I began to understand that some of my activism had been experienced as violence and erasure by Black and Brown sex workers. It was necessary for me to stop emceeing and cede the space to QTBIPOC, to play a support role and keep my mouth shut. And one year, I experienced violence in my own relationship and realized that holding space for survivors and mourners while your own survival is at stake is not possible.

In 2018, after four years of not attending a December 17 event, I felt like I needed it again. But instead of performing feelings in public, I wanted to be with friends and acknowledge the hard truths of the day while also making a space that might feel like healing. I had come to understand that I could not be in service to other people's healing while my own trauma was untended.

I invited a small crew of friends and comrades to my Brooklyn apartment. We surrounded ourselves with framed photos of sex workers we had known or had advocated for, who had died by murder, suicide, overdose, or lack of access to health care. We lit candles. We talked about the movement and about our lives over platefuls of puttanesca, the pasta sauce reputed to have been created by Italian sex workers who needed to prepare quick meals between clients. Someone performed a sound bath and I listened to my friends breathing deeply.

The feelings of empowerment and invincibility that I had those first months as a sex worker will never return. Those feelings were rooted in denial, inexperience, and a lack of understanding of my relative privilege. Reckoning with violence, including both naming it and understanding how it impacts other sex workers, particularly trans women of color, has complicated everything. Violence is complex and wiggly. And if we allow our definitions to be large enough, we can acknowledge the painful reality that it has impacted us all.

My early understanding of how violence impacted sex workers was that it happened to and among strangers: I believed that lone-wolf, scary clients did violence, and the sex workers I knew—who looked whole and fine to me—had not experienced it. I believed that there was a set of tips I could follow that would protect me. When violence happened to me, with men I knew, I didn't recognize it, couldn't name it. Over the following months and years, I began to understand that it wasn't that I didn't know this was violence—it felt bad, sent me spinning, I needed to recover—but that if this was violence, then violence was so common that it was unremarkable to everyone but the survivor. I had expected something else from violence. I didn't know it could be so intimate, that I would have to struggle to acknowledge that it was real, that two acts that cumulatively took place over less than an hour would shape my experience of my body and my truth for years to come, long after that crescent-shaped scar had faded.

# HEALING

# Going from Homeless Trans Youth
## to Holistic Caregiver

CEYENNE DOROSHOW with ZACKARY DRUCKER

C eyenne Doroshow is the daughter, and I am the granddaugh-
ter, of legendary drag queen Mother Flawless Sabrina, a.k.a.
Jack Doroshow. So, in the lineage of chosen queer family, Ceyenne
is my aunt.

I met Flawless Sabrina when I was an eighteen-year-old queer
kid who had just migrated to New York City. Flawless guided and
supported me through my entire adult life until her passing in 2017.
She did the same for Ceyenne many years before my arrival, inviting Ceyenne into her home when she was a homeless teen sleeping
in Central Park in the 1980s.

After I left New York for Los Angeles, I continued to visit
Sabrina regularly and spent stretches of summer stowed away
in the magical escape of her home. Filled with smoke from her
slender MORE menthol cigarettes and decades of queer history
embedded in the walls, Sabrina's salon was a gathering place for
people of all stripes. Her door was never locked in my sixteen years
of knowing her.

It was a stiflingly hot summer night about a decade ago when
I first met Ceyenne. I was visiting Sabrina's salon and she swept
in from New Jersey like a tropical storm. She brought groceries
and immediately started frying food in the kitchen while updating
"Ma"—only Ceyenne called Mother Flawless Sabrina by such a

familial endearment—in the next room about her organizing in the trans community, providing support and advocating for the rights of sex workers.

After listening to their wild banter for a while, I dozed off, twisted into the balmy sheets of Flawless's cubbyhole bed, lulled to sleep by the sound of their cackles in the next room. When I woke hours later, long after the sun rose, they were still at it, shrieking and cracking each other up. They were so loud, so full of stories.

I can never return to that summer night, but this memory is pressed into the deepest terrain of my psyche. I can feel the humid, smoky air, see the glowing amber haze of the room, and hear the sound of their love; mother and daughter adoring and entertaining each other through the night.

Today, Ceyenne is still advocating, still speaking out about the lack of opportunities for trans women in society. She's the founder of the organization G.L.I.T.S.—Gays and Lesbians Living in a Transgender Society—which provides holistic care to transgender sex workers, and sits on multiple boards for LGBT community organizations. Like Sabrina, Ceyenne is someone for whom family is expansive; who, no matter how hard things get, can't help but offer care. Ceyenne is a mother figure now too, delivering Sabrina's nurturing legacy of generosity and judgment-free love into the future.


**ZACKARY DRUCKER:** Tell me about your journey early on.

**CEYENNE DOROSHOW:** I couldn't hide femininity like some people could, or wish they could. I didn't have that. I was just feminine. I didn't know how to turn it off. So, a lot of my problems came from that.

You ever see the version of Carol Burnett when she cuts up the curtains? Well, sweetie, I cut up every curtain in the house. It was because I wanted to make a dress. When [my parents] would leave the house, I wanted to have those girly moments.

And because I figured out that I can't keep getting punished over cutting up the curtains, I trickled down to, *I'm going to wear mommy's outfit around the house.* And, again, being a child not smart enough to put it back . . . I got punished for that. "What are you doing with my clothes? What are you doing with my shoes?" It was a constant.

Then not having a school to identify that there's a problem there, not really concentrating in school because gender identity was certainly looked at from both sides—from the students and the teachers—as a no-no. When I was a young person, they would run through the halls singing my name attached to "gay boy." And it would ring throughout the hallways and shit. I hated school.

And then high school came and that was like a real obstacle course. Because now I'm with an older group of people who are gonna discriminate. So, it was always levels of discrimination around sexuality that made me feel super uncomfortable. And, ending high school in that waffley area of being a young adult and wanting to go out and wanting to explore community, of course, my mom was not having it. Not having the clothing, not having any parts of gender identity. I began to miss curfew; she threw me out, over and over again. It seemed like it was easier to have me outside than in. As long as I was away, they didn't have to identify what was going on.

I was literally in Central Park with my suitcases just trying to find a place to sleep. I was still in communication with my childhood friend, and one of my girlfriends was like, "Oh, I want you to come with me to [the club] Bentley." I was like, "Girl, they not gonna let me in Bentley." She said, "Oh, yes they are. We're gonna dress you up and you're gonna be fine."

Well, sweetie, that night changed my life. Because that night I met this old lady on the dance floor with white hair and a bob and a football jersey and leather pants. And I was like, "Ooh, she's fabulous." And she was like, "Oh, my god, I love you young people. You should come back to my house." And I looked at my girlfriend and my girlfriend looked at me. Her name was Ronnie. And she said, "Girl, we're gonna go back to her house and we're gonna have some more wine and we're gonna drink and we're gonna talk and this is gonna be fabulous." We jumped in the car with this lady and we go up to Seventy-Third Street. And, I'm like, *Okay, Seventy-Third. Girl, you hit big time.*

We get in her apartment and she says, "Listen, I gotta do a long-distance conference call. Give me an hour. There's wine, there's food; make yourself comfortable and when I'm off we're gonna party some more." We waited. Me and Ronnie was high as hell. We're sitting on the floor. I'm like, "She must have the world's biggest cat . . ."

We're just laughing and she finally gets off the phone and comes in the living room and sits in her throne, her little chair, behind her desk. I says, "Excuse me, what kind of cat do you own?" And she says, "Cat?" I said, "Yeah, the white hair on the rug." She starts to peel this cemented wig off her head. I almost faint, 'cause you can hear it ripping from the skin.

I said, "No, no, no. What are you doing?" And she said, "Sweetie, you thought this was mine? Oh, no, no, no. Go in the bathroom, look, there's racks of hair." And, I am weak to my stomach, laughing. And, she says, "Child, illusions are everything and a little pain is beauty."

So, Ronnie went home. And then she said, "Tell me about you."

And I said, "Okay."

I started to tell her my mom threw me out and she started to get dressed. And, she says, "Well, you take a little nap and when you get up we're gonna have breakfast at the diner on the corner. And, then I'm gonna take you home." I said, "Sweetie, home to me is Brooklyn, Bushwick." And she said, "We're going home to Brooklyn, Bushwick." And, we went and had breakfast and we came back upstairs and she called the garage and told them to pull out the old station wagon. And she drove me home and had the conversation I had never had with my mom about my gender identity.

I mean, my school had sent me to therapists. They sent me to the Gay and Lesbian Center downtown. It was horrible. Those queens and the facilitator told me there was no room for me in there because I wasn't femme. Imagine a child trying to be someplace where they feel like they belong—and you get in this room and you find out you don't belong in that room either.

I couldn't have imagined it: an old, white, Jewish woman taking a Black girl home. It was priceless, but it also gave my mom a heads up to what was happening. Did it work? No, 'cause within a couple of weeks after that I was thrown out again.

But it at least set the precedent for my mom to know that this wasn't just a gay thing, as she was just ringing the chimes on. It was a gender identity thing. And I didn't even realize or recognize or know that, because there was no words for it.

Then I went to Covenant House. And Covenant House told me, "Oh, no, no, no. We cannot house you. We're a Catholic charity and we don't condone what you're doing." Well, it led to the question, *What am I doing?* And they went, "Oh, you have on a bra." And I said, "Well, yeah." And, they were like, "No, you can't stay here."

So, once again, I'm homeless—and on Forty-Second Street, no less.

Then I found out about the Port Authority, which was a hotbed of steamy shit for a teenager, and found out I can make some coins there. That worked a for a little while because I was able to get a hotel room. But, how long would I be able to do that before someone kills me? And there were some moments with clients. Back then there was a real epidemic with crack. Clients would get cracked out and I didn't know how to handle that. And, of course, if they're paranoid and I'm trying to leave, they're trying to hold me down and I was like, "This is not good." So, once again, I find myself at the door of Flawless.

**ZD:** Had you seen her since?

**CD:** Yeah. Oh yeah, and she made it a requirement. You call me, you beep me. Back then, we had beepers. And, [she said], "Let me know your progress, and it's mandatory that you stay in school. If you stay in school, I'll help you."

**ZD:** You were a high school student?

**CD:** Yeah, I was a high school student and still scared; scared that I didn't have family support; scared that my family would find me and hurt me. So, I stayed terrified.

When I graduated, now I'm in a whole new world, in a whole new bracket, because I'm definitely an adult now; a young adult who's homeless, who has to navigate society and try to figure this out and it wasn't good. It just wasn't good to try to be me and get a job. Clearly they were not hiring a young person who identified as a young woman, who wasn't a young woman, who had no support for being a young woman and no name. I remember I went to apply at McDonald's and the manager said, "Here's a cross-dresser that wants to apply," out loud.

I tried the shelter systems and they were a mess, and dangerous. I don't know whether it was wrong being me, or they were wrong for being themselves. They were able to live in their skin, I was not able to live in my own, and was persecuted for being me.

So, I stayed on many people's couches, including some of the people I knew it was toxic to be around; but if I could have a place to stay for the night, it was a good thing.

Would I have to get up in the morning and travel with all of my stuff? Yes. But there were also times when I would fall asleep on the train with all my stuff, and be physically attacked by grown people, by children. I would be asleep and get punched in the face and I'll be like, "Oh god. My life is really not worth anything." Some people would say, "Oh, you know, this is what you asked for when you decided you wanted to do this, you had to know that was going to happen to you." It just was not good.

Off and on I would stay at my grandmother's until she couldn't take it, but at least my grandmother wasn't transphobic or anything. She tried to tell me, "Listen sweetie, that makeup—wrong. Wrong. You gotta go find something that matches you." Of course, my grandma was very light skinned; I'd be trying to put on her makeup, looking all two-toned and just crazy, and just trying to fit in. I didn't even fit in in my own community, so how was I going to fit in in society?

Finally, I did get a good job.

I was staying in a shelter then, and the shelter didn't even know I was in the shelter. They thought I was staff, because I was very well dressed. They just assumed that I was a new, young, hired staff. And finally they found out I wasn't a staff and one of the caseworkers was like, "You know, you was meant to do this," and I was like, "Do what?" And she said, "Be an institutional lead." And I said, "Really?" She said, "Yeah, you're helping people in here, and you're not even working here. So I'm going to give you an address and a number, you're going to go apply for a new shelter opening up in Midtown."

I went to Flawless, and I got a jacket and shirt and we went and bought me a pair of khakis, and I went and applied [presenting as a man] for the job, [under the fake name] Edward Morales. They hired me.

On my first day I was very nervous, and very scared. I tried to hide my sexuality, and I did. So I was worried that people were going to find out my gender identity, and I was just scared all the time. Well, the first duty that they gave me was bathroom monitor. So, I had to supervise naked men in the shower, and I stayed in fear the whole time. But I also gave these men respect. I stayed within eye contact, I never looked down at their privates. I tried to keep eye contact at all times because I realized,

"Oh my god. They're going to know what I am, and they're going to kill me in the shower." I didn't have to stay in the bathroom, but I had to do a walk-through every fifteen minutes. This went on for six months.

Finally, I passed my evaluation, and I said, "After I pass my evaluation, I'll spring it on them: I'm gay." Once I passed my evaluation, I went for a makeover at Macy's. I went shopping. I went and had my hair done. I used my next couple of days because I worked four days for ten hours and had three days off.

Well, that Monday afternoon when I went to work, I was Ceyenne. I walked down the block in sunglasses and perfume, and I smelled good and I looked fabulous. I walked into the building and I walked past security, and security was like, "Miss, miss, you can't walk in this building. Miss, miss." I just kept walking, and I went to my station, and I grabbed my clipboard. Security came running downstairs, and they were like, "Miss, we told you, you cannot be in here." I pulled off the sunglasses, and they went, "Eddie?" And I said, "Yeah, about that."

They ran upstairs and they got the manager, his name was Reverend Peacock, and he comes downstairs, and he turns and he looks at me, and he goes, "I knew it." And I go, "You knew what?" And he goes, "I knew there was something that you wasn't comfortable with. I couldn't put my finger on it." I went upstairs, and I just sobbed. He said, "Why you didn't tell me?" And I said, "I didn't want to not have this job." He said, "Let me tell you. These clients love you. I would have second thought it, but I would have still gave you the job." And he was like, "You could have been honest with me." I said, "I've been honest with everybody and had been denied." He said, "I get it." He said, "Here's your clipboard. Go downstairs. Go do your job. How do you think the clients are going to receive you?" I said, "I don't know. This is all a test."

I went downstairs and some of the men did have a huge

problem with it, but it was the other men in the shelter that actually handled them:

"Has she ever disrespected you?"

"Yes, she didn't tell us."

"But has she ever crossed the line with us?"

And they were like, "No." So they said, "Then, what the fuck is the problem? She's still the same person."

There was the one time Flawless had came down to the shelter, and she was so proud and she was like, "Oh my god. I love it. And they love you." They respected me, and I respected them.

But we kept having suicides and stuff like that and [eventually] I realized, by then, I had developed a wee bit of a cocaine problem. And I realized that cocaine in this job was not helping me. So, I quit the job and I moved to New Hampshire, Maine. Imagine, a Black trans girl in Maine! . . . Survival looked so different from what it looks like now.

ZD: Yeah, what do you think about that?

CD: I think there's so many opportunities. At the same time, opportunities for who? As a Black trans woman I see progress, but not that much. It's like that song, "God bless the child that has their own." We're living in a world of opportunity, but we have a government fighting against our very existence.

So we're facing some real serious times just being a part of this community. We're living in a marginalized government where we stand to be erased. I'm sorry, I'm not going nowhere.

I don't know what it would be like. Are we gonna go back to the Stonewall days where you need to have on two male articles [of clothing]? I remember Flawless telling me them stories of how she would take a shirt tie and tie it around her underwear or sew it on—she would have these articles of clothing sewn into her clothing because they were gonna get her. That's determination. I'm gonna be who I wanna be and you're not gonna tell me who I can't be.

I will never go back to those times, I'm sorry. When I had to be Eddie Morales, it was for survival. When I had to do sex work, it was definitely survival. Because even working a part-time job for a nonprofit where I'm saving lives was not paying me enough to sustain in life. Yeah, I'm doing the work. I'm working almost twelve, thirteen hours a day but not being paid like I should be paid, not valued like I should be valued.

And we're still seeing that today in not-for-profits. We're being tokenized.

And we see this way too often: "Oh, but by the way, we stipend women of color. We're giving them a stipend and lunch and a MetroCard." Oh, that sets the tone for survival. Let me go buy hair and makeup and wig—oh, there goes my stipend. So now I still have to get to work. So what am I gonna do to eat? Oh, let me become a part of the system. Now I get to be not only systemized by your system, I still gotta go to work. And I gotta work for the system, work for the stipend. It's a lot. But society wants us to have to go to them to sustain.

We can systematically turn people off when we let a government ordain what femininity looks like, what women's rights looks like, what protection looks like. Man, we're a messed-up society.

**ZD:** What is your advice right now to young trans people?

**CD:** That they should reach out. When you're faced with abuse, tell somebody. When you're finding an obstacle to make it through—and I mean make it through society, through school—reach out, educate yourself. As community, we need to uplift the younger generation to be everything we couldn't. That means I want to see images of us in everything. I want to see us in media, I want to see us as lawyers, doctors, judges, politicians, congressmen; there needs to be more reflections of us out here for us to be taken serious.

We need to be images and reflections. We need to have scholarships out here for young people. We need to create jobs so our kind can be a part of the process. It starts somewhere, and by employing our own, we're able to uplift them. I'm not talking just employ them—build them up for sustainability. In this climate, we need to be sending kids to school. By educating them, we have such a better chance to see a better tomorrow.

This divided sense of who we are; now this needs to be a connective. It's not only gay white men that deserve to be at the table. It's all of us. It is the collective, the GLIBQTIABNC—all of it. It's going to be a full alphabet soon. Everybody deserves to be at the table, and they need to be uplifted. We need to be uplifted. And if we are elders, we're supposed to encourage the best.

**ZD:** Yeah. That has been crucial to our survival—supporting each other and being each other's family.

**CD:** Without our alternative family, we'd have never had support. Because these were the ties that bind. It was that outside family. It was Flawless Sabrina. It is Miss Major Griffin-Gracy. It was Rose and Sweetie who were able to pinch me and tell me, "Get it the fuck together."

I remember, one day, me and Flawless went to the board of education meeting to meet with Sweetie. I don't know what was going on with me, but my eyes looked like a rainbow. I had fifty-two colors up on these eyes. And Sweetie said, "Girl, girl, meet me in the bathroom." I've never seen Sweetie as her normal self. And I was like, *Well who is this big queen telling me to come in the bathroom?*

Finally, in the bathroom, she said, "Yeah, we're just going to wipe some of that off, because you're speaking on the behalf of young people for the board of education, so we're going to tone this down a little." And I said, "Well, wait. Why?" She said, "Because you need to present yourself proper at meetings like this. They already know the deal, but take it down a notch."

I never understood that and I got it that day: if I want to earn their respect, it's not me being who I am, it's how I present myself that could make or break a meeting—or how society sees me.

I had never actually thought about my presentation as a trans woman. What the girls were teaching—they said the uniform was a mini skirt, a pushup bra, and a wig. If I'd have listened to that scenario, I would never have a job and I would never be taken seriously.

It was odd to look across that room and see Sweetie with no makeup and well-manicured eyebrows. And I was like, *Oh, there's a time and place for everything.* I didn't know that, because these were not lessons taught to me before. But they were damn sure important.

I was like, *Wow, I took a lot for granted.* I had to look [back] on some of the attention I was getting in some of the places I was going. Yeah, maybe I should not be there, maybe I should listen. And it made sense because I was putting myself in these high-risk situations.

We're not having these conversations when girls get attacked, that—you know—presentation is everything. The idea is, as a youth, I didn't ever get well because I didn't know. As an adult, I'd learned to navigate and get respect in areas where I certainly wouldn't have because—*pay me no mind.* Why? Because I blend in. I'm tall as shit and I'm bigger than life, so it's not like they don't know the situation. But presentation is everything. And that changes the narrative on how you waffle through society, how you just navigate these waters of oppression and discrimination.

I see so many of these horrible videos where girls are being jumped. And one issue with one person turns into three or four people attacking this trans woman. And I can't watch the video. I turn them off because they're so disrespectful; how society will just jump in. It ain't got nothing to do with whatever the situation is, but they will jump into the fight and just attack this trans woman because of who she is. Did she do something wrong?

Probably not, probably not at all. What was her crime? Waking up and going out. That was her crime.

She didn't do anything, didn't say anything. But what we don't teach and we need to be teaching is conflict resolution— how to deflate a situation. I already know who I am, and what I am, so I don't need to clap back when somebody says something. Even if it's gender different and somebody says, "Oh, that's a man." Sweetie, I'm okay with that. I am totally okay with that. But what you're not going to do is put your hands on me. And could I make it through that? I could live another five fucking minutes if I just walked the hell away. You don't have to fight every fight. It's not meant for you to have to answer for every idiot's discrimination.

*Interview has been edited and condensed for clarity. Originally published on* Vice (Broadly) *on December 17, 2018.*

# The Belly of the Beast

LOLA DAVINA

My client is getting dressed after sex. It's an ordinary Wednesday afternoon at my downtown San Francisco studio in-call apartment. He's a typical client—he called from his office to make an appointment to swing by at two p.m. Midfifties, business suit, wedding ring, an envelope stuffed with twenty-dollar bills from the ATM. The sex act and the man blur together—sweaty, meaty, perfunctory.

I have my Sade playlist memorized—he has about five minutes left in the hour. I'd slipped into a robe while he was taking a shower, and now I'm lounging on the bed. Getting a client dressed and out the door is delicate. I need to keep up the illusion that I'm still languid from the sex and not impatient to get rid of him, but I'm fine with seeing him go.

"My wife doesn't know that I do this." His confession is unsolicited. It, too, is typical. I say nothing. I'm thirty-four years old, back in the escorting game after a seven-year hiatus. Listening is part of the job.

"She doesn't have the same needs I do," he says. I grin widely to override a smirk. After all, this man just paid to have sex with me, so I know a few things about his technique. I'm guessing his wife doesn't love it any more than I did. I'm guessing she's had enough.

I'm escorting in order to earn my way out of out of a financial hole it took me ten years to dig. Divorce, personal bankruptcy—I need this man's money. I need clients to come back again and again, so I'm not here to make trouble for myself. These are the early days of prostitution review boards, and clients are just learning how to flex their collective power to punish sex workers they don't find sufficiently pliant. I could stay quiet—in fact, I most certainly should. And yet I can't let this slide.

"Well, I just have to wonder about that . . ." I drawl, a little too slowly. "We all have needs." As if dish soap had dropped on the oily surface of our polite postcoital conversation, the goodwill in the room scatters. His posture becomes defiant. He buttons up his dress shirt, radiating displeasure.

"You don't know my wife. I keep her satisfied."

There is a pause. I know my role as dutiful whore. Rush in to gush, placate, smooth any misunderstanding over with proclamations of his girth, his prowess, his stamina. I know the script to flatter a man like the back of my hand. I might very well have played the part he was paying me to perform had he not added, "I need variety and excitement. All she needs is me."

No curiosity, no imagination about the erotic life of the woman he is closest to—again, typical. But this crime I cannot forgive. Complicity had been, up until that point, a standard service included in my fee. But my hostility to providing cover for male entitlement, hypocrisy, and delusion had hit the limit. I could no longer look away. There's a distinct chill that descends on my limbs when I decide a certain man will never again be allowed back inside me.

"Give her five hundred bucks and an afternoon to fuck the pool boy. I bet she'd take it."

My client knows he's been fired and accepts it like he's been fired before. "This was fun. Got any girlfriends?"

THIS EPISODE WAS not the first time in my life that the adult industry had left me queasy. I grew up in a white, middle-class, educated home, but alcoholism and chaos shaped my upbringing, my parents pitched in a schizophrenic battle. My mother found any sexual image or discussion abhorrent; my father would leave his pornographic magazines strewn throughout the house.

I must have been about ten when I realized I would never look like any of those perfect Playboy bunnies. Their velvety airbrushed perfection left a tight knot in my stomach, a mixture of lust and dread. The notion of ever being treasured as they were, to have the power they exuded—over me, over my father—seemed impossible. A ruthless education: *This is what sexy looks like. This is what men desire.* Like a cutter's blade, I'd pick up those magazines when I wanted to punish myself, slowly turning the pages, their beauty burning into my skin.

I left my parents' house to attend a hippy college in the era of Andrea Dworkin and Catharine MacKinnon and the Meese Report, at the height of the feminist anti-porn wars. Alongside my women's studies classmates, I protested Miss America pageants, calling them "meat markets." At the same time, I stepped into my own adult sexuality, which softened some of pornography's crueler edges. I found myself craving knowledge, a more complex understanding: How did sex work *work*? Who really was in charge? Curiosity, but also defiance. I knew I was never going to appear in the pages of *Playboy*, but I wanted to break free of the shame and inadequacy porn invoked in me. I wanted to claim some piece of this electric world of fantasy and pleasure for myself.

Right out of college, I auditioned at a peep show strip club and was hired. It was a revelation. Despite my cellulite and the bump in my nose, mere mortals such as myself could strip. Getting paid a whopping twenty dollars an hour to dance, I found the peep show world captivating. Gorgeous goths and riot grrrls with pixie wigs on their bald heads. Piercings, tattoos, and armpit hair, these women were nothing like the unapproachable beauties of the magazines—inspirational, in the flesh and on fire. I felt like I had stepped through a magic door to become a member of an underground society.

I've heard stripping referred to as a gateway drug. Fellow strippers introduced me to professional domination, making lesbian porn, and finally, escorting. I bounced along from call to call, accumulating adventures from the demimonde for my memoirs and enough money to retire with a few thousand dollars in the bank. In my twenties, I'd never considered sex work my calling; it was more like a rebellious detour from reality. Seven years later, in my early thirties, shipwrecked by financial and marital failure, sex work was my salvation.

Escorting gave me the resources to pursue a master's degree in human sexuality. My intent was to develop skills in order to explain my sex work experiences to the wider world. Monday, Wednesday, and Friday afternoons, I'd entertain gentlemen callers; Tuesdays and Thursdays, I'd listen to lectures on Foucault and Butler and Derrida. But the semioticians and deconstructionists left me cold— sex and gender were no mere abstractions in my world. Ringing in my ears was Audre Lorde: find uses for the erotic. Petition for survival.

As graduate school trained me to be critical of power, I found it more difficult to justify my job. It no longer felt radical or daring— it felt more like abetting in crimes I could not rationalize. What would Lorde have thought of my career stroking the egos of clueless businessmen? I suspected I had the answer, her diamond-cut critique from *Sister Outsider* admonishing me: "For the master's tools will never dismantle the master's house. They may allow us temporarily to beat him at his own game, but they will never enable us to bring about genuine change." No longer an outsider nor a dilettante, I recognized myself as deep in the belly of the beast, laboring at the intersection of capitalism and patriarchy.

Now I would spend my waking hours wrestling with what it meant to be a part of a clearly fucked-up system. I was no longer sure it was possible to navigate the adult industry's corrosive dynamics and yet still be a conscious sexual being. After all, I was profiting from a racist, misogynist, transphobic, fatphobic, ableist, ageist system perpetuating impossible standards of beauty—hard to call that life-affirming labor. Even as I did sex work out of financial need, I struggled to reconcile accumulating wealth when so many others suffer from not having enough.

If an economic system is structured to keep a subset of the labor force underresourced and disposable, then poverty is the point. Members of the underclasses find it difficult to protest, agitate, organize, or disrupt for change because they struggle to survive. Haves and Have-Nots are not random. Racism and patriarchy define which bodies are full citizens and which are conditional, under threat from cradle to grave. Nowhere is this more blatant than in the sex industry, where the color of skin and the size and shape of body parts regulate marketability. Relentless dictates determine who "gets to" and who "has to": who gets to screen clients and who has to service everyone who walks through the door. Who gets to charge thousands of dollars, and who has to take what they can get. Who gets to set limits, and who has to do as they're told. Lorde and other feminist and queer thinkers made it so I could no longer work with one eye open, the other closed, only half-awake.

And so that ordinary Wednesday afternoon, with that utterly ordinary client, marked a turning point in my working life. I vowed to cull the worst offenders and cultivate a more mindful clientele. Whenever a client displayed his entitlement, I'd smile and nod in the moment, then never take his calls again. I poured myself into those who fed me: virgins needing instruction. Trans folks exploring their bodies and desires. Sexual adventurers motivated by generosity and reciprocity and gratitude. I was fortunate enough to be able to take the financial hit, but it kept me from burning out. Two years later, my debts paid and six figures saved in the bank, I retired.

I HAVE HAD a long and fraught relationship with the sex industry, finding it endlessly fascinating and honest, revealing, and repulsive.

I have hated it while needing it desperately. Those motivations have, at times, overlapped and intensified each other. Writing now, I am fifty-one, my sex work career behind me. No longer focused on keeping clients happy, I now have space and scope to see the adult industry more clearly.

As an author focused on sex work and self-care, I spend hours every day following the social media of sex workers: their advertising, their shit-talking, their flirting, their public service announcements, all their gorgeous, raucous humanity. As long as sex work remains work-of-last-resort for women and gay men and queers, I'm committed to promoting harm reduction to make it not just survivable, but thrivable.

Additionally, in the past few years, as a married woman with very different needs than my partner's, I've spent a few lovely afternoons idling with paid-for pool boys with my husband's blessings. The sex industry certainly looks different when it services the female appetite—especially the aging female—softening its patriarchal imperatives. At the same time, I recognize how extraordinarily fortunate I am to have the health, wealth, free time, and sensibilities to be a client—only a handful of women in history have had the fun I'm having. Realistically, the sex industry caters primarily to men—we're still a long way off from anything resembling gender parity. But the opportunity is there.

In her essay "The Uses of the Erotic," Audre Lorde wrote, "The erotic is the nurturer or nursemaid of all our deepest knowledge." While the crushing prerogatives of the demand side remain deeply ugly, that only tells half the story. It is the supply side—the workers themselves—where I see positive change.

The most gorgeous, raw, authentic emerging sexualities aren't born out of Hollywood or Madison Avenue or the runways of Paris. It is sex workers who are the embodied erotic, choosing both truth *and* dare. Our culture's sexual imagination is no longer top-down, dictated by white, cisgender, heterosexual male tastemakers. Hugh Hefner died an irrelevant relic, *Playboy*'s supremacy a distant memory. The adult industry has become ferociously do-it-yourself, an explosion of vitality and creativity from the ground up. Workers display their bodies and fantasies to anyone who will look and listen: *See me for who I am. Come play.* No longer hidden in the shadows, spend any amount of time on sex work Twitter, and you can learn about workers' daily lives—their families, their hopes and sorrows, their kids entering kindergarten, and cats with ringworm. Unairbrushed, unvarnished, not just the stuff of fantasy.

My bullishness on the current and future state of the industry doesn't end there. Sex work is a radical redistribution of resources to women, the LGBTQ community, people of color, the disabled, and big beautiful folks for precisely what disenfranchises them—unruly bodies, genders, and identities that cannot be conquered nor contained. These are the uses of the erotic marketplace I can heartily support.

The ethics of the sex industry remain vexing and complex. Now, with both eyes open, I make no apologies for its inequities, hypocrisies, and exploitations. And yet, and yet. The sex industry may well have been built for the master's pleasure, but he is but a paying guest. Sex workers are the ones who live here. Laboring under crushing cultural forces, finding ways to step into our authentic selves. Tearing the world down to build it anew.

*A version of this piece appears in Lola Davina's* Thriving in Sex Work: Sex Work and Money, *published by The Erotic as Power Press in September 2020.*

*Searching for Foxy*

GODDESS CORI

Age seventeen: I'm wet and my clit is throbbing. I open my laptop to find some porn that will guide my fantasies to a place of climax. I start on Pornhub—the YouTube of porn—and immediately I'm bombarded with titles like "Tiny Flexible Teenager Gets Pounded by Huge Black Stallion" and "Blacked Down Terrified [insert white porn actress] Gets Ripped Open by 10 bbcs." My hard-on is fading, my vulva is drying up, but I am determined. I search "dyke porn"—it's a risky move, but I'm optimistic. The titles are immediately disheartening. "Kinky Girl Next Door's First Time" and "Gay Dyke Hoe Said We Couldn't Fuck Her but We Showed Her" were among the top listed videos.

I make a decision to switch it up. I had heard of a queer porn site and decide to check it out. I open up the website to find every single preview clip featuring white performers having soft, slow, intimate moments. I search through the performers list and only see hypermasculine images of Black folx. The majority are small white femmes or white dyke daddies. At this point I am bored and frustrated. I try one more site: Shine Louise Houston's Crash Pad series. I have a debit card, but there is no money in my bank account, and even if there were, my mom would definitely see the charge. I retreat into myself, defeated and frustrated, initially with my lack of orgasm and eventually with the lack of accessible queer of color content.

RACE IS COMMONLY fetishized in pornography: it's used as a way to separate and categorize bodies so that viewers can search for and consume the types of performers they desire and filter out the types of performers that challenge their desires. This fetishization of race is clearly more acceptable in this form of media than in any other. Pornography provides us with immediate gratification and this immediacy makes fetishization more likely; the viewer's access to racialized bodies is quick and easy.

While porn itself is easy to access, the violence in porn is far more complex than one might notice upon quick observation. Not only is there sometimes personal violence between performers on-screen but symbolic and structural violence as well—which is much more difficult to spot when you have your dick in your hand. Far too often, we overlook the symbolic violence that occurs in pornography because porn is already outside the realm of "acceptable" sexual behavior, and those who consume it want to do so discreetly and quickly, without thinking too deeply about the racial, cultural, and sexual implications of their media consumption.

Even though mainstream companies are starting to produce pornography that is filled with more positive images (i.e., women being the subjects of their own sexuality as opposed to the objects of others), the overwhelming majority of porn films still support the sexual narratives of white, heterosexual, cisgender men who have been socialized to be aggressive and violent toward femmes, and especially femmes of color. The majority of mainstream pornography is filled with uncontextualized images of forced blow jobs, hardcore penetration (with no lube), and fantasies of unwilling "teenage" girls being coerced into sexual acts with white cisgender men. When we look at Black women in mainstream porn, the picture is even more bleak. *Booty Quake #6* is a feature by Pulse (Candy Shop) productions, starring pornographic legend Naomi Banxxx and Julius Ceazher, among others. This film is advertised as a film about ass and it does not disappoint. One scene focuses in on Julius Ceazher, in sagging pants and no shirt, gazing at Banxxx's butt. The camera spends extensive amounts of time surveying her butt as she is bent over, not showing her face. Julius grabs a hose and begins to squirt water on Banxxx's backside, as she wiggles and moans under the water. There is no need to focus on Naomi's face, or even on Julius's: the pleasure derived from a hose-down is solely the viewer's. The scene proceeds into intercourse, and like most mainstream pornography, focuses on the cis man's pleasure and the customer's gaze. This company produces various racist tropes of Black and Brown bodies: *Ba Dunk A Bounce, Bubble Bursting Butts, Alone in the Dark, Once You Go Black You Never Go Back,* and *Black Ass Attack.* All these films fetishize Black bodies and hold the butt as the most attractive feature of the Black woman. It's no surprise that audiences fetishize Black women's asses (or Black men's cocks) when they are the sole focus of mainstream porn featuring Black performers.

While the performers committing these acts may be willing and able to participate in these scenes and personally enjoy these fantasies, these images have the potential to be damaging and leave a lasting effect on the viewer without proper context. The stereotypes that are embedded in these videos and images have the potential to taint public perception of entire genders and races. This is especially true because the American sex education system is failing and the internet introduces most children to sex.

While this may seem like an indictment of porn, it's not my intention. The industry's problems actually leave this form of entertainment wide open to innovators interested in changing the sexual narrative. Mainstream porn companies are not always incentivized to do so, but when Black queer folx direct productions and run production companies, the narratives of Black bodies often lack the violence and objectification that is prevalent throughout mainstream pornography and media. Black bodies are allowed the space to express their sexualities freely, without judgment or persecution. Black femme porn becomes a space to bring our own fantasies into fruition, for the gratification of our performers and our communities.

As a stark departure from the mainstream, *Foxy Strikes Back* from BEYONDEEP Productions is a retelling of the infamous Blaxploitation film *Foxy Brown*. In this particular short film featuring Honey G as Foxy and K Rivers as Sapphire, the couple stands out not only because they are truly queer, very Black, and at least one of them is trans or nonbinary but also because they are an actual nonmonogamous couple outside of pornography. The scene begins with some classic Blaxploitation funky music and Foxy tied to a chair, facing away from the camera. The shot reverses and you see Sapphire open the door and taunt, "Right where I left you . . . my little fox." Sapphire turns Foxy around and we see that she is blindfolded and gagged. Sapphire takes off the gag and Foxy immediately spits on her and shouts, "Fuck you." Sapphire takes off her silky robe, takes out a crop and beats Foxy with it. Foxy whimpers and Sapphire takes off Foxy's blindfold, turns her around and slides her pants down. The camera uses a POV shot for this—that way the ass is not being centered, but still used as a way to entice the viewer. Black people can acknowledge our bodies are beautiful, sexy, and enticing, but Black femmes who have been subjected to the degradation that comes with having a Black femme body can bring that consciousness into their films. Throughout the film, the shots cut between POV and wide shots, but generally always capture the performers' full bodies.

Both these scenes tell significantly different narratives about Blackness and the way Black bodies operate in a sexual context. It is evident that the master narrative of the Black butt being the prime and most desired aspect of the Black body drives the first scene. Movies that are directed by femmes of color tend to be less focused on racially driven labels, while mainstream queer pornography companies label their pornographic films that star Black bodies as "ebony edition" or include "Black" in the title. This is because

categorization is the ultimate tool used by the pornographic industry to separate and sell content.

AGE TWENTY-TWO: I chose to become the change I wanted to
see in the industry. However, in my own work, I have experienced
a lot of racism, both overt and covert. In the beginning, I didn't
have enough financial stability or social status to define how I was
going to do sex work. It was purely dependent upon whoever would
pay me and what they wanted to do (to a certain extent). Most of
the time, that looked like a lot of older white men asking me to
show them my butt or make twerking videos. It looked like being
grossly underpaid, or not paid at all, for hours of labor. It looked
like expecting me to submit even though they paid me to take the
role of Domme. In *A Taste for Brown Sugar: Black Women in Pornography*, Mireille Miller-Young talks about this exact phenomenon:
she uses the term "illicit eroticism" to describe how "black women
use, manipulate, and deploy their sexualities in the economy."
"Commodifying one's own sexuality," Miller-Young writes, "is part
of the strategic and tactical labor black women use in advanced economic capitalist economies." I work within the capitalist system to
propel myself into a different place financially. Working within the
constraints of capitalism always comes at a price for Black femmes.

I remember at the very beginning of my endeavors in the sex
industries, getting at least five private messages from men telling
me I was their "slave nigger" and I was to do whatever they told me
to do or they would hurt me or expose me to my friends and family.
I was eighteen. It's difficult to determine how much of those threats
I internalized and how much of them I believed. But I was scared
nevertheless. I'm still scared. Now that I'm more well established,
I don't get these kinds of threats any more, but I know that could
change at any time.

I've learned how to protect myself, and I understand that I can
only do that because of my privilege. When I say "privilege" as a
dark-skinned, Black, queer, nonbinary sex worker, it comes nowhere

close to any of my non-Black counterparts. I am still underpaid and sometimes not paid at all. I receive far less work. I am seen as a submissive before a Domme. I am seen as not sexually valuable unless I am centering my ass. My privilege is recognizing my own worth and value. It's having a civilian job that pays me more than minimum wage, even if it's only part time. It's having a high school diploma and some higher education. My privilege is my access to community. I have taken those privileges and used them to better my community through restorative BDSM and guiding others in unlearning racism through Black femme worship and sadism. That's where I've found my path, making the change I want to see in the sex industries.

AGE TWENTY-TWO: I give a white cis male client instructions— the furniture in a room must be rearranged to fit specific dimensions. He has never seen the room. He won't see it for several days. When he arrives, I tell him that he must take all the furniture out and move it according to the specifications I gave him in fifteen minutes or less. This is an impossible task. If he doesn't complete it, he will sit in a cage for the duration of the session and explain to me how, symbolically and practically, Black folx are forced do this every day of their lives. Before he goes, I carve "cracker" into his skin with a razor and tell him to take a picture of it every day until the carving heals. I save them all and send them back to him sporadically. I love having him say thank you. Not just "Thank you, Goddess" but "Here is the money I have. Your labor has bettered me and I will carry what you have taught me into the rest of my life."

## We All Deserve to Heal

### YIN Q

"I want to be punished," Gerry stated, as a Bach fugue serenaded from speakers above and candlelight flickered across the lenses of his wire spectacles. His brow furrowed to convey gravity and I nodded, but not without a smirk. This was not an unusual post-cocktails request for me to hear, as at that point I had been a dom-inatrix for close to two decades. Gerry had been a regular client since my first year practicing as a professional in the Bay Area. As many sex workers can attest, client relationships with longevity of loyalty and good behavior can often evolve into something akin to friendship. There are clients we keep at bay and those with whom we relax our boundaries.

Gerry was what I deemed a personal client. Someone whom I allowed to know me beyond the professional, controlled S&M top service I offered as job. I was also familiar with a greater part of his life, having met with his wife at social occasions several times with full disclosure of our relationship. However, I made no illusions that the social downtime is still supported by the monetary rela-tionship—a wad of cash or something like it.

That particular evening, we had met as usual at my private S&M studio, a spacious loft in the Financial District of New York City with bespoke bondage furniture for the immobility aficionado. With natural light pouring through ten-foot windows and grand mirrors poised to reflect one's image ad infinitum, I had created my studio to be a space where one could feel an abeyance of time and identity. There, we enjoyed a playful session with rope bondage, spanking, and a bit of delectable whipping, ending with a prodigious strap-on cock, so gargantuan in size that I actually had to lean back on my heels to accommodate the lolling weight. Gerry was a tall, rotund figure with the plump face of a man-boy. He was an IT programmer by day and a size queen by night. I was a dominatrix by day and by night, betwixt sessions I was a writer, yogi-cyclist, drunk, and sex workers' rights advocate.

Unlike many of my other clients, Gerry had never divulged any stories of acute trauma. We had talked about his childhood, particularly about how his father had been a flagrant womanizer and adulterer, as we were transforming his daddy issues into scenes of kinky play. Gerry was proud that he had his (second) wife's permission to engage with sex workers, rather than cheat behind her back. He was almost sanctimonious in regards to the payment for erotic services. In his eyes, the monetary exchange upheld the respectful equality between client and service provider, in judicious contrast to his father's misogynistic philandering. I couldn't agree more.

"I need to tell you something that I've never told anyone before . . ." Sex workers hear this all the time. We carry the secrets that men never tell their wives, their friends, not even their therapists. As whores, we are entrusted with the most profane and, I believe, the most precious personal stories. I have listened to stories of bones broken, of violent incest, of suffering war crimes from victims who are brave enough to come through my doors and seek ritualized reenactment. Some seek to reface the trauma for closure; some seek to transform it into affirmative kink.

Kink sex work was a perfect career for me. It suited my personal inclinations of bondage, control, and sadomasochism and channeled my zealous sexual expression into cash. It also was a daily therapy for me to address violence in a consensual manner.

Sexual violence is part of my history. I was and am vocal about it. I learned the word "rape" when I was eight years old. As a daughter of Chinese immigrants, there was an abundance of words I had to look up in the dictionary, as my parents were learning English at the same or slower rate as my brother and me. My mother often recollects learning her English numbers from *Sesame Street*, which might be the root of her slightly comical pronunciation. "Rape," however, was a word from my mother's own mouth. She had used it in the story every child wonders about: How was I born?

I was conceived by rape. Though horrific sounding now, this truth was less so for me at the time. The word just doesn't carry as much weight to most children as the word "homework" or the presentation of a dark staircase. At eight, I didn't even understand the mechanics of sex. I understood from my mother's voice that it was a terrible thing, something that made her body curl up next to me in my bed, hiding from my father. The meaning of rape gathers its due thorns as we mature into beings who have either experienced it ourselves or have the empathy of decent humans. I later entered into the full understanding of the word "rape" first through the latter door, then the former.

A few months into our freshman year at college, Jen, a close friend from high school, called me from her Syracuse dormitory. A boy she had been smitten with had raped her after a party. I can't recall all of our conversations, and there were many, but I know that I had urged Jen more than once to go to the authorities, to press charges. It seemed imperative that she try to stop this guy from inevitably doing the same to another woman. I feel ashamed now that I didn't place her needs and safety first before a hypothetical future victim. I also realize now that I was experiencing her rape as an excruciating epiphany.

The sound of Jen's voice, her tears and soul-ripping sobs, unearthed the deep memory of my mother's story, the same hollow tone, the utter devastation of safety. I felt more than empathy for my friend. I felt my body shatter, fully coming into the understanding that this act was the seed that had planted me in the world.

It would be years later when I'd learn "rape" again. In 1994, my junior year of college, I was studying feminist theory and gender politics in the classroom by day. I spent my evenings with the drag queens, fire-eaters, and strippers of the Blue Angel Cabaret in Tribeca, where New York City Neo-Burlesque was blooming.

I performed an S&M vampire lesbos act that showcased my sexual goth fantasies to a basement of strange men and swank hipsters. And though exposed through kitsch choreography, complete with fake blood that tasted like cherry cough syrup, I felt confused by these roles in private: Top, bottom, Sadist, masochist. These urges seemed to be regressive replicas of a childhood steeped in domestic violence: abuser, victim. I hurt and sought hurt with no rules.

One night, after a performance, I met my friend's older brother. He was visiting the city, a beautiful man with full lips and a mane of dreadlocks. After my first drink, I grabbed his head by its ropes and drew him in for a biting kiss. I wanted to show him that this little Chinese girl was fierce and I was pleased when he grabbed me at the wrists, locking them by my side. He had just seen my act; he "got" what I was into. My friends phased in and out of our barroom foreplay. After the second drink, his thick hands seemed to multiply. By the third, my face was flushed and I felt like a sea plant, being pulled by a hard current back to his hotel. In the confines of the stark, anonymous room, all the rules of how far one could play in public vanished and I was naked. The man was rough and frightening and I had wanted it that way.

Then all of a sudden he was hitting me too hard. He smashed my cheek to the side and gripped my throat. I was caught in the undertow and I didn't want it anymore but my playful wrestling just moments before had clearly meant "yes." There was no safe word.

When he was done, I pulled on my clothes as though I were dressing a mannequin. I hovered over my body, watching. I remember that he escorted me downstairs in a bright, fluorescent-lit elevator, that he kissed me and said, "You're bleeding," in a gentle voice as though he were simply saying "good evening."

When I got home, I showered and the water seemed to glaze off of me. I slept on my floor, unable to crawl into the loft bed. I hid in my apartment for days before picking up the phone and calling my mother for help. Later, while I was being examined by the family doctor, I uttered the word "rape," but I felt I was lying. Though my friends encouraged me to contact the authorities, just as I had encouraged Jen, I refused to press charges. That man had beaten me and fucked me, but I didn't think it was rape because I had asked for it.

Many twists, turns, and several deep annihilation dives ensued in the following years of my life, including depression and addiction. I stopped dancing but was drawn to the sex industry again in my quest for control.

There is another reason that I fought with the word "rape." It truly means victim. It means that I was not in control. If I was not in control, then it could happen again. I sought control and instead found consent. I began a career as a dominatrix.

Conducting kink sex work allowed me to interact with clients in a sensual and erotic manner, and though it reflected my sexuality, the commercial contract simultaneously reserved personal desire. Sex work can detach emotional vulnerability from physical intimacy in a way that allowed me to observe myself—the various desires of sadism and domination—and how my actions affected others. It taught me control over my inclinations for violence.

I am not the first or only person to declare my path of kink and BDSM to be one of healing, but in early 2000 it was not yet common in the professional field to be out about one's own journey as a masochist and abuse survivor. The fear of stigma and assumptions of pathology are still so daunting in the business of erotic domination; exposing one's personal rape history can feel even riskier. More from accident than from courage, I spilled my story onto my LiveJournal, writing into a dark screen with no analytics to comprehend where my words were landing. But my truth drew in certain clients—many of them abuse survivors as well as queer and trans people who were dealing with everyday trauma. A few of them had also suffered rape.

While BDSM/kink and many other arenas of sex work can provide therapeutic experiences, reeducation of consent, and facilitation of cathartic rituals, they are not replacements for therapy and community. For clients who were dealing with a history of acute trauma or suffering from depression and anxiety, I urged outside counseling with kink-friendly therapists. Kink clients are often not involved in the Leather community and so their professional providers may be the only people they have to talk to about their sexual orientation. This lifeboat dynamic is then loaded with so much more emotional gravity than the power exchange contract.

Even when we are not providing the sympathetic ear for personal stories, the work of sex work is active listening. The emotional labor involved in not only being empathetic to the most confidential sexual fantasies but also then choreographing the enactment is profound and widely unacknowledged. But as a storyteller, I usually enjoy this part of my job immensely, and so I sat with Gerry in my kitchen during our post-session decompression and urged on his confession, not at all prepared for what was to come.

Gerry told me that he had raped his first wife one night, after she had clearly refused to explore anal sex. He told me that, with a few drinks fueling his rage, he had held her down and forced his way into her body from behind. He told me that she had cried in pain, that she'd cried for him to stop, that she'd kept crying for days after. It was, he swore, the only time.

"I want to do some kind of ritual with you," Gerry said, "I can't ask my ex-wife for forgiveness (she had since passed away), but I can ask you, as a rape survivor. Could you . . . beat me, carve it out of my flesh—whatever anger you may have for your rapist?" Tears were pouring from his eyes. He fell to his knees with outstretched palms, repeating the words, "I'm sorry . . ."

I had once observed a similar confession. I was a child playing quietly at the underbelly of my mother's baby grand piano behind the foliage of houseplants, my stuffed animals and myself unseen. My father walked into what he thought was an empty room and fell to his knees, weeping. It was just days after he had committed a horrific act of cruelty in our home. He was sorry, he said in Chinese, he was sorry again and again, but it was said to no one and no one answered.

An unknown witness, I didn't forgive my father as I watched him supplicate to the emptiness around him. Fear and anger hardened my young heart into a fist. I hated him and wished him dead. The violence I had witnessed was enough, but it was also the everyday silent threat of violence, the stone face I had to assume outside the household walls—those tensions were wires that tightened across my chest and allowed no room for forgiveness.

Decades later, as I was bound in a web of rope, my naked back burning from the pounding of leather floggers and unrepentant whips wielded by a dominatrix I had paid for a ritualized pain session, those wires were broken. As air expanded my lungs, space rushed in, and I was allowed to forgive, to let go. I had done my digging, uncovering my father's own fatherless childhood, the abusive treatment by his adoptee uncle, and came to understand what it meant to live in a brown Asian body in an America where he was called a "gook," a "slant-eyed," a "ching-chong Chinaman." I had realized that there was an undiagnosed illness within him and a world of brutality that had shaped him.

"Please forgive me," Gerry said after a long silence as I took in his story. One of the tea lights had extinguished, his round face waned to the darkness. A tendril of smoke floated upward and along with it, I felt myself unhinge from my body and hover above, watching my hands that had just been holding this man's body so close to my own, connected by a penetrating silicone shaft.

"No," I said. I remember saying no, I could not share my anger for my father or my rapist with him. I would not punish him and I could not be his dominatrix for that scene. "It's not my place to forgive you. I am not the woman you raped."

"But," I may have said, looking into his face, though not his eyes, "as a woman who has been raped, I am sorry for you."

"We all deserve to heal," a friend said to me recently. "Even rapists." But it is also not the responsibility of the victim to heal the abuser. In our society, it is often those who are most vulnerable and victimized who bear the cross of educating the greater population on what it means to be humane, what it means to be tolerant, what it means to be kind. As a rape victim, as a daughter born of rape, as a sex worker who has helped victims heal, as a mother of two girls, I hold both these positions: what it is to forgive and to not forgive.

I don't remember the rest of my conversation with Gerry that night, but we floated along without disruption to our professional relationship. I believe I must have drunk quite heavily afterward, as I was prone to do those years. Perhaps a better woman, a stronger feminist, a more professional dominatrix would have stopped seeing him, cut him off. Or perhaps she would have created a soulful ceremony of mercy. But I did neither. I shelved his secret in the same dark corner where I'd stashed a load of memories that pop out from time to time to wreak havoc as PTSD episodes. Healing is never done.

We met again for sessions, but never with the intention to address his confession. I also met him several times after we ceased professional sessions. We met to talk, as people who had shared time on earth together, as he was dying of cancer. The October morning I learned from Gerry's wife that he had passed away, I cried with grief but also with immense relief, the same that had washed over me when my father had died.

*May your suffering and that which you inflict upon others end. May your dust grow better things.*

## How to Build a Hookers Army

VANESSA CARLISLE

By the time I was in college I'd already been called a whore. I had been followed down the street, had my car broken into by a boy I'd rejected, been harassed by a boss who "liked to see me sweat" while I stocked shelves. The first time I remember fighting off a physical attack, I was eighteen years old, and wouldn't become a sex worker for another year. I was at a college dance in the large student union building. It was the end of the night, the room had mostly cleared out, and I was crossing the floor to meet up with my friends. I was grabbed from behind, a huge arm encircling my neck, another around my waist. A menacing voice whispered in my ear, "I'm taking you home with me." Instinctively, I elbowed as hard as I could, broke free, and ran. Within seconds, my friends, many of whom had seen the attack, were with me, and the boy who had grabbed me had run out of the building. I knew violence was part of the world I lived in, but that was the first time I viscerally under-stood it could happen so quickly, in a room full of people, without my seeing it coming.

As a sex worker I have worked in strip clubs, done out-calls with clients in their homes and hotel rooms, performed on cam-era, and taken in-calls in private dungeons. I began a self-defense training path after years of both successfully and unsuccessfully fighting off boundary-crossing behavior from my sex work clients, schoolteachers, friends, friends of friends, and intimate partners.

I've been through all of the common aggressions: following, stalking, grabbing, yelling, etc. I've also experienced some of the more horrible forms of violence including rape, a rough arrest and illegal detainment, and being choked out. Over the years I've read the best-selling self-defense literature and taken a variety of self-defense classes ranging from popular nationwide programs like Rape Aggression Defense (RAD) to a small local program called the Super Hero Experience (SHE). I've mostly found women's self-defense training to be triggering, exhausting, and ultimately unhelpful as I forgot the techniques, struggled with PTSD, and felt alienated as a queer sex worker in classrooms full of heteronormative non–sex working women who expressed casual prejudice against me and my communities when they complained that men treated them "like whores." Still, I wanted to feel safe in my body, to trust my capacity to perceive and respond to threat, and so I kept searching for training.

Despite finding my own path to a traditional martial art, I never stopped wanting to pass self-defense techniques on to my community. I began to envision a self-defense training by and for sex workers that was trauma-informed and did not rely on high-adrenaline scenarios with techniques that were difficult to remember—and also did the transformative work of real empowerment by offering techniques for violence prevention, support for our survival of violent encounters, and care for the trauma after the violence had ended. I knew I was starting a big project when I thought of it, but I had no idea what an incredible adventure the Hookers Army would become.

## WHY WE NEED HOOKERS ARMIES

Let's start with what's wrong with women's self-defense classes, in general.[1] Imagine a world in which there are affordable, accessible classes for cis men, trans men, and masculine-of-center people that teach how boundaries are communicated and respected, alternatives to boundary-crossing behaviors, and how to self-regulate intense emotions. Imagine there were as many of those as there currently are women's self-defense classes. As a culture, we still behave as if our current rates of rape and violence against women and LGBTQ people are natural, biological effects of testosterone, and therefore unpreventable on a large scale. There is something wrong with this. We locate the responsibility of preventing individual violent experiences in the victims, after the fact, and then provide "women's self-defense" as another level of responsibility that vulnerable populations are expected to take on. At the same time as I offer this critique, given the high rates of violence that do currently exist, I believe anyone who wants self-defense training should be able to get it. And the market for women's self-defense classes has certainly bloomed.

From my perspective as a femme-presenting queer sex worker, the women's self-defense industry can be understood as roughly: 50 percent victim-blaming cops (or instructors who like to act like cops) teaching heteronormative women to rely further on the carceral state; 40 percent anti-violence activist feminists, some of them lesbians/queer people, sincerely trying to empower women but lacking analysis of how race and class intersect with gender violence or LGBTQ issues; and 10 percent absolute snake-oil bullshit that arrives with any money-making industry. In other words, women's self-defense, as a profit-driven industry, is a reactionary entity that relies on an unquestioned belief in the gender binary and all the nonsense that arrives with it; and, it continuously reinscribes some of our most insidious cultural programming about why women are so vulnerable to violence while eliding the reality of queer, transgender, and nonbinary experience.

Women's self-defense is mostly taught as a response to "realistic scenarios," which often rely on an implicitly racist, classist cliché of "stranger danger." Most women who have taken a self-defense class have been prompted to practice their new groin-kick and hammer-fist skills on a man wearing a large padded suit who has just cornered them at the imaginary ATM, broken into their home, or blocked them from getting to their car. This approach does not adequately address the most common forms of interpersonal violence.

Obviously the surprise stranger-danger type of attack does happen, and it is worthwhile to train for it. However, the majority of self-defense classes for women perpetuate a myth that the most dangerous person is a man (of color, or poor) out there in a "bad" neighborhood, who you could avoid if you just don't go to "dangerous" places by yourself, and especially not dressed like *that*. While no one speaks of it directly, often the attackers in stranger-danger scenarios perform aggression in racialized ways. They put on voices and personae of men of color, such that women are attacked in scripts like "Give me that money—I know you got enough, white girl," or "Come here, baby, you Asian girls look sweet but I know there's a tiger in there." Instructors often call their model attackers "bad guys," and encourage self-defense students to see themselves as warriors, soldiers in a war against rampant "urban" attacks.

Consider the fact that the vast majority of violence against people identifying as women, transgender, queer, and nonbinary— of all races—comes from intimate partners, family, coworkers, friends, and other people we know. A philosophy of self-defense training that takes this into account would begin with psychological preparation for the precursors to physical violence: behaviors that exhibit control, the crossing of personal boundaries, possessiveness, a devaluing of the student's capacity to make their own choices about their body, betrayals of trust, isolation, and so on. While many self-defense books do spend time on these issues, they still often resort to victim blaming that can sound like a bad country song: "Decks are loaded. Wild cards are scattered across the board. Big-time gambling is going on. Life and death are the stakes."[2] Even the best-selling Gavin de Becker writes in *The Gift of Fear*, "An axiom of the stalking dynamic: *men who cannot let go choose women who cannot say no.*" He and many other self-defense industry writers exhort women to cut people out of their life or leave troubling relationships without any analysis of how financial dependence, addiction, family dynamics, or other cultural factors may be adding complexity to their decision making.

A favorite refrain from self-defense instructors is to "trust your gut." The goal is to get students to listen more to the signs of fear in their bodies, to stop talking themselves out of taking steps to protect themselves. While we definitely all need more somatic intelligence, more connection to our bodies, and more awareness of our feelings and sensations, our guts don't always tell us the truth about our safety. Simply telling people to trust their gut fails to address the concerns of many people who have experienced violence and felt like they didn't see it coming. (*There must be something wrong with my guts!*) After getting attacked at my college dance, I spent months berating myself for not feeling my attacker approach, not sensing his intention before he grabbed me. That self-criticism was a hindrance to my healing.

Another twist: the command to trust your gut also erases the ways in which racism and classism are *felt experiences*—for example, the way white women unconsciously hold their purses tighter to their bodies or cross the street when they cross paths with Black men. Structuring women's self-defense programs around a belief in "women's intuition" gives permission for women to *both* cling to unconscious prejudice *and* blame themselves when they are surprised by the onset of violence.

As if all of this wasn't enough—as a rule, mainstream women's self-defense writers and teachers have *absolutely nothing to say* about violence against LGBTQ people or within LGBTQ communities, against sex workers, or violence that comes from the police. A philosophy of self-defense that demands I reduce my risk of violence through preventive measures like staying in packs, not going out late, not wearing revealing clothing, and so on, is not only a recipe for victim blaming and slut shaming, it is structurally unsound advice for sex workers. Because most women's self-defense involves this implicit blaming of the victim, sex workers are positioned to be the most blameworthy of all victims. Not only do we deliberately wear skirts like that, we want a safe exchange of money for our performance of sexiness, an act already stigmatized and criminalized. The models of self-defense that rely on purity narratives about women's sexuality or fragility simply do not allow for sex workers to be protectable, especially under the current regime of criminalization in the United States.

Of course, not all sex workers are equally vulnerable to violence. For example, Black women are vastly overrepresented in arrests for prostitution in Los Angeles.[3] Police have historically been a major source of violence in the lives of sex workers, and there have been verified accounts of police using "No Humans Involved" to classify murder cases involving Black sex worker victims. It may seem like training sex workers to defend themselves is asking for trouble. Many sex workers already carry weapons and plan to defend themselves because they know no one will value their lives more than they do. At the same time, studies show that self-defense training does work to reduce incidences of violence, which is why I want anyone who desires the training to be able to get it.

Thus, developing a self-defense system for sex workers requires more than compiling a list of techniques that can be performed in close proximity, in heels, with nails, or in a car. It requires a philosophy of self-love for sex working populations that asserts our right to bodily autonomy and self-protection in a culture that treats many of us in media and in law as disposable people.

## THE BIRTH OF HOOKERS ARMY LOS ANGELES

Outside the for-profit women's self-defense industry, there are radical queer collectives teaching each other how to use kitty knuckles in cute, home-printed zines. There are women, nonbinary, and queer martial artists who exit the mainstream path and create their own LGBTQ-inclusive intersectional feminist spaces. And there are occasional grassroots groups and nonprofits like Girl Army in Oakland, California, that teach self-defense for women, queer, trans, and nonbinary people from both a martial arts and anarchistic organizing perspective.

The mission of Girl Army is to offer peer-taught and affordable physical and psychological self-defense for women and trans folks. I was in recovery from a relationship that had ended in violence, while also experiencing the fallout from an intentional community that had broken up because of violence, and was searching for ways to heal during a temporary stay in the Bay Area. For a year, I took every class Girl Army offered, went to their anarchistic collective meetings, and learned to teach middle schoolers how to throw an elbow while yelling "NO!" at the top of their lungs.

What Girl Army did differently from mainstream women's self-defense classes was create space for scenario-based training that involved truly uncomfortable situations that weren't physically violent. Girl Army makes a practice of introducing the notion of a continuum of violence that begins with basic boundary crossing. For example, you practice keeping your boundary when a friend who wants to borrow your car pressures you after you've already said no. Instructors with Girl Army acknowledge that most violence occurs between people who know each other. While we did role-play a few stranger-danger situations—including sexualized and transphobic catcalling, getting cornered at a bus stop, and other common aggressions—what stood out to me was the way Girl Army prioritized processing the difficult reality of violence between intimate partners and family members.

I remember sitting on the mat at one of my last Girl Army classes, looking at the circle of people I'd come to feel such affection for, and realizing that I wanted something else; something specific that had been inspired by my training there. I wanted to be in a room of sex workers, to offer these techniques to sex workers, and to get a collective of sex workers together who functioned as a peer support network dedicated to each other's safety and well-being in an ongoing, sustainable way. The key was that we would care for each other in a holistic way via peer support—not just training. The self-defense training was to be a part of a larger vision of sex worker community skill shares. It felt huge and absolutely impossible to create.

After moving back to Los Angeles, I decided to continue my training in the martial art from which Girl Army drew their techniques. I found a dojo and came out as a sex worker to my sensei. I shared my dream to train sex workers in self-defense. My sensei made it clear that self-defense was a specific use of the training, and that what I'd be doing in the dojo was a classical martial art with some self-defense application. Although I didn't yet understand this distinction, what mattered was that I had found a teacher who was a true ally to me and to my project. I started training as hard as I could so I could quickly and effectively pass on self-defense techniques to my community. Now, I consider myself both a student of jujitsu and of self-defense, and they are related but separate spheres of training. I consulted with a few community organizers whom I respected, and they advised me to just hold a meeting and see what happened. I pitched the idea to a few other sex worker friends, we decided on a day and time to meet at a park, and Hookers Army of Los Angeles—HALA—began.[4]

Danny Cruz, one of HALA's founding members, remembered the list of names we went through, trying to decide what to call our experiment. One was "Prostituted Persons of Los Angeles," a dig at the way sex workers are often characterized by those who want to "save" us— as if we have no agency, as if the action of prostitution has been done to us, rather than by us of our own bodies. We joked, "Prostituted Persons: trafficking each other, together." Danny said with a wink, "That phrase will never leave me."

We have to laugh, or we'll break something—because under the currently overbroad laws, what we're doing to protect ourselves *could* be considered trafficking. We share safety information. We talk about our work. We buy each other food and offer each other rides. In order to receive the meeting location information, you have to be vouched by a current member, so the group grows slowly. HALA is not a policy advocacy group or a nonprofit; while many of the participants are sex workers' rights activists, many are not. Being an activist is not a prerequisite to participation. The only requirement is that someone has to self-identify as a person with lived experience in any facet of the sex trades.

The HALA statement of purpose was cocreated early on with founding members:

> Members of Hookers Army take active steps to care for ourselves and each other in this climate of predatory policing and sexist, racist, classist attacks on our bodies. We meet twice a month to offer each other peer support and exchange self-defense skills, which we take to mean any skill that protects us, enhances our capacity to live as we choose, furthers our healing from past trauma, and strengthens our community. We are committed to enjoying our sex working lives. In a spirit of honest, open kinship building and mutual aid, we help each other.

In the words of Lauren Kiley, another founding member, "We work to actively take care of and be good to whoever shows up, however they show up. And we ask people what they need from the group and try to meet them based on what they say."

Our first meeting was at Kenneth Hahn Park in South Los Angeles. Three of us sat on a blanket in the late afternoon light during the first week of June. We checked in with each other, asked each other questions about work, chatted, and then practiced a set of wrist escape techniques and went over some basic principles of breathing, finding a stance, and using your voice to set boundaries. We've met in three parks, three homes, a community center, a coffee house, an art gallery. Sometimes the group is very small, sometimes it's up to eight people. I'm grateful for the times when only one participant shows up—I get to know that person much better. HALA met the night Trump was elected. The light was strangely orange in Plummer Park that night, and one member remembers me saying, "Welcome to the apocalypse. I'm glad to be with you all." HALA met the night FOSTA-SESTA sailed through Congress. We cried and processed and went out for drinks and supported each other through our fear.

When someone new joins the meeting, we have a special check-in to welcome them. Everyone shares something of what brought them to the group, including the new person. We learn what everyone's needs and expectations are. If someone has self-defense or martial arts training, they are invited to share their techniques. Depending on the level of energy and comfort with training in the room, on someone's first day we usually go over a series of basic moves to escape a few common attacks—being grabbed by the wrist, for example, or a choke hold.

When I first started training with Girl Army, and even at the beginning of my more dedicated dojo practice, I would have an uncomfortable adrenaline response to feeling a training partner's hands around my neck. Just a few years before, I had been violently choked to the point of passing out by an intimate partner, and my body held that traumatic memory very close to the surface of my skin. Sometimes I couldn't even do the technique without needing to sit down and fight back tears. My sensei allowed me to go at my own pace, to train choke escapes slowly and carefully, until I learned to feel safe doing them. It turns out that escaping a choke is not only doable, it's one of the simpler sets of techniques to teach. One can raise an arm, turn to the side, and drop their elbow down on their attacker's arms. One can hit the middle of their attacker's neck and then turn to the side to escape. There are so many options. Once I'd moved beyond the painful intensity of my trauma symptoms, I felt grief and sadness doing the technique. If only I'd known how easy it is to break a choke hold *before* . . . I blamed myself for my lack of preparedness until I realized I was continuing the harm of the attack. The fact is, I didn't stop that person from choking me in the past. However, now I know how; and when I imagine someone coming at my throat today, I think, "What an idiot." To me, this is a major healing benchmark, achieved through dedicated, slow, repetitive practice and supportive training partners. This story also illustrates an important part of physical self-defense: there are always more options, and the main predictor of your survival is that you keep trying stuff, keep going, until you are safe.

Many women's self-defense classes acknowledge that there are likely survivors of violence already in the room, but do not treat the presence of those survivors as a gift to the collective. HALA prioritizes the experiences of the people in the room: when someone has a triggering experience or a painful memory, the group shifts to support them in whatever way feels best to them. The support for healing that HALA has provided me and others has been remarkable.

Since HALA has been meeting regularly, I've started to receive feedback from participants about how the group has affected them. Some of the stories involve the use of actual self-defense techniques—one member stopped a person from choking her, another used her training to get out of a hug she didn't want, many have been able to hold physical boundaries through their stances. Other stories are about the effect of HALA's peer support component. On our two-year anniversary of regular meetings, I asked everyone to share something about what HALA meant to them. One person said, "I feel better just knowing this group exists, even when I can't come." More said, "I am grateful to have something to look forward to." This was one silent promise I had made to myself after years of other activist work had burned me out: I had to look forward to HALA. I had to want to do it. And I can say now that I have never left a HALA meeting without feeling better than when I went in.

At HALA meetings, we don't simply insist on "trusting your gut." We talk about ways to *train* our guts to be more trustworthy—to balance our desire to believe in our own feelings with our capacity to analyze risk factors and take responsibility for our choices.

We listen to each other's stories and uplift one another. We notice when a person is blaming themselves for another person's behavior and we intervene, gently. Sometimes, we just eat chips and laugh, relaxing together and swapping stories the way people in other jobs take for granted.

Danny says that since HALA began, "the worlds we navigate in sexy time are a little less dangerous and a lot less isolating." Even if only one other soul shows up, it's a place where you know someone will. People keep showing up. And telling their friends. And this mission of HALA—to provide real-world, self-defense training for sex workers—continues to spread.

## NOTES

1. I do not wish to offend the people who have gone through these trainings and felt helped and empowered by them, and I'm glad any time I hear that's happened. But for many of us, these classes cause some harm and I'd like to explore why they are not a workable model for a self-defense system designed specifically for sex workers.

2. Lori Hartman Gervasi, *Fight Like a Girl . . . and Win: Defense Decisions for Women* (New York: St. Martin's Press), 129.

3. Amira Hasenbush, Bianca Wilson, Ayako Miyashita, and Madeleine Sharp, "HIV Criminalization and Sex Work in California from 2017," Williams Institute (October 2017), https://williamsinstitute.law. ucla.edu/wp-content/uploads/HIV-Criminalization-Sex-Work-CA-Oct-2017.pdf.

4. Sex workers who feel comfortable using the word "hooker" started this group, but we've always maintained that we'd change it in an instant if someone in the group didn't feel good about it. We settled on the name "Hookers Army" because we intended to keep much of the vision of Girl Army and wanted to offer an homage. Also, it is an acknowledgment of the fact that we intended to build a real fighting force in an oppressive system. We do not seek to emulate a state-sponsored military; we seek to appropriate "army" imagery for our ad hoc guerrilla resistance movement. We use "HALA" to refer to the group outside of our sex workers–only space. This way, "hooker" remains a reclaimed, insider word.

# Contributor Biographies

**NORMA JEAN ALMODOVAR** has been a sex workers' rights activist since she left the LAPD in 1982. She is the cofounder of the first sex worker nonprofit organization, the International Sex Worker Foundation for Art, Culture, and Education, and the author of an autobiography, *Cop to Call Girl*.

**SONYA ARAGON** is a writer and artist who lives in New York. She works at the intersection of intimacy and capitalism.

**femi babylon**, formerly known as suprihmbé, is the author of the well-received queer poetry book *libra season* and a zine titled *heauxthots: On Terminology, and Other [Un]Important Things*. She is on the board of Sex Workers Outreach Project.

**LINA BEMBE** is a Latinx performer, filmmaker, and writer based in Berlin who has been featured in a diverse range of pornographic narratives. Lina works in front of the camera and behind the scenes at Sex School Hub and often writes, speaks, or curates screenings about feminism, culture, sex education, and explicit sexuality.

**VANESSA CARLISLE** holds a PhD and has worked in the sex industries for over twenty years. She is a founding member of the Hookers Army of Los Angeles and author of *Take Me With You*. She also teaches workshops and classes on a variety of topics on sexuality and gender.

**CHRISTIANNA CLARK**, a.k.a. "Selena the Stripper," is a sex worker, writer, podcaster, and community organizer. After graduating from MICA in 2015, fae felt out of place in the elitist world of institutional art. Through stripping, fae found financial stability and a community of incredibly strong, radically free thinking artists. Fae is a political commentator for *The Doe* and hosts the podcast *Heaux in the Kneaux*.

**GODDESS CORI** is an educator, dominatrix, and artist in Los Angeles who focuses their work on community healing and community justice centering BITPOC. They have taught at CSU Northridge, Pitzer College, and CSU Channel Islands.

**ANTONIA CRANE** is the author of the memoir *Spent* as well as a writing instructor, stripper, and performer in Los Angeles. Her screenplay *The Lusty* is a recipient of the San Francisco Film Society & Kenneth Rainin Foundation Grant in screenwriting, and she is a producer for several episodes of *DRIVEN*.

**REBELLE CUNT** is an indie scholar, whorestorian, and sex workers' rights advocate from the Chicago area. Dedicated to examining and documenting the connections between race and the desire industry, they are also the creator behind the Heaux History Project—an archival effort that centers Black and Brown erotic labor and heaux culture and movements.

**LOLA DAVINA**, author of *Thriving in Sex Work*, has spent more than twenty-five years in and around the sex industry working as a stripper, dominatrix, porn actress, and escort. She earned her MA in human sexuality and her MS in nonprofit fundraising, and writes a self-care and wellness column for YNOT Cam.

**CEYENNE DOROSHOW** is a performer, activist, organizer, community-based researcher, and public figure in the trans and sex worker rights' movements. She is the founder and executive director of Gays and Lesbians Living in a Transgender Society, and coauthored the Caribbean cookbook *Cooking in Heels* while incarcerated on prostitution charges.

**ZACKARY DRUCKER** is an independent artist, cultural producer, and trans woman who has performed and exhibited her work internationally in museums, galleries, and film festivals. Drucker is an Emmy-nominated producer for the docuseries *This Is Me*, as well as a producer on Golden Globe– and Emmy-winning *Transparent*.

**DIA DYNASTY** is a Shamanatrix: a professional dominatrix who incorporates spiritual and healing modalities into her BDSM practice. She and her Dommewife, Lucy Sweetkill, founded La Maison du Rouge on similar compassionate and principled BDSM interests after meeting at a commercial BDSM house.

**JUNIPER FITZGERALD** is the author of the first children's book with a sex working mother, *How Mamas Love Their Babies*. She is a mother, writer, and former sex worker.

**APRIL FLORES** is a muse, model, performer, and writer. She was the first BBW to win two consecutive AVN Awards for her groundbreaking work. She has modeled for fine art photographers, appeared in adult films in every genre of the adult industry, and spoken out about body image through her presence, powerful sexuality, and her activism.

**MELISSA GIRA GRANT** is a staff writer covering justice at the *New Republic*. She is the author of *Playing the Whore: The Work of Sex Work* and was a senior staff writer at the *Appeal* as well as a contributing writer at the *Village Voice* and *Pacific Standard*.

**MILCAH HALILI** is a nonbinary writer, web developer, and performer. They write about intersectionality, cannabis, sexuality, and web development. They've been published in the book *Coming Out Like a Porn Star*, *Witch Craft* magazine, the *Rumpus*, and *Filthy Media*. He lives in Los Angeles with his wife, April Flores.

**TINA HORN** hosts and produces the long-running kink podcast *Why Are People Into That?!* She is also the creator and writer of the sci-fi sex-rebel comic book series SFSX (Safe Sex). Her reporting on sexual subcultures and politics has appeared in *Rolling Stone*, *Hazlitt*, *Glamour*, *Jezebel*, and elsewhere. She is a Lambda Literary Fellow, the recipient of two Feminist Porn Awards, and holds an MFA in Creative Nonfiction Writing from Sarah Lawrence.

**LAUREN KILEY** works in the sex industries as a fetish porn performer, digital marketer, production assistant, and content manager. She has over a decade of experience organizing in sex working communities and is a founding member of Hookers Army. Lauren currently lives in Miami with her partner and pets.

**LORELEI LEE** is a sex worker, writer, and community organizer. Her fiction, nonfiction, and poetry have appeared in *Salon*, the *Rumpus*, *WIRED*, the *Los Angeles Review of Books*, *Hustling Verse*, *$pread*, *n+1*, *The Feminist Porn Book*, and elsewhere. She owes her life to other sex workers.

**MAGGIE McMUFFIN** has been getting naked for art and money since she was nineteen. In her spare time, she fights TERFs on Twitter and runs an Instagram for her cat. She is not only bisexual but bicoastal, and splits her time between New York and Seattle.

**CYD NOVA** first appeared in a truck stop magazine in 2004 and has since been blessed by the family and the highs of the sex industry while also being a witness and prey to the shit surrounding it. He now lives in New York City, where he works as a consultant for Transgender Equity Consulting and writes about all the sexual encounters that have shaped his life.

**ASHLEY PAIGE** is a Professional Dominatrix, queer fetish porn performer, BDSM educator, and sex worker advocate based in New York City. As a well-rounded sex worker with more than thirteen years in the adult industry, she possesses a wit and work ethic that create and inspire change in every community to which she belongs.

**REESE PIPER** is a stripper, writer, and art model whose work explores sex work, labor rights, class, and autism. She lives in Brooklyn and organizes for sex workers' rights with Sex Workers Outreach Project. In her free time, she frequents burlesque shows and hangs out in lesbian bars.

**YIN Q** is a BDSM educator and writer based in New York City. Their media work includes the dramatic web series *Mercy Mistress* and the short documentary *Yang Song: Fly in Power*. Yin is founder of the production collective Kink Out and codirector of Red Canary Song, a grassroots Asian American sex workers organization.

**ARABELLE RAPHAEL** is of French nationality, currently based in the Bay Area. She is an award-winning adult film actress and artist. Arabelle continues to produce her own content while working on her photography, poetry, short films, and other writing.

**AUDACIA RAY** is an advocate and writer based in New York. She currently serves her LGBTQ community as director of community organizing and public advocacy at the New York City Anti-Violence Project, and is a founding member of the Decrim NY Coalition. She was the executive director of the Red Umbrella Project, a sex worker media, storytelling, and advocacy group, and executive editor at *$pread* magazine.

**IGNACIO G. HUTÍA XEITI RIVERA** holds a master's degree and is the founder and director of the HEAL Project to end child sexual abuse. They are an internationally known gender nonconforming speaker, educator, writer, performer, and healer. Ignacio has over twenty years of experience on multiple fronts, including economic justice, anti-racist and anti-imperialist work, as well as feminist and LGBTQI movements.

**HELLO ROOSTER** is an intersectional feminist and a member and activist of the Sex Worker Advocacy and Resistance Movement. They are a nonbinary performer of color currently training as an intimacy coordinator. Hello Rooster has also been a panelist on labor rights and ethics, and is a cinematographer and a Feminist Porn Award winner.

**CHRISTA MARIE SACCO** holds a PhD from Pacifica Graduate Institute and has worked as a peer counselor and advocate with human trafficking, sexual assault, and domestic violence survivors. She is a professor, project consultant, writer, circle facilitator, public speaker, and performing artist in Southern California.

**JESSIE SAGE** is a sex worker, writer, and organizer. She writes a weekly sex and social justice column in the *Pittsburgh City Paper* and cohosts a podcast about the sex industry called *Peepshow Podcast*. Her writing can be found in publications including the *Washington Post*, *Men's Health*, *VICE*, and the *Establishment*.

**AK SAINI** is a sex worker, storyteller, and activist whose advocacy work has been featured on the cover of the *New York Times Magazine*, and *Marie Claire* listed them as a sex worker better suited for the presidency than Donald Trump. They have curated sex worker storytelling events and film festivals in numerous cities and played a lead role in the passage of statewide legislation to end the use of condoms as evidence of prostitution-related offenses in New York State.

**BRIT SCHULTE** is an adjunct lecturer, activist archivist, curator, community organizer, and sex working art historian based in New York. They are a current collective member at Bluestockings Bookstore & Activist Center and also coordinate the Justice for Alisha Walker defense campaign.

**JUDY SZURGOT** is a mother, daughter, and sister to a wonderful family, and an advocate for formerly incarcerated women. She's currently based in Illinois.

**ALISHA WALKER** is a multimedia visual artist, poet, inside organizer, (former) sex worker, and criminalized survivor. She is a member of the Support Ho(s)e Collective. Alisha is currently (forcibly) based in Decatur, Illinois.

**NATALIE WEST** is a writer and educator based in Los Angeles. She worked as a professional dominatrix while obtaining a PhD in gender studies, and she learned as much about gender and sexuality from her sex work as she did in the classroom. Her personal essays have appeared in *Salon, Autostraddle, Kink Academy, Columbia Journal*, and *them*. She moonlights as a sex work, BDSM, and queer community authenticity consultant for film and television.

# More Activist Anthologies from the Feminist Press

**$pread: The Best of the Magazine That Illuminated the Sex Industry and Started a Media Revolution**
edited by Rachel Aimee, Eliyanna Kaiser, and Audacia Ray

**All the Women Are White, All the Blacks Are Men, But Some of Us Are Brave: Black Women's Studies**
edited by Akasha (Gloria T.) Hull, Patricia Bell Scott, and Barbara Smith

**The Crunk Feminist Collection**
edited by Brittney C. Cooper, Susana M. Morris, and Robin M. Boylorn

**The Echoing Ida Collection**
edited by Cynthia R. Greenlee, Kemi Alabi, and Janna A. Zinzi

**The Feminist Porn Book: The Politics of Producing Pleasure**
edited by Tristan Taormino, Celine Parreñas Shimizu, Constance Penley, and Mireille Miller-Young

**The Feminist Utopia Project: Fifty-Seven Visions of a Radically Better Future**
edited by Alexandra Brodsky and Rachel Kauder Nalebuff

**I Still Believe Anita Hill: Three Generations Discuss the Legacies of Speaking Truth to Power**
edited by Amy Richards and Cynthia Greenberg

**Queer Ideas: The David R. Kessler Lectures in Lesbian and Gay Studies**
from the Center for Lesbian and Gay Studies at CUNY

**Radical Reproductive Justice: Foundation, Theory, Practice, Critique**
edited by Loretta J. Ross, Lynn Roberts, Erika Derkas, Whitney Peoples, and Pamela Bridgewater Toure

**Still Brave: The Evolution of Black Women's Studies**
edited by Stanlie M. James, Frances Smith Foster, and Beverly Guy-Sheftall

**The Feminist Press** publishes books that
ignite movements and social transformation.
Celebrating our legacy, we lift up insurgent
and marginalized voices from around the
world to build a more just future.

See our complete list of books at
**feministpress.org**

**THE FEMINIST PRESS**
AT THE CITY UNIVERSITY OF NEW YORK
FEMINISTPRESS.ORG